Reward for High Public Office

Asian and Pacific-Rim states

The way states reward their top public officeholders – prime ministers, presidents, top bureaucrats, legislators and judges – reveals a great deal about political values and assumptions about governing. This book uses reward for high public office as a window into the working of seven Asian and Pacific-Rim political systems (Australia, China, Hong Kong, Japan, South Korea, New Zealand and Singapore). The seven cases include some of the most generous and some of the most meagre top reward packages in the world, as well as some of the cleanest and most corrupt political systems on orthodox indicators, and very different official philosophies about rewards at the top. They offer a particularly rich opportunity to explore the causes and consequences of different ways of rewarding top public officeholders – a subject that has engaged political philosophers from Confucius and Plato to Spinoza, Hegel and Bentham, yet has been surprisingly little explored in empirical research.

The book starts from a careful comparative analysis of top public officeholders' rewards over two decades, then probes beyond the data to tell the political and institutional stories that lie behind the numbers. It shows that the level and structure of top-level rewards is better explained as a product of politics and history than of economic development. It shows that democracy and democratisation make a difference to patterns of top-level rewards – and vice versa. And in spite of received arguments in 'good governance' debates, it shows there is no simple relationship between top rewards and levels of corruption. Top-level rewards are a mirror of political life, raising fundamental issues for governance debates, and this book is important for students and observers of politics, public administration and Asian studies.

Christopher Hood is Gladstone Professor of Government and Fellow of All Souls College at the University of Oxford, and currently chairs the Politics Section of the British Academy. **B. Guy Peters** is Maurice Falk Professor of American Government at the University of Pittsburgh and has published and lectured extensively in comparative public administration and public policy.

Routledge research in comparative politics

Reward for High Public Office

Asian and Pacific-Rim states

Edited by
**Christopher Hood and
B. Guy Peters,**
with **Grace O. M. Lee**

Routledge
Taylor & Francis Group

LONDON AND NEW YORK

First published 2003
by Routledge
11 New Fetter Lane, London EC4P 4EE

Simultaneously published in the USA and Canada
by Routledge
29 West 35th Street, New York, NY 10001

Routledge is an imprint of the Taylor & Francis Group

© 2003 Christopher Hood and B. Guy Peters for editorial material
and selection; individual chapters, the contributors

Typeset in Baskerville by
Newgen Imaging Systems (P) Ltd, Chennai, India
Printed and bound in Great Britain by
MPG Books Ltd, Bodmin

British Library Cataloguing in Publication Data
A catalogue record for this book is available from the British Library

Library of Congress Cataloging in Publication Data
A catalog record for this book has been requested

ISBN 0–415–30349–4

Contents

Figures

Tables

Contributors

Jostein Askim has a Master's degree in Public Administration and Public Policy from LSE and has recently completed a two-year Master's degree in Political Science at the University of Oslo. He is currently extending his experience of policy and management analysis by working for Asplan Analysis, a consultancy firm in Oslo that specializes in public management development.

John P. Burns is Professor of Politics and Public Administration at the University of Hong Kong. His publications include *Civil Service Systems in Asia* co-edited with B. Bowornwathana (Cheltenham, Elgar, 2001) and 'Governance and Civil Service Reform in China,' in J. Howell (ed.) *Governance in China* (London, Rowman and Littlefield, 2002).

Kosaku Dairokuno is Professor of Comparative Politics, School of Political Science and Economics, Meiji University, Tokyo, Japan. His publications include *Hikaku-Sijigaku to Demokurasi no Genkai* (*Comparative Politics and the Limits of Democracy*) (Tokyo, Toshindo, 2001) and *Muruyama Seiken to Domokurasi no Kiki* (*Muruyama Government and the Crisis of Democracy*) (Tokyo, Toshindo, 2000).

Robert Gregory is Associate Professor of Public Policy and Administration in the School of Government at Victoria University of Wellington, New Zealand. His main fields of interest are public administration and state sector reform, and public policymaking theory. He has published widely on these topics and his recent work includes 'Accountability in Modern Government', in the 2001 Sage *International Handbook of Public Administration*.

Christopher Hood is Gladstone Professor of Government and Fellow of All Souls College Oxford, UK, and currently chairs the Politics Section of the British Academy. Recent publications include *The Art of the State* (Oxford, Clarendon 1998), *Regulation inside Government* (with C. Scott *et al.*, Oxford University Press 1999) and *The Government of Risk* (with H. Rothstein and R. Baldwin, Oxford University Press, 2001).

Pan-Suk Kim is Professor of Public Administration in the College of Commerce and Law at Yonsei University, Korea. He is co-author of seven books in Korean and one in English on human resource management, government reform and organization development, and has published in journals including *Administration and Society*, *Public Administration Review* and *Australian Journal of Public Administration*.

Grace O. M. Lee is Associate Professor of Public and Social Administration at the City University of Hong Kong. Her research interests are in executive government, public management and public policy, and her recent books include *Managing Public Services: Crises and Lessons From Hong Kong* (2000, with A. S. Huque) and *The Civil Service in Hong Kong: Continuity and Change* (1998, with A.S. Huque and A.B.L Cheung).

Akira Nakamura is Dean of the Graduate School and Professor of Political Science at Meiji University, Tokyo, Japan. He has published widely in English and Japanese on government reform and crisis management in Japan and is working on a new theoretical approach to Japan's public management. Recent works include 'Preparing for the Inevitable: Japan's Ongoing Search for Best Crisis Management Practices,' in U. Rosenthal, R. A. Boin and L. K. Comfort (eds.) *Managing Crises* (Springfield, IL: Thomas, 2001) and (with A. Ichinio *et al.*) *Kokka no Yukue* (*The Demise of Nation States*: Ashi Shobo, 2001).

Martin Painter is Professor, Department of Public and Social Administration, City University of Hong Kong. He is researching administrative and policy capacities of governments in East and South East Asia, and his recent books include *Collaborative Federalism* (Cambridge University Press, 1998) and *Public Sector Challenges and Government Reforms in South East Asia* (RIAP, University of Sydney, 2001).

B. Guy Peters is Maurice Falk Professor of American Government at the University of Pittsburgh, USA, and Honorary Professor of the City University of Hong Kong. He is actively involved in research on administrative change and institutional theory. His most recent books are *The Future of Governing*, 2nd edn (University Press of Kansas, 2001) and *Success and Failure in Public Governance* (Edward Elgar, 2001).

Jon S. T. Quah is Professor of Political Science at the National University of Singapore and co-editor of the *Asian Journal of Political Science*. He publishes widely in international and regional journals on public administration in Singapore and other Asian countries, and specializes in administrative reform, personnel management and anti-corruption strategies, on which he is a leading international expert.

Foreword

The topic of rewards at the top of government administrative and political systems has been poorly understood both by academic researchers and international development agencies alike. True, efforts to reform civil service pay and employment practices in borrower governments have been part and parcel of multilateral development bank (MDB) programmes for nearly two decades. But until the 1990s, the emphasis was more narrowly technocratic, focusing on the supply-side of public-sector management and working predominantly with government through provision of technical inputs and advice. These efforts have focused exclusively on administrative cadres, ignoring important links with the political class and largely dismissing citizens' 'demand-side' pressures for accountability and transparency in public rewards policies. And, although international donors have frequently exhorted governments to decompress civil service salary structures to skew rewards toward the top grades, salary reforms proposed by MDBs have typically comprehended the entire civil service, rather than targeting the higher bureaucratic echelons specifically. As such, they have not taken the care, as this volume does, to examine the intricate details of rewards for high office holders. This has often prevented international donors from getting a clear grasp of the real incentives that drive the behaviour of government leaders.

The relative neglect of this topic flies somewhat in the face of the growing investment multilateral donors have been making of late in the 'good governance' industry. Several factors may help explain this lapse. First, rewards for high public office in most developing countries conform to the construct developed in this book of a largely invisible, compensation 'iceberg'. Opaque remuneration mechanisms that include both legal and extra-legal allowances and rents for high office holders proliferate in developing countries around the world. In democratic contexts, governments fear upsetting constituents who favour egalitarian basic wage structures, and the 'real' rewards are thus obscured beneath the water's surface. In authoritarian settings, such as the one described by John Burns for China in this volume, incompletely developed market mechanisms and largely secretive elite competition may produce a hidden web of non-wage rewards. The sheer difficulty of obtaining accurate information about these non-transparent rewards and the sensitivity associated with the extra-legal components of this invisible 'iceberg' have precluded aggressive exploration of this murky area of rewards to top-level officials.

Another factor that explains the reluctance of multilateral development bodies to delve deeply into questions of rewards to top-level officials, especially for political-office holders, is the prohibition on development bank political activity. The charters of both the Asian Development Bank and the World Bank explicitly proscribe direct political interference in member country political affairs, leaving economic considerations as the only legitimized basis for their decisions. Many borrower governments regard (both executive and legislative) rewards at the top as an internal political matter, and MDBs fear exceeding their mandate by treading too heavily in this area. The interdiction of political interference has traditionally led development agencies to steer clear even of political analysis that might be seen to breach their articles of agreement. The domination of the operational and research functions within these institutions by economists has also inhibited work on the political features of governance. The result has been a dearth of empirical analysis of these issues until recently.

Third, there is the concern, only now being investigated vigorously, that international agency funds themselves may figure (sometimes significantly) in the rewards 'iceberg' of borrower governments. Attention to MDB fiduciary responsibilities has only recently been intensified with public disclosures about fraudulent use of public – and internationally financed – monies in high profile cases, such as Russia or Indonesia. In East Asia, accusations of cronyism in the aftermath of the late-1990s financial crisis have spurred MDB worries about the hygiene of their own investments in the region. Along with the political will to undertake detailed analysis of this issue, the technical competency to 'follow the money' is still to be developed in these agencies, so much work remains to be done to anchor the high rhetoric about 'good governance' to more grounded, empirical analysis of rewards to top-level officials as carried out in the chapters of this volume.

Finally, as the cases explored in this volume suggest, the theoretical underpinnings that would argue for further intellectual investment by MDBs in this topic are far from robust. While popular assumptions about the relationship between pay and corruption or performance may still operate on an *ad hoc* basis within these organizations or among developing country policy-makers, what little analysis has been carried out by MDBs debunks the facile conclusion that low government pay leads causally to corruption. Efforts to document the relationship between performance and pay in the public sector have been similarly inconclusive, though the effects of low remuneration on the ability of developing country governments to attract and retain talent have been better analysed.

This much-needed book breaks new methodological ground in its careful estimation and analysis of rewards for high public office. More applied work of this kind could significantly enhance the ability of international donors and policy-makers to design governance programmes based on the basis of political realities and in-depth understanding of the particulars of individual country historical inheritance. Hopefully, the lessons learned from this research can be extended to other Pacific-Rim countries and, eventually, to other regions.

Barbara Nunberg (World Bank) and
Clay Wescott (Asian Development Bank)[1]

---

1 The views expressed here are our own and do not represent those of the ADB or the World Bank.

Preface

Using rewards at the top of political systems as a window into their ways of working seems such an obvious idea that the relative lack of attention paid to rewards to top-level officeholders in contemporary political science has long puzzled us. Surely this is research territory that should be intensively examined and heavily fought over by researchers from a range of different analytic perspectives? Why, for example, is it not central to the concerns of the various schools of rational-choice theory for which it ought to be a central preoccupation? Why do contemporary political theorists take so little interest in something that so many of their classical counterparts put at the heart of reasoning about politics?

Such neglect seems hard either to explain or to excuse. If war is too important to be left to the generals, the rewards of top public-office holders are too important to be left to pay consultants, and this book is our second foray into this territory, since it follows up an earlier study of European countries and the USA that we published almost a decade ago. As we explain in Chapter 1, the political systems of Asia and the Pacific Rim offer more variety than the established democracies of Western Europe and North America, in the range of published money rewards, levels of corruption and degrees of democratic scrutiny over rulers. They include some of the highest-paid as well as some of the lowest-paid top public-office holders in the world, as well as some of the cleanest and most corrupt political systems on the orthodox indicators, and very different official philosophies about rewards at the top.

This book is the product of two years of data gathering and analysis. We set out to put together some basic data about rewards to top-level officeholders and then to probe beyond those data by trying to tell the political stories that lay behind the numbers. This beguilingly simple plan proved to be easier to formulate than to execute. The work we did over those two years taught us the hard way that even apparently simple questions about who gets what at the top can take even experienced researchers a surprisingly long time to answer, even in what is supposed to be an age of 'transparency'. Over time we learned to take less for granted and every one of the chapters that appear in this book went through a major transformation as our ideas developed. Pooling our efforts to produce this study was hard, long-drawn-out and often difficult work, but it proved an experience that was intellectually (not financially) rewarding.

The basic plan of the book took shape in two intensive workshops in a departmental conference room at the City University of Hong Kong that developed our shared fascination with the subject and our endeavours to understand the politics of rewards in the seven political systems that we were exploring. Trained as students of political science and public administration, we found ourselves grappling with issues that would be challenging even for international tax accountants, and we struggled to reconcile what was practically researchable with what was analytically meaningful across a set of very different political systems. Over the course of the project some of us also met in other places, including cities as various as Oxford, Phoenix and San Francisco, to discuss drafts and develop parts of the analysis. But, as is the way with this type of research in the present day, most of our exchanges were 'virtual', in that they were conducted across continents through cyberspace, and at times the volume of traffic was such that it challenged the limits of our email inboxes, to say nothing of our own cognitive capacity to absorb and analyse the data we were assembling.

Most of our thanks are due to the City University of Hong Kong, which helped us to generate this project in at least three different ways. One was by giving Christopher Hood the opportunity to work and teach in the Department of Social and Public Administration as Visiting Professor of Public Management for a semester in 1999–2000, a sojourn that led to a series of conversations with Grace Lee and which in turn produced the impetus for this study. City University of Hong Kong also helped by giving Grace Lee a grant for cross-national comparative research on institutional developments, a grant that supported our meetings in Hong Kong and allowed us to employ Jostein Askim, who worked part-time with Christopher Hood in London and Oslo at the essential task of helping to build, cross-check and analyse the pooled data that the study produced. The work demanded a mixture of patience, careful sifting of data and repeated dialogue with those who produced it for each political system. A third invaluable source of help from City University was the loan of some of its facilities for the two intensive workshops in 2000 and 2001 that we used to develop our ideas into a common framework and exchange our preliminary research findings.

We have other major debts to acknowledge as well. We greatly benefited from the advice and interest of several scholars, including Anthony Cheung, David Lindauer, Bidhya Bowornwathana and Joergen Christensen (as well as the anonymous reviewers commissioned by the publisher, who gave us valuable feedback) and we also gained from the experience and perspectives of Barbara Nunberg (of the World Bank) and Clay Wescott (of the Asian Development Bank), who both attended one of our workshops. We are grateful to LSE's Government Department for additional research funds and facilities, to Hong Kong University for financing a visit by Guy Peters in 2002 that helped to consolidate the project in its final stages, to Michèle Cohen of Oxford University's Department of Politics and International Relations (and based at All Souls College) for her help in turning a collection of papers into a single manuscript, and to Gillian Hood for her help in preparing the index. Several of our contributors used other assistants whose help is acknowledged in individual chapters.

Christopher Hood
B. Guy Peters
May 2002

Part I

Rewards for high public office

An overview

1 Introduction

Christopher Hood and B. Guy Peters,
with Grace O. M. Lee

Place your duties before reward ...

(Confucius: see Huang 1997: 130)

Appointing good people to government *and paying them well* is an ancient Confucianist concept ...

Goh Chok Tong, Prime Minister of Singapore,
National Day Rally Speech, 20 August 2000: 44 (emphasis added)

Humphrey ... explained that he saw the rewards of his job as the knowledge that one has been of service to the nation. I'm sure he was telling the truth ...

(Lynn and Jay 1986: 152)

Rewards for high public office in Asia and the Pacific Rim

This book examines the rewards that go to those at the top of the state structures – in the political, bureaucratic and judicial domains – in seven Asian and Pacific-Rim societies, namely Australia, China, Hong Kong, Japan, South Korea, New Zealand and Singapore. Lasswell (1936) once famously defined politics as 'who gets what when how', and in that vein the politics of reward for those in the topmost positions of the state concerns who gets what rewards, when and how – and with what consequences.

As we shall see, the seven societies chosen are strikingly varied in how and how much they reward their top leaders. So, they can be used – in a limited way, at least – as a basis for examining the causes and consequences of different approaches to rewarding those in high public office. Asia and the Pacific Rim include numerous countries (like China, Indonesia, Thailand) whose leaders' published salaries are in the poverty league. What these leaders are officially paid puts them well below what welfare recipients obtain in many affluent western welfare states, and China is included as one of those cases. But the region also includes cases at the other extreme, including the small city-state of Singapore, which seems to have the highest-paid public officials in the world (see Quah 1999: 492). The Prime Minister of Singapore has a basic salary approximately 500 times higher than the leader of the largest and most powerful Pacific-Rim state, China.

The variation can be striking even among societies with similar levels of Gross Domestic Product (GDP) per head. For instance, if the Australian Prime Minister and the Chief Executive of Hong Kong were to have lunch together, the latter would be better placed to pick up the tab, since his published salary is more than double that of the Australian leader, even though the two economies are at a similar level of GDP per head.

At the least, such variation prompts questions as to what political conditions produce what sorts of reward structures to the top-level officials in the public sector and how much – if any – difference it makes to the working of the economy and political system. Is Singapore 10 times better governed than Australia, for instance? Are Hong Kong's lavishly paid top bureaucrats far more capable than their more modestly paid counterparts in Japan? What accounts for the differences?

As we shall see later, such comparisons of published salaries tend to conceal as much as they reveal, for at least two reasons. To use a well-worn but still useful analogy, one can think of the rewards to government leaders as icebergs floating in the sea, with basic salary as the part that can be seen above the water. In cases like Singapore, the earnings 'iceberg' seems to be largely above the water, whereas in cases like China the basic salary forms a tiny tip, scarcely visible above the water. Moreover, in many cases hidden or semi-hidden extras comprise the most important part of the reward package. In some cases, these 'extras' consist of earning opportunities in the private sector, during or after public office, while in others they come from allowances or other payments from public funds.

Moreover, as we shall see in the next chapter, salaries of top officeholders need to be related to the income levels of the society concerned. For instance, the published salaries of top public officeholders in Singapore and Hong Kong seem stratospheric compared to those from other cultures even in the affluent developed world. But these salaries have to be assessed against the extraordinarily large amounts earned by top professionals in these societies. Indeed, Jon Quah shows in this book that Singapore in the early 1990s was steadily losing its bright young civil servants to other more lucrative occupations in spite of what for bureaucrats from almost anywhere else would be the stratospheric level of civil service pay in Singapore.

Equally striking as the range of published basic earnings is the variety in the way public-sector leaders are rewarded, including features such as openness, base-salary salience, distribution of rewards over time and the way rewards are decided. For instance, as we shall see in Chapter 2, the formal rewards for all the top positions in Japan are published and fairly easily accessible, at least for industrious and knowledgeable observers. But for others – including New Zealand, which made 'transparency' the watchword of its much-discussed state-sector reforms of the 1980s – some or all of those rewards are difficult or impossible for such observers to ascertain. As the chapters in Part II will show, in some cases, like that of Singapore, those at the top of the state hierarchy directly decide their own pay and conditions. But in others, such as Australia, this delicate decision is partly or wholly entrusted to quasi-independent bodies aspiring to be above 'politics'.

Further, what different public-sector elites do after they leave office – the rewards that accrue after rather than during their terms of office – is equally revealing.

Why – or to whom – do rewards to top public officials matter?

The reason for exploring such variations is more than a voyeuristic interest in the lives of the powerful and famous. There are at least three reasons for looking carefully at rewards to top-level officials in the state structure across a set of Asian and Pacific-Rim countries. First, the issue of how to reward those in the topmost offices of the state – judges, top bureaucrats and politicians – is a central and recurring preoccupation of political theory and institutional design everywhere. That is because the level and structure of such rewards is ordinarily assumed to have major consequences for the working of government and politics, and hence it figures prominently both in traditional political theory and in contemporary ideas about the design of government. As the first two epigraphs of this chapter indicate, political philosophers from Confucius and Plato to Spinoza, Hegel, Bentham and beyond have laid heavy stress on the rewards and conditions obtained by the leaders of the state as a key design factor in good governance and offered a variety of 'best practice' recipes. In contemporary political science, the influential rational-choice school that has developed since the 1960s portrays top-level rulers as self-interested egoists (Niskanen 1971; Bates 1999), and a growing literature concentrates on state predation and kleptocratic rule (North 1981: 20–32; Schleifer and Vishny 1998). So, the way rulers reward themselves ought to be central to those analytic perspectives in both classical and contemporary political science. In fact, as we said at the outset, little serious cross-national comparisons have been made of such rewards, none have come from the rational-choice school of thought and such comparisons have not been made across Asian and Pacific-Rim societies up to now.

This gap deserves to be filled, not just because of the substantive importance of such societies but also because of the range of conditions they encompass. As already noted, our seven Asian and Pacific-Rim cases show considerable variety in rewards to top-level officials, and they also comprise a range of different political systems and varying state performances. So, they offer an opportunity for critically examining the various claims that have been offered about the consequences of different levels and structures of reward to top-level officials. Indeed, each of the seven cases has been presented as a form of 'tomorrow' or future model for the rest of the world over the past 50 years or so, from the Australasian countries, once regarded as models of democratic innovation and other pioneering reforms, to the East Asian 'little tigers' that racked up levels of economic growth and performance up to 1997 that were the envy of the rest of the world. Though a small-*n* comparative study of this kind does not allow for conventional multivariate testing, such variations allow us to probe for explanations of what shapes the size and structure of rewards for high public office and to test propositions about the consequences of such rewards.

Second, there are some specific traditions and established ways of thought about rewards to top-level officials in the state in the Asia-Pacific region against which contemporary patterns and trends can be examined. One is the Confucian tradition recalled in the epigraphs to this chapter – the official philosophy of imperial China and still pervasive in much of East Asia, particularly for China, Japan and South Korea within our set. The Confucian tradition is associated with the idea of inequality of rank (based on inequality of merit), but, as the epigraphs show, what Confucian ideas actually mean for rewards to high-level officials is ambiguous in Asian politics today. Goh Chok Tong, probably the highest-paid Prime Minister in the world in published salary at the time of writing, interprets Confucian ideas to mean generous reward for top talent. But others, for example, in the Korean and Japanese *samurai* tradition, read Confucian ideas to imply frugality and self-sacrifice by rulers, who are expected to put the interests of those they rule ahead of their own interests. Even for the latter interpretation, however, 'self-sacrifice' can be construed, in practice, in more than one way. As Chapter 6 in this book (by Akira Nakamura and Kosaku Dairokuno) argues, in Japanese tradition, bribery or insider trading affecting those in the topmost positions of the state has not been regarded as serious 'corruption' if the proceeds were largely distributed to followers rather than staying in the leaders' pockets. Also, top bureaucrats have concentrated on gaining the most lucrative positions after they leave office ['descending from heaven' (*amakaduri*) in Japanese parlance and 'parachuting' in the Korean one], meaning that any degree of Confucian self-sacrifice during their public service career can be matched by greater wealth afterwards.

In contrast to the ideal of knightly frugality at the top (or Japan's 'Confucian compromise' of modest pay in office and lucrative positions thereafter) are very different ideas about how and how much the highest-level officers of the state should be rewarded. One is the continuation (or accentuation) of colonial traditions of lavish rewards to top state officeholders, originally designed for expatriate governors and racially exclusive colonial civil services. Another is a more egalitarian strain of thinking about the rewards appropriate to those in the highest offices of the state. Such ideas include the hyper-egalitarian Maoist tradition (arguably linking back to older Chinese egalitarian traditions as well as to the ideals of the 1871 Paris Commune), holding that the top-level rulers of the state should be rewarded in the same way and at the same level as ordinary people. They also include an Australasian populist version of egalitarianism that is not associated with revolutionary socialism but holds that the leaders of the state should be rewarded at a level that is not too far out of line with the position of ordinary citizens. Such traditions are part of the institutional and cognitive backdrops against which the politics of reward to top-level officials play out in the seven cases.

Third, the rewards of those in leading positions of the state are central to several recurring ideas about good governance that have particular resonance in the Pacific-Rim region. For instance, a decade or so ago (in 1993) the World Bank produced a much-quoted report on the East Asian miracle arguing that there was a clear connection between rewards at the top of the bureaucracy and economic performance. The claim was that the fine-tuning of the economy necessary to sustain high economic growth levels depended on bureaucratic competence and integrity in policy-making and implementation. Such competence and integrity, in turn, depended on selection and compensation practices. According to the World Bank, the 'High Performing Asian Economies' had followed principles for bureaucratic improvement that were 'readily applicable to any society' (World Bank 1993: 174). Among these principles was the idea that 'total compensation, including pay, perks and prestige, must be competitive with the private sector' and that 'those who make it to be top should be amply rewarded' (World Bank 1993).

In the following year, the Singapore government boldly produced a landmark White Paper, titled *Competitive Salaries for Competent and Honest Government*, that approvingly quoted the 1993 World Bank report. The document suggested that integrity and competence in government could only be achieved by paying salaries to officials those at the top of the state that were at least comparable to those of top private-sector earners. It was noticeably silent on the Japanese 'descent from heaven' tradition, but noted with disapproval some of the circuitous methods that other countries used to deal with the sensitive politics of rewards to top-level officials. (The methods it referred to included: hiding substantial elements of pay in non-transparent perks like expense accounts or paid holidays, allowing top officeholders to earn money for themselves in other ways or by simply accepting second-rate people at the top.) It argued for high visible salaries for those at the top, claiming that such an approach was 'more transparent and accountable, and more honest to the electorate' (Republic of Singapore 1994: 2). It accordingly introduced a system of salaries to top officials of the public sector based on private-sector benchmarks (described in Chapter 9 by Jon Quah) that puts top state positions in Singapore – with the notable exception of its MPs – at the top of the international league for public-sector pay.

How far such apparently unexceptionable doctrines of top public-sector pay are indeed 'readily applicable to any society' as the World Bank so confidently claimed, or even across Pacific-Rim states, are questions explored later in this book. In fact, the World Bank later heavily revised the simple assertions of its 1993 report, and the development establishment today is more sceptical about the idea of higher pay at the top as a sovereign go-anywhere remedy for cleaner and more capable government. This book shows that the relationship between rewards to top-level officials and state performance may neither be as linear nor as universal as the World Bank and the Government of Singapore were asserting in the mid-1990s.

What are rewards for high public office?

A 'reward' in its most general sense denotes anything of value to any individual that comes as a result of holding high public office.[1] As Akira Nakamura and Kosaku Dairokuno suggest in Chapter 6, it is useful to distinguish between intangible and more tangible rewards, and between formal and informal rewards.

Intangible rewards are those that have no immediate money value, such as the satisfaction of believing oneself to be working for the common good of society (as in the third epigraph from the egregious Sir Humphrey Appleby of the famous *Yes, Minister* sitcom), the pleasure of being able to exert influence, the intrinsic interest derived from involvement in high-level affairs of state among a governing elite, or less 'mentionable' elements such as the sexual allure that is often claimed to attach to those with power. Such intangible rewards are often said to go with high public office, but they are not universally valued. What counts as a 'reward' to some individuals (such as always being in the media spotlight or spending long hours locked up in political discussions) may be considered as a punishment by others. For that reason, we take the more tangible rewards of high public office as the starting point in this book – salaries, allowances and fungible in-kind benefits. But even then there are numerous cases of reward that are in some ways intangible but in other ways potentially 'fungible' either while holding office or at a later date. For example, in a media age, the 'famous factor' can be used for financial reward (as in the case of those Australian ex-Prime Ministers who have appeared in TV advertisements after leaving office) and working with the governing elite can be used to build up a network of contacts that can be put to profitable use after leaving office.

As with tangible rewards, some intangible or semi-intangible rewards are formal. Examples include the coveted lapel pin worn by members of the Japanese Diet, the various other medals, ribbons and titles high public officeholders may obtain and entitlements to wear particular clothing, as in the Chinese mandarin tradition and the white suits worn by top Thai officials today. But many rewards of high public office – both tangible and intangible – are informal, in the sense that they are not, or cannot be, laid down in law or any formal document. For instance, public respect for high public officeholders could be taken as the key informal tangible reward obtained by such people, and one that seems to have declined over the past 30 years in several of the established democracies. However, many tangible rewards can also be informal, ranging from the expectation of being able to secure a remunerative job after leaving office, through the capacity to profit from insider knowledge (for instance, in money market dealing) to outright bribes.

As the later chapters show, views about the public acceptability of such informal tangible rewards are variable, and appear heavily influenced by cultural traditions. In many – perhaps all – societies there is some distinction between what is regarded as 'honest' and 'dishonest' corruption. For example, Western notions of insider trading as a form of corruption have not traditionally been widely regarded as such in Asian countries. Also what is 'acceptable graft' at one time period may lose public favour at another point in time, as in the case of the apparently declining public acceptability of the Japanese 'descent from heaven' and 'migrant birds' practices as discussed by Akira Nakamura and Kosaku Dairokuno in Chapter 6. The convention of pursuing highly paid second careers after early retirement from the higher ranks of the civil service is not illegal (unless officials have engaged in bribery or extortion to secure lucrative post-retirement positions), but according to Nakamura and Dairokuno, such practice is increasingly being seen as a form of 'sleaze' as Japanese public attitudes change, particularly with the advent of a new generation of more independent women.

The chapters in Part II include consideration of the informal and intangible aspects of reward for high public office and how they may be changing. These aspects of reward are of crucial importance, since changes in the informal/intangible aspects of reward may lead to change in formal/tangible rewards and vice versa. However, in the next chapter we start with the more tangible and formal aspects of reward for high public office – those that take the form of salary, allowances and in-kind benefits that can be 'cashed out' in some form either during or after public office. Some of these additional forms of tangible reward are very significant, as Chapter 2 shows, but the value of in-kind or on-demand benefits is not always easy to pin down and may well vary according to individual tastes and circumstances as well as culture more broadly. For instance, being housed in a palace, plied with elaborate food and drink and driven around in a limousine is not necessarily a 'reward' for those individuals of ascetic tastes who would rather live in a cottage on simple fare and ride a bicycle. Indeed, some cases (such as Singapore or Australia) seem to be 'self-drive' cultures even for people in the highest public offices, while for many of the others it would be unthinkable for ministers, high officials or anyone of any importance to be seen driving their own car.

In spite of such conundrums, we follow as far as possible – and that is not very far – the culture-free approach of income tax inspectors, and try to put a rough cash value on a few of the more readily fungible perks and allowances of top public officeholders, as well as taking account of the way tax obligations intrude into their salary packages. We adopt this approach in Chapter 2, when we compare the formal money rewards (and some near-cash substitutes) available to the topmost bureaucrats, politicians and judges in the seven societies included in this study. Such analysis can only be pursued to a limited extent, for reasons already noted and some of the complexities and information barriers found would deter even the most determined and capable tax inspector, as we will show.

Why these cases? Seven political systems, four varieties of 'yesterday's tomorrow'

These seven Asian and Pacific-Rim cases are compared in several ways. Part II of the book juxtaposes the available quantitative data on rewards to top public office-holders in these political systems, together with available indexes of economic performance, corruption and 'good governance'. But for the purpose of eliciting the politics behind the numbers and bringing out the more intangible and informal aspects of reward for high public office, a set of more qualitative chapters is offered in Part II. As already noted, each of the political systems has been presented over the last 50 years or so as the wave of the future for the rest of the world, and together they comprise three or perhaps four main types of 'yesterday's tomorrow', namely the world's largest remaining formally Communist state, two antipodean settler-capitalist democracies with a strong egalitarian ethos, the Japanese model of capitalist democracy, which built one of the world's most successful economies in the decades after Second World War, and three rather different variants of the Asian 'little tiger' societies that achieved phenomenal economic success in the two decades up to the Asian crash of 1997 – the Singaporean 'administrative state', Hong Kong as the inspiration for Reaganite 'supply side' economics in the 1980s and South Korea, where dramatic industrial and urban development under authoritarian regimes that fostered the interests of big-business *chaebols* gave way to an era of democratization from the later 1980s.

Yesterday's communist tomorrow: China

China is an important case in this study for at least two reasons. One is that it is the world's most important remaining communist state, still officially committed to the Leninist doctrine mentioned at the outset that even the top members of the state hierarchy should earn little more than the average worker [though as John Burns shows in this volume (Chapter 3), the practice departed sharply from that official doctrine in the 1950s]. Second, it is a major specimen of a group of developing countries that rate fairly low in world competitiveness rankings and high in Political and Economic Risk Consultancy and Transparency International rankings for corruption levels (even though, as John Burns notes in Chapter 3, there are severe formal penalties for major corruption). In China, as in several other Asian developing countries like Thailand and Indonesia, the base salaries that go to top public officeholders and bureaucrats appear tiny by comparison with the other cases in our set, as noted at the outset. But the comparatively low salaries earned by top public officeholders in China are the tip of a rewards iceberg that is largely below the surface, with a high proportion of total compensation coming from other, less visible, sources. Indeed, China seems to be a country of a type common in Asia and elsewhere in the world, where high public office is valued not so much for the formal salary as for the other earning opportunities it provides for officeholders and their families. Moreover, top leaders' formal salaries are insignificant in China compared to the semi-submerged allowances and in-kind benefits available to those individuals and their families.

Australasian settler-capitalist democracy

Australia and New Zealand are cases of antipodean settler-capitalist societies that have often been considered as models of democratic innovation and social reform for the rest of the world, especially the United Kingdom. New Zealand was among the first to open the votes to women and adopted a comprehensive welfare state earlier than most other countries. Likewise, Australia was the first major case of the Westminster systems to formalize that style of democracy in a written constitution. Both countries have long achieved first-world status in economic development, though their economic position was widely seen as having become much more precarious in the 1980s and they did not match the rates of growth achieved by Japan and the Asian 'little tigers' at that time. Both countries tend to figure in the second quarter of the 'world competitiveness scoreboard' compiled by International Institute for Management Development (IMD) and like Singapore and Hong Kong they rate low on international ratings for the extent of corruption, making them critical cases for the idea considered earlier that high salaries are the way to keep corruption low.

Both countries are governed under variants of the Westminster Model (and arguably have longer traditions of thoroughgoing democracy than the United Kingdom from which their state structures derive) but they differ substantially in size and in the details of their government systems. Australia, with nearly six times New Zealand's population, is a federal state whose politics is shaped by an upper legislative house not normally controlled by the party in government, while New Zealand is a unitary state with a unicameral legislature. Though they share a British administrative inheritance with Singapore and Hong Kong, these Australasian cases recruited their bureaucrats from the local population and hence have no tradition of lavishly paid colonial nabobs. Indeed, what may differentiate these two cases from many other versions of the Westminster tradition is the anti-elitism of their politics. As Martin Painter and Robert Gregory argue in this volume (Chapters 4 and 5), egalitarianism is strongly entrenched in the popular culture of both countries. This cultural trait is represented by public scepticism about elites in general (with the much-discussed antagonism to 'tall poppies'), and about political elites in particular, though they traditionally rated much higher than Japan on public responses to questionnaires about trust and confidence in government. Nevertheless, in such conditions, public opinion might be expected to be hostile to the Singapore-government doctrine that political and administrative elites need to be generously paid to ensure honest and competent government. This generalized scepticism about the public sector also means that any indirect benefits for public employees are likely to be considered illegitimate – or as 'rorts' in the Australian colloquialism (meaning petty corruption or abuse of office) used by Martin Painter in his account of the Australian top rewards 'game' in Chapter 4.

In the 1980s and 1990s, these two countries, and especially New Zealand, again became models for the rest of the world, in the eyes of some who saw managerialism as the future for public bureaucracies. Both countries vigorously adopted doctrines of the so-called 'new public management' from the 1980s. While the much-discussed merits and shortcomings of managerial approaches to public administration are not the central concern in this volume, we shall see later that the rhetoric of managerialism in both cases was used to support an 'escape route' for senior bureaucrats from being linked with politicians over salary and rewards (see Christensen 1994). Managerialist ideology presses toward differential, and substantial, rewards for managers in the public sector, a tendency that runs counter to the populist and egalitarian hostility towards bureaucratic 'fat cats' in these counties.

The Japanese model: machine politics and 'Confucian capitalism'

Japan's 'economic miracle' in the decades after Second World War put the country into the top league of first-world affluence and sent the rest of the world scurrying to learn lessons from Japan, including its organizational practices (in some cases reimporting the very Total Quality Management practices that American engineers established in post-Second World War Japan) and its methods of orchestrating industrial development as a 'developmental state' through the once-legendary industry ministry (MITI). Japan is our important case of a large affluent democracy, and has affected many of the other cases in our set, including Korea, which was a Japanese colony until 1945, and Singapore, which strove to imitate various Japanese public policies in the 1980s. Japan traditionally combined a distinctive style of machine politics ('money politics') with a key role for the civil service in economic development and a special style of public administration that reflected various international borrowings before and after Second World War but also important indigenous traits.

As already noted, 'good governance' ideas in Japan were often linked to the Confucian tradition, with an ideal of government by ascetic knightly 'generalists'. Patrimonial and group ties are conventionally argued to be relatively strong in Japanese society, compared to other systems, and the country rates higher than the antipodean cases or Hong Kong and Singapore on international estimates of the incidence of corruption. Further, as already noted, one of the traditional ways that the civil service has adapted to the Confucian or *samurai* ideal has been by means of the 'descent from heaven' by which senior bureaucrats move to more remunerative positions in their 50s. As we shall show in the next chapter, although Japan is often claimed to be 'hierarchist' in its cultural traits,[1] the published pay of its top-level leaders is surprisingly modest in comparative perspective.

Variants of Asian 'little tiger' newly industrialized countries: South Korea, Hong Kong and Singapore

The fourth category of cases consists of three Asian 'little tiger' economies that were widely heralded as the wave of the future in the 1980s and 1990s as they propelled themselves into first-world affluence within a generation. These countries are all instances of the state as an active player in mobilizing resources (Johnson 1982; Wade 1990), but there are three very different variants of that model.

One, the largest of the three, is South Korea. Korea was a Japanese colony until 1945, and it is no coincidence that Japan and South Korea have a number of common administrative traditions, including the 'descent from heaven' by senior bureaucrats, patrimonial styles of organization, a shared Confucian ideal of government by ascetic generalists and other Confucian conceptions of public management (Kim and Kim 1997: Chapter 4), and a state sector that was central to economic development in the international capitalist world. Further, South Korea followed Japan a decade or so later in becoming an international manufacturing giant in the world economy in the late twentieth century.

However, South Korea differs from Japan in at least two ways that makes it a critical case in this study. First, in spite of its dramatic development since the 1980s, its GDP per head is still substantially lower, and it ranks lower than Japan in world competitiveness rankings and substantially higher in international corruption survey scores. Indeed, it was a critical case for the World Bank's 1993 argument, discussed earlier, that high public-sector salaries can reduce corruption. Yet, as Pan-Suk Kim shows in Chapter 7, rewards for top-level officeholders were not a central concern in Korea's substantial anti-corruption drive after 1993, in spite of the World Bank's recommendation. Second, while Japan democratized after Second World War, South Korea's political history was more varied, with a relatively liberal political regime during the 1960s succeeded by authoritarian government up to 1987 (with a brief return to a more liberal position in 1980). It, thus, offers an opportunity to assess the effects of democratization on rewards for high public office.

Our other two 'little tiger' cases are those of Hong Kong and Singapore, the two richest trading cities of Asia. These two systems have several features in common. They are both geographically small but densely populated cities, and could loosely be considered as city-states, though Hong Kong has never been an autonomous state. They also share a common inheritance from the British imperial tradition, having been ruled by generously paid and racially exclusive expatriate bureaucracies during their colonial period, and that common inheritance can be seen in many aspects of their administrative systems. Further, these two societies have developed as major business centres in Asia, and in both cases have moved through an industrial phase to 'post-industrial' structures dominated by banking, trade and commerce rather than traditional manufacturing. They share the property of being rated low on corruption ratings and high on competitiveness ratings by international business institutions (though Hong Kong showed some movement on both indicators in the most recent period) and stand out from all our other cases in the lavish scale of the published salaries available to their top public officeholders.

Despite these similarities there are also some important differences in these two cases. Singapore, as an autonomous state, is limited only by domestic public opinion and international competitiveness considerations in deciding how much (and how) to reward its top public officeholders. Hong Kong, as a special administrative region of China since the end of British colonial rule in 1997, is formally autonomous under the Basic Law one-country/two-systems regime, but subject, in practice, to influence from Beijing over a range of political issues that are considered sensitive. The two systems also have different systems of welfare state provision, with Singapore using a common savings and retirement fund for all employees, including top public officeholders, but Hong Kong having a segmented system of retirement pension arrangements (undergoing substantial change at the time of writing, as Grace Lee explains in Chapter 8). Further, while both are largely Chinese cities, the two cases are different in ethnic composition. Hong Kong is overwhelmingly Cantonese while Singapore traditionally comprised several Chinese language groups as well a substantial and politically significant Malay minority (and to a lesser extent Tamils), meaning that it must consider who receives what types of rewards from office in a way that does not apply to Hong Kong.

Analysing the causes and consequences of different rewards for high public office in Asian and Pacific-Rim states

As noted earlier, this study of rewards for high public office across seven Asian and Pacific-Rim cases can help to throw light on the causes and consequences of different reward patterns. Chapter 2 shows that rewards to top-level officeholders vary both in their level and in their shape or structure, so what needs to be explained is why the 'icebergs' are the size they are (relative to the income level of the society), why lifetime earnings patterns vary and the relative amount of the pay 'iceberg' that is under water relative to the visible tip. For analysing the consequences (if any) of reward patterns to top-level officials, what needs to be explored are links between corruption, democracy, government performance and reward levels and structures.

This book suggests at least three interrelated propositions about the causes and consequences of different levels and structures of reward for high public office. First, the level and structure of rewards at the top seem to be better explained as a product of politics and history than as a simple function of economic development or performance. Second, as Alexis de Tocqueville suggested long ago in his *Democracy in America*, democracy and democratisation seems to make a difference to patterns of rewards to top-level officials, but in these Asian and Pacific-Rim cases this effect does not invariably seem to operate as Tocqueville expected. Third, in spite of the passionate conviction with which the neo-Benthamite arguments of the 1993 World Bank report and the Singapore government have been advanced – that high rewards offset and deter corruption – the seven cases in this study suggest there is no clear relationship between high rewards and corruption.

Causes of different patterns of reward

This book argues that politics (in a broad sense) shapes the rewards of those at the top of the state at least as much as economic conditions. As will be shown in Chapter 2, rewards to top-level officials are not a simple function of GDP per head. Nor can orthodox wage-theory explanations readily fit the observed patterns. For example, in general discussions of public-sector pay levels, pay is often seen as reflecting a risk–reward tradeoff, with the greater security of working in the public sector (relative to the private sector) often said partly to compensate for lower public-sector pay levels. When greater risk is introduced into top public-sector work – for instance with the abolition of permanent tenure for department heads in Australia and New Zealand in the 1980s – that risk is typically claimed to justify substantially higher rewards. But it is hard to argue that risk–reward factors wholly account for top public-sector pay levels, particularly across countries and types of office. For instance, the difference between the salary of the Singapore Prime Minister and his Australian counterpart can hardly be convincingly explained on the grounds that the Singapore leader's job is more risky, given the People's Action Party's iron grip on political power for over 40 years. Judges are often more secure than top bureaucrats or politicians, but that greater security is rarely reflected in substantially lower pay. And when politicians seek to transfer more political risk to bureaucrats (as in the New Zealand case after its 1980s public-service reforms) their own salaries are seldom reduced to reflect the new distribution of risk between politicians and bureaucrats. We can conclude that economic conditions form a background to the rewards game, but politics heavily shapes how those in the topmost offices of the state are rewarded.

There are several other possible analytical angles of vision on top public-sector rewards. From the viewpoint of a rather simple view of culture, for instance, there might be arguments of a distinctively 'Asian way' of running government. The stereotype of such an Asian way might be might be thought to include a Confucian respect for rank and age, and with that the use of seniority in defining rewards, as in the case of Korea. This Asian stereotype might also be thought to manifest itself in a devotion to family, and with that some nepotism in assigning positions and rewards, or at least the clientelism that characterizes several of these systems. As we will see later, however, such simple cultural stereotypes do not stand up well to empirical examination across this set of cases.

Another angle of vision sometimes claimed to be an alternative to a 'rational' view of politics, historical institutionalism (Steinmo *et al.* 1991) could also be invoked to explain patterns of rewards to top-level officials. This approach to political phenomena commonly assumes that once a policy or institutional pattern is path dependent it will tend to persist (through patterns of 'path dependency' and 'punctuated equilibrium'), at least until some significant political force produces a non-linear change. It is doubtful whether such an approach really contradicts the rational-choice approach (since few exponents of the latter approach are really so blinkered as to deny that historical points of departure affects the type of game that rational players must engage in) and it tends to be indeterminate as an explanation insofar as it argues that historical patterns are all-important up to the point of punctuated equilibrium where seismic changes occur. As we shall show later in this book, different historical patterns are certainly associated with different levels and types of reward to top-level officials, but those historical traditions often go together with income-maximizing strategies by the players, and political pressures may well override them at critical points, such as the combination of regime change and severe fiscal change affecting Hong Kong after its transfer from British to Chinese rule in 1997.

From a rational-choice perspective, it is almost axiomatic to understand reward outcomes as the product of lifetime income-maximizing strategies pursued by top state officeholders in the face of various constraints, including institutional rules that are costly to change and moves made by rivals or opponents. However, such an approach risks being a tautology or truism unless the ecology of, or constraints on, the 'rewards game' can be specified in such a way that explains the observed variety in the level and structure of rewards across the cases examined here.

In earlier work (Hood and Peters 1994: 9), we suggested that rewards for high public officeholders might be viewed in soft game-theory terms as a product of strategic interactions – between state leaders and citizens on the one hand, and between various political or bureaucratic actors on the other. The assumption was that state leaders would prefer greater rather than lesser rewards for themselves, while citizens (who have to pay for those rewards) would have the opposite preferences, although citizens form a large diffuse group who individually have less at stake over the rewards outcome than the smaller group of actual or potential high public officials. (Both sides might vary in their attitudes and beliefs as well. For example, if citizens are fatalistic they may have no expectation that their rulers will be open about their rewards. If they are hierarchists their respect for those rulers may be positively linked to the visible trappings of office, but egalitarians will have the opposite pattern of preferences.) Nevertheless, at an orthodox and broad-brush level of analysis, one would expect the degree of effective party or elite competition to be the key restraining factor on high public officials' rewards, since citizens' preferences for lower rewards for their leaders can ordinarily be realized only through such competition.

The active players in the rewards 'game' for top public officeholders include politicians, bureaucrats, judges and representatives of lower-level employees. The more these groups can form an effective 'cartel' of politico-bureaucratic producers against citizen 'consumers' of government, the higher their rewards are likely to be. But if citizen preferences for restraining top public-sector pay are strong, individual actors may gain payoffs from resisting higher rewards for themselves or other high public officeholders. For example, politicians may choose to be 'tough' rather than 'tender' on top bureaucratic salaries to appeal to voters in general or organized labour in particular (as part of more general attempts to keep wages in check). Politicians, judges and bureaucrats may work collectively, by agreeing to linkages among their rewards, or follow separate approaches to reward. They may all seek to institutionalize 'automatic' systems for increasing rewards, linked to pay in the private sector, as in the case of Singapore's famous 'benchmark' system. Politicians themselves may function as a group, or compete for lowering of their rewards to please citizens or voters. Hence, one can conceive the level of base salaries of top public officeholders as the result of a precarious co-operation game whose outcome is likely to be significantly affected by the strength and organization of organized labour and the extent to which electoral rules encourage party competition.

This analysis is broadly compatible with the early nineteenth century ideas of Tocqueville (1946: 143–4), based on his classic observations of the early development of the United States against the European countries of that time. Tocqueville's argument was that democratization tended to produce pressures to pay relatively low salaries to those in the topmost positions in the state. The presumption is that 'the politics of envy' tends to bring about such a result in democracies and one of the ironic and unintended implications of such democratic parsimony over state rewards to top-level officials is that only millionaires or criminals may be able to afford to fill such offices. If the Tocquevillian presumption is correct, it implies that democratization may be expected to have a depressing effect on base salaries of high public officeholders, and may also increase the pressures to increase the less visible parts of the high-rewards 'iceberg'.[3] It may suggest multiple causes for high base-to-tip ratios of the high-rewards 'iceberg' among different states, since we can observe low basic salary levels relative to GDP levels in different types of state.

A similar type of rational-actor reasoning can be used to explain the *shape* of high public-sector rewards – the amount of the pay 'iceberg' that is below the surface – as opposed to the size of base salary. Again, we have advanced this argument in previous work, and Table 1.1 presents a modified version of this approach. The assumption is that top public officeholders can choose to be open or devious over their reward patterns, with 'open' denoting a pay 'iceberg' that is largely above the surface and 'devious' a pay iceberg that is largely under water. Citizens for their part can choose to be cynical or respectful of their leaders. If both parties are viewed as self-interested in conventional rational-choice terms, citizens might prefer leaders to be open and leaders might prefer citizens to be respectful, according them high legitimacy. In such a structure, one can imagine circumstances in which state leaders' rewards are visible and citizens are respectful, in contrast to circumstances where citizens are disrespectful and state leaders' rewards are invisible, or both. Such a 'game' can be considered as a variant of the orthodox Prisoner's Dilemma, with a potentially tragic dynamic, in that leaders might be expected to seek to increase their rewards by putting more of the rewards 'iceberg' below the water, moving from cell (1) to cell (2) or from cell (3) to cell (4). But if top state officeholders move from cell (1) to cell (2) to increase the total size of the rewards 'iceberg', citizens may respond by becoming less respectful, moving the 'game' into cell (4). Similarly, if citizens are disrespectful even when top leaders' rewards are visible, the latter may conclude they have nothing to lose by moving from cell (3) to cell (4) by pursuing a more devious strategy. Such an analysis would suggest that popular respect and trust in regimes might be expected to link to the openness with which leaders reward themselves.

Such an analysis may seem abstract, but it can form a useful starting point for understanding the 'rewards game' and the different ways it plays out in different contexts, as shall be see in later chapters. For example, Martin Painter suggests in Chapter 4 that competitive pressures within the Australian political system served

Table 1.1 The politics of rewards to top-level officials – interaction between citizens and state leaders

		Top public officeholders	
	Strategy	'Open' (Rewards iceberg largely above water)	'Devious' (Rewards iceberg largely below water)
Citizens	Respectful	(1) Rewards: visible Legitimacy: high	(2) Rewards: invisible Legitimacy: high
	Disrespectful	(3) Rewards: visible Legitimacy: low	(4) Rewards: invisible Legitimacy: low

to reinforce citizen preferences for keeping top public officeholders' rewards down, while top bureaucrats sought to raise their rewards by adopting managerial strategies instead of a traditional 'grand cartel' among top-level officeholders. Robert Gregory argues in Chapter 5 that New Zealand's bureaucrats are moving from cell (1) to cell (4) as a result of the rewards game they played during the era of managerial reform. However, any such approach can only be a heuristic and the key challenge is to work out how the reward-maximizing 'game' plays out in different historical and political conditions, to identify what exactly the actors seek to maximize – the nature of their preferences – and against what historical and institutional backdrop. This issue will be discussed in Chapter 10 after observing some of the nuances in Part II of the book.

Consequences of different patterns of reward

Turning from causes to consequences of reward patterns to top public office-holders, this study suggests some qualifications to the conventional wisdom that the level of rewards for high public office will be reflected in economic growth and performance. The ideas of the World Bank in its 1993 report and of the Singapore government as discussed earlier [echoing though in neither case quoting Jeremy Bentham's (1825) doctrine 'By emoluments exclude corruption'] imply that rewards to top public officeholders will be closely linked to corruption levels and the quality of state leadership. Corruption levels are in turn commonly held to be related to economic performance because they affect the levels of transaction costs in the economy. Transaction costs are said to be related to overall economic competitiveness against competing states because they affect the transparency of business costs. Also, levels of competence of state leaders are held to relate to economic growth and development because they affect the extent to which economies can be regulated or fine-tuned for maximum performance.

The idea that the rewards of top-level leaders is linked to a country's economic performance is a state-level equivalent of the 'immodest theory' that the pay of business leaders will be reflected in the profitability or growth of the firms they direct. This theory has proved hard to sustain in practice for the corporate world, following Broom and Cushing's (1977) early analysis (and later work for New Zealand, noted by Robert Gregory in Chapter 5); but its state-level equivalent is an idea widely held both at the level of 'tacit theory' and in explicit formulations like those of the World Bank in its 1993 report on the East Asian miracle. This idea is laid out diagrammatically in Figure 1.1. If rewards for high public office are as important for economic performance as the conventional argument suggests, we ought to be able to find evidence of a clear link, in contrast to Broom and Cushing's findings for corporate rewards to top-level officials.

In fact, we find no clear evidence for the link suggested by this beguiling orthodoxy, as shall be shown in Chapter 2. A 'null hypothesis' that there is no discernable relationship between levels or structures of rewards to top-level officials and economic performance seems more consistent with our observations for some aspects of economic performance, though the ideas put forward are better supported by data on economic competitiveness (as compiled by IMD 2001). Several

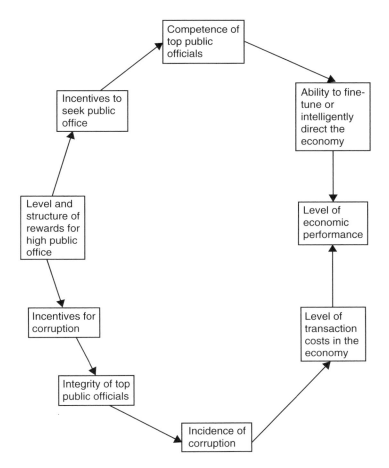

Figure 1.1 Rewards for high public office and economic performance: the 'high pay' orthodoxy.

of the links in the chain of argument depicted in Figure 1.1 appear problematic. For instance, high levels of corruption as ordinarily conceived do not necessarily seem to preclude high levels of economic growth, at least from a low base, as the cases of contemporary China and South Korea show. On the other hand, low levels of rewards to high state officials also do not necessarily seem to lead to high corruption, as the cases of Australia and New Zealand show. Indeed, Robert Gregory argues in this volume (Chapter 5) that sharp increases in top public-service pay in the Australasian countries have helped to launch a 'culture of greed', which strengthens rather than weakens tendencies to corruption.

The plan of the book

This chapter has introduced the cases and the analytic issues at stake in the comparative examination of high public officeholders' rewards in selected Asian and

Pacific-Rim societies. It is followed by a chapter that puts together the available data for all seven cases in the set to explore systematically the propositions about the causes and consequences of state rewards for top-level officials that have been discussed here. Part II of the book consists of chapters on each of the seven societies included in the analysis, discussing the politics behind the numbers that are set out in Part II in the light of the analytic themes that have been introduced in this chapter.

For instance, John Burns shows how successful income-maximizing strategies pursued by China's leaders in the 1950s were followed by an era of sharply reduced official salaries at the top as the constraints on the income-maximizing strategy altered. Martin Painter shows how Australian politicians' visible rewards are restrained by party competition in the face of citizen preferences for politician pay restraint and historically powerful labour unions, while top bureaucrats have tried to escape from being linked to the politicians' fate by casting themselves as a new managerial class whose rewards are to be determined in a 'business-like' way. Robert Gregory offers a similar analysis of the New Zealand case, but as noted earlier he adds the argument that substantially higher pay for bureaucrats may have unintentionally added to corruption, albeit at a low level, rather than the reverse. Akira Nakamura and Kosaku Dairokuno show how Japan's top bureaucrats have developed lifetime earning strategies that combine generous post-retirement rewards with public expectations of relatively frugal *samurai* behaviour by the bulk of bureaucrats while they are in office. Pan Suk Kim shows how a variety of forces, including democratization, reshaped South Korea's top public reward pattern from its traditional emphasis (deriving in part from Japanese colonial rule) on a high ratio of allowances to basic pay and on attracting the best and brightest to public service by the mandarin prestige rather than high salaries that went with high public office. He also shows how, in sharp contrast to many other political systems, Korean legislators achieved pay parity with ministers in the wake of democratization. Grace Lee explores the contradictory pressures of colonial inheritance and regime change allied to fiscal stress in reshaping the high rewards pattern of post-1997 Hong Kong, producing a system in which the top officeholders remain very highly paid in comparative perspective, but in ways that increasingly diverge from the colonial pattern and involve a new class of politician–bureaucrats at the top. John Quah analyses the (probably unrepeatable) political circumstances that lay behind Singapore's adoption of the highest top public officeholders' salaries in the world, and concludes from the narrative of that case that high salaries at the top are better understood as a consequence than as a cause of the dramatic reduction of corruption in Singapore after the city-state became independent in 1959.

As these chapters show, each of the seven cases in this study can be considered 'critical' for ideas of what shapes such rewards and what consequences these rewards have. In Part III of the book, comprising the concluding chapter, we return to the issues raised above, identifying the unanswered questions raised by this study and drawing out what has been learnt about the causes and consequences of rewards for high public office in Asia and the Pacific Rim and what difference they make for governance and democracy in that region.

Notes

1 The *locus classicus* is Bentham's (1825: 192) definition of reward as 'a portion of the matter of good, which in consideration of some service supposed or expected to be done, is bestowed on some one, in the intent that he may be benefited thereby'.
2 For a discusison of this cultural type and the others to be used in this chapter, see Hood (1998).
3 Our earlier study of state rewards to top-level officials mainly in Western Europe and North America (Hood and Peters 1994) concluded that the Tocquevillian presumption did seem to explain some of the observable variety in public-sector rewards, though culture and institutional arrangements were hard to disentangle.

2   Alike at the summit?

*Christopher Hood and Jostein Askim, with
John P. Burns, Kosaku Dairokuno, Robert Gregory,
Pan-Suk Kim, Grace O. M. Lee, Akira Nakamura,
Martin Painter, B. Guy Peters and Jon S. T. Quah*

> The summits ... of the various kinds of business are, like the tops of mountains, much more alike than the parts below ...
>
> (Bagehot [1867]1964: 198)

Introduction

In Chapter 1, we explained why rewards for the topmost offices in the state in Asia and the Pacific Rim deserve some attention. As we saw, rewards at the top are commonly thought to be central to 'good governance' issues (both in classical political theory and in current debates about development and public-sector reform), and they go to the heart of ideas about culture, self-interest and institutions in the working of political systems. In this chapter, we turn from general philosophy and broad scene-setting to comparative observation. We present a general overview of the reward patterns and trends for the seven political systems considered in this book, against some of the analytic issues considered in Chapter 1.

We leave it to the chapters in Part II to give a more detailed account of the institutional and cultural traditions shaping top-pay politics in each political system, and also some of the finer points of how the 'top-pay game' works and who are the key players. As we explained in Chapter 1, the political systems we examine here vary widely in the values they are commonly supposed to encompass and in their point of departure into the modern age (including settler capitalism, colonial trading ports, agrarian feudal societies, revolutionary regimes). What we aim to do in this chapter is draw an outline of the overall pattern, putting together the data collected from the seven political systems into comparable terms, expressed as far as we can in cardinal or ordinal scales. This overall analysis is necessarily limited, largely because even with patience and assiduity there are sharp limits to the sort of data that can be collected in comparable form. But it is also necessary as a starting point, because we cannot fully grasp what is distinctive or normal in each case without surveying the general background.

Surveying data of rewards to top officeholders in the seven Asian and Pacific-Rim political systems over the 20 years to 2000, this chapter shows three main things. First, we identify the range of variation that can be observed in rewards for the topmost offices of these political systems and assess how much of the observed variation can be attributed to politics and culture. Starting with base salaries, we show that rewards at the top are not simply a function of overall levels of income per head in each society, and we indicate how much these rewards diverge from what might be expected on the basis of per capita income. We also show some of the major differences that can be observed in relativities: how the rewards of those in the topmost offices of the state compare to those at the bottom, how they compare with Gross Domestic Product (GDP) per head, and how they compare with whatever is known about the rewards of top business people in the private sector.

Second, we look at the relationship between rewards at the top and some of the other factors (discussed in Chapter 1) that are commonly expected to shape or be shaped by rewards to top-level public- officeholders – particularly democracy, economic performance and corruption. Our analysis shows that the link between pay at the top and the working of the society – particularly in terms of economic performance and corruption – is far less determinate than might be expected from some of the bolder 'good governance' doctrines of a decade or so ago that we discussed in Chapter 1. The 'immodest theory' that we reviewed in Chapter 1 – that social performance is a function of how well top-level leaders are rewarded – appears to work only sometimes, when we examine data for corruption and economic growth. Rewards to top-level officials seem to be important everywhere as a key element of symbolic politics, but their connection with social performance appears to be variable, and often casual rather than causal. More modest theories seem to be needed.

Third, we use rewards to top-level officials as a 'window' into the working of political systems, to learn about their levels of transparency, egalitarianism, the relative positions of different sets of actors at the top of the state and the way the rules of the game over pay and reward to top-level officials shape the behaviour of those officeholders during and after their time in office. This analysis challenges some stereotypes, as we shall see. For instance 'Communist' China did not consistently have a more egalitarian reward system than several developed capitalist states; top bureaucrats in supposedly egalitarian Australia and New Zealand were paid more than their counterparts in supposedly hierarchist (and much richer) Japan; and those leaders who came out as most highly paid in international comparisons (notably in Hong Kong and Singapore) can look much less opulent in relative terms within their own societies than others who are further down the international pay league. We explore these issues at the end of the chapter.

Who gets what? Variations in pay of top-level officials

Base-pay comparisons

Figure 2.1 shows what a set of selected top-level state officeholders were reported to be paid in base salary in the year 2000 across the seven political systems in our

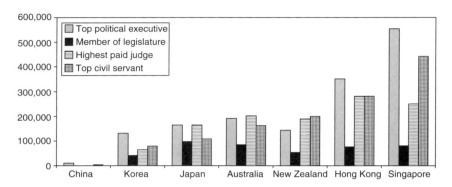

Figure 2.1 Top public-sector base salaries in seven political systems (figures for 2000, in US$ at PPP rates).

study. To make the numbers as comparable as possible, they are all expressed in US dollars, modified for variations in purchasing power parities (PPPs). PPPs are exchange rates designed to take account of differences in price levels for a given set of goods and services in different currencies (see OECD 1992: 143). So the numbers shown in Figure 2.1 are not simply what the high public officials in the seven political systems discussed here would get if they exchanged their entire annual salaries into US dollars at an ordinary bank or *bureau de change*. Instead, as we put it in an earlier study, 'we have to imagine them exchanging their salaries at a special bank, which converts those salaries not at the ordinary exchange rate, but at an exchange rate which would allow them to buy the same basket of goods and services with US dollars in the USA as they do with [the currency units] in their own countries' (Hood and Peters 1994: 29). The reason for using the apparently artificial concept of PPPs instead of simple exchange rate conversions in Figure 2.1 is to give an approximate picture of what high public officeholders can actually buy with their salaries in their own societies, and to control for exchange-rate fluctuations. But, of course, there remains an unavoidable element of distortion in using any common currency unit for comparison across diverse societies, and we shall discuss more of these complexities later on.

As we noted in Chapter 1, globalization has apparently not produced anything like a uniform 'going rate' for state leaders in the seven political systems considered here. In fact, the range of variation in base salaries is striking, as we have already noted, with the highest-paid holder of chief executive office (the Singapore Prime Minister) paid over 500 times more than the lowest-paid officeholder in our set (the Chinese President). The epigraph to this chapter is Walter Bagehot's oft-quoted remark that institutions are like mountain-tops, more alike at the top than at the bottom, but that does not seem to go for the official salaries of these mountaineers. Some of the leaders seemed, in pay terms, to be at the top of Himalayan peaks while others were barely above sea level.

Besides the marked differences among countries that Figure 2.1 reveals, there are also some notable differences in the base pay of different kinds of public office. The most obvious, and from the standpoint of democratic theory probably most important, feature is that the reward systems of all these political systems seem to be heavily executive-biased and in all cases legislators are paid less than topmost bureaucrats or the topmost political executives. Only in Japan and Korea do they even come close, and in Singapore the ordinary members of the legislature receive only an 'electoral allowance' that is intended merely as a supplement to their professional incomes from other sources (the same applies to most members of Hong Kong's legislature). Even Australia and New Zealand, often cited as early twentieth-century pioneers of democratic development, give their parliamentarians a level of base pay that is one half or less than that going to high-level bureaucrats and top executives. The executive domination of reward systems indicated by these salary patterns raises important issues about democracy in these cases to which we return in Chapter 10. Does it imply a low value placed on the representative institutions of government rather than its executive or bureaucratic parts, as part of some 'development state' mind-set? Does it reflect a (negative) auction among parties and candidates for office, bidding down their own salaries as a strategy for winning votes? Does it impoverish democratic government by encouraging the best and the brightest away from the representative roles that are often taken to be central to the effective working of democracy?

Politics and economics: pay to top officials relative to GDP per head

Such an analysis cannot be more than a limited snapshot, and it is limited in several obvious ways that we mentioned in Chapter 1. To penetrate beyond a simple league-table of basic pay, we need to pay attention to the less visible aspects of pay and reward, and we also need to give some attention to pay relativities and the effects of taxation. Further, even leaving those complexities aside, any comparative snapshot may turn out to be taken in a year that is somehow unrepresentative for some political systems in a set of cases, and cannot portray trend changes over time. Accordingly, Figure 2.2 presents the base salary data depicted earlier over two decades, comparing the selected positions over four data points (with a few missing cases).

Figure 2.2 shows three things. First, a widespread pattern of 'erosion' in pay for high public office (in constant-price terms) that has been noted for the western democracies (Peters and Hood 1995) does not apply widely to these seven countries. Indeed, even in the immediate aftermath of the 1997 Asian crisis, we see only fairly modest dips in the PPP-value of salaries of top officeholder for two of the cases in our set (Hong Kong and Singapore[1]), and the overall pattern is one more of accretion than erosion.

Second, the relativities among the seven countries alter to some degree over the two decades from 1980 to 2000. Singapore rose sharply up the league for the pay of the top political executive and top civil servants, far outstripping all the other cases, while Japan and Hong Kong slipped slightly down the league for the same

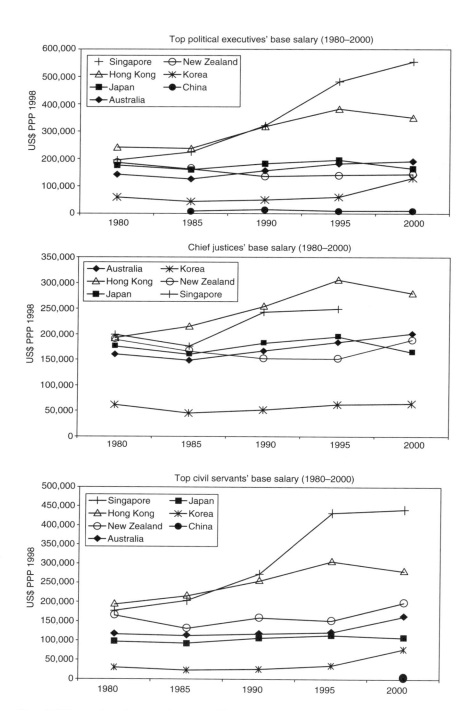

Figure 2.2 Rewards of selected top public officeholders in seven political systems, 1980–2000.

Note
Data for Singapore's Chief Justice was not published or available for 2000.

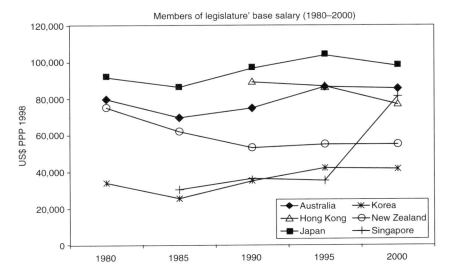

Members of legislature' base salary (1980–2000)

Figure 2.2 (Continued).

positions and Korea closed the gap at the lower end of the league. For top political executives, top bureaucrats and judges, we observe a striking increase in the range over the two decades, with the cases far more bunched in 1980 than they were 20 years later. There are no homogenizing effects of 'globalization' to be seen here.

Third, not all of the top state offices that we consider in this book show the same pattern. The big gainers tended to be found among the top political executives and bureaucrats (and judges to a lesser extent) rather than legislators, particularly since Singapore did not extend its policy of very high pay for top civil servants and Ministers to ordinary members of the legislature. As we noted earlier, legislators tend to have been poorly paid at the outset relative to other high public officeholders, and their pay has tended to fall further behind. Nevertheless, Figure 2.2 suggests that there was nothing very unusual about the year 2000 for top public-sector salaries for most of our cases, meaning that the figures shown in Figure 2.1 are no 'flash in the pan' arising from some special and unrepresentative year.

The top people's base-pay league depicted in Figures 2.1 and 2.2 can only be the beginning of our inquiry. Before we can say very much about the political and institutional significance of those rankings, we need to know at least three things. The first is how much politics matters as against economics – or, to put it in another way, how much variation is left in pay patterns when we take account of the large differences in GDP per head among our seven cases. The second question, harder to answer, is how far the 'base salaries' depicted in Figure 2.1 represent the total pay package, and consequently how much variation would be left if we analyse total rewards rather than base pay, or if we take tax deductions into account. The third question is how the rewards of top-level state leaders relate to others inside and outside the public service, since the rewards of high public office depend, in part, on what everyone else gets.

To explore the first question, Figure 2.3 presents a scatterplot of the base salary of each political system's top political executive (i.e. the Prime Minister, or President if the latter is the active chief executive) in each of our political systems against GDP levels. (Again, the figures are for the year 2000 and expressed in US dollars, adjusted for PPPs for the salary figures.)[2] What that figure shows is that differences in GDP per head account for only some of the observed variation in basic salaries and leave a substantial amount of variation (51 per cent, to be precise) to be explained. We can conclude that economics matters up to a point, but politics in a broad sense is important too, since something other than the general level of wealth in their country accounts for at least half of the variations in these top-level leaders' base pay.

Another way of presenting the same information is to look at the base salary of the seven leaders as a multiple of GDP per head, as is shown in Figure 2.4. If variations in salaries of top-level officials were simply a product of variations in national income levels, we would expect their salaries to be more or less the same multiple of GDP per head. But as Figure 2.4 shows, the highest-paid leader's base pay is more than six times higher than that of the lowest-paid leader as a multiple of GDP per head. So, if we used GDP per head as the sole predictor of what

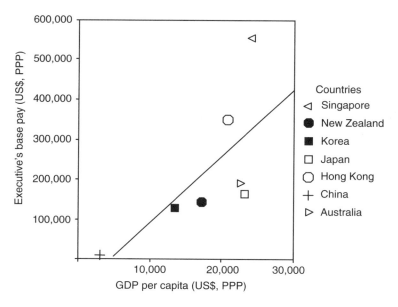

Figure 2.3 Scatterplot of top political executives' base pay against GDP per capita (figures in US$, PPP-adjusted, 2000).

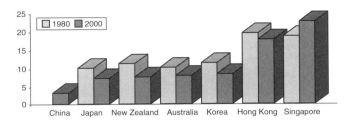

Figure 2.4 Top political executive's base pay as multiple of GDP per capita, 1980 and 2000.

top-level leaders are paid, our predictions would be inaccurate at least 50 times in a hundred, on the basis of this analysis.

If a simple GDP-based economic explanation cannot explain at least half of the variance in these rewards, there must be other factors at work. Evidently, there is a substantial 'politics' factor (taking politics in the broadest sense, which can embrace cultural differences and historical legacies) at work in shaping these variations. Indeed, the analysis of salaries of top-level officials in these cases presents an opportunity, unusual in political science, to go beyond the obvious, hackneyed and banal claim that 'politics matters' and show just how much it matters. But this still leaves open the question of what kind of 'politics' shapes what.

Iceberg tips and submerged bases: transparency and pay supplements

There could, of course, be less to the differences we have been discussing than meets the eye, for several reasons. For example, the variations shown in Figure 2.1 might simply reflect differences in the proportion of base to total reward among the various political systems in our study. Readers will recall that in Chapter 1 we used not the Bagehotian imagery of mountains for the rewards of top public officeholders, but instead that of icebergs floating in the sea, with base pay as the visible component that is above the water, and the rest as the invisible submerged component.

In some cases, most of the reward iceberg is floating on the top of the water and what you see is largely what you get. That is, published base salary forms the main part of the officeholders' rewards, supplemented by minor add-ons in the form of other allowances, information about which is readily accessible. Out of our set of cases, the New Zealand Prime Minister's rewards perhaps came closest to that pattern. Logically, the opposite extreme of reward transparency consists of a pattern in which most of the iceberg is under water. At that end of the transparency scale, the overwhelming bulk of an officeholder's reward comes from sources other than base salary, but the details of those supplements are neither published nor available. Out of our seven cases, the reward pattern of top officeholders in the People's Republic of China came closest to that pattern, but it is common in other Asian countries such as Indonesia or Thailand, as we noted in Chapter 1. In between these two extremes are cases where supplements to base salary form a substantial addition to the base, but the base is still a major part of the total reward pattern. We can further sub-divide this class of cases into those where information about the supplements are published, those where they are available to the assiduous inquirer and those where they are neither published nor available. Such a first-order analysis gives us five broad levels of reward transparency, which are briefly described and illustrated in Table 2.1.

Table 2.1 A ladder analysis of reward transparency

Transparency level	Step	Features	Cases
High	5	Published base salary as the main part of officeholders' rewards, supplemented by 'minor' add-ons ($\leq 50\%$)	NZ Prime Minister; Korean President and civil servants (2000); HK Chief Executive and civil servants; Japanese civil servants and judges
Medium high	4	Add-ons constitute major but not overwhelming part of officeholders' rewards (50–150%) but are published	Australian civil servants and judges; Singapore civil servants before 1995
Medium	3	Add-ons as above but not published – available only to assiduous and well-informed inquirers	Korean and Japanese judges
Medium low	2	Add-ons as above but neither published nor available to inquirers	Parts of New Zealand public service after 1988 and Singapore civil service from 1995; Japanese MPs
Low	1	Add-ons constitute the overwhelming part of officeholders' rewards ($\geq 150\%$) but are neither published nor available	Top-level officeholders' rewards in China

Table 2.2 itemizes some of the most obvious perks that may accrue to top officeholders, with an illustrative notional 'score' and examples drawn from the cases in our set. It should be explained that we have here excluded the sort of perks that anyone in the upper reaches of government service can expect, like free postage or free travel on business, and focused only on the sorts of perks that produce variations. The scores are intended to be illustrative, not definitive, and any such scoring exercise raises at least seven problems, none of which can be completely overcome. First is the sheer difficulty, even for pertinacious, well-connected and locally based researchers, of finding out everything that is available in many cases. The second is the difficulty of cashing up all of the supplements

Table 2.2 'Little extras make a difference': some selected additions to basic salary for top public officeholders

Field	Type of supplement	During office	For life
1 Transport (top perks score: 6)	Chauffeured limo or superior car at free disposition for officeholder and officeholder's family	Perks type: 1a Perks points: 1 Examples: all HPOS in China and HK (except legislators), Singapore President and PM only (all others self-drive)	Perks type: 1b Perks point: 3 Example: China
	Free air travel		Perks type: 1c Perks points: 3 Examples: Australian MPSs life gold pass for domestic flights
2 Housing (top perks score: 6)	Free apartment or mid-to-high quality accommodation	Perks type: 2a Perks points: 1 Examples: Japanese MPs and judges, NZ ministers	Perks type: 2b Perks points: 3 Examples: top office holders in China
	Free 'palace' (i.e. type of housing only available to the super-rich in a market economy)	Perks type: 2c Perks points: 2 Examples: Australian and NZ PM and HK Chief Executive	Perks type: 2b Perks points: 6
3 Health care (top perks score: 6)	Free top private-type health care (i.e. exclusive premium service by top professionals) for officeholder	Perks type: 3a Perks points: 1	Perks type: 3b Perks points: 3
	Free top private-type health care (as above) for officeholder and family	Perks type: 3c Perks points: 2 Examples: top HK officeholders	Perks type: 3d Perks points: 6
4 Other superannuation (top perks score: 6)	Non-contributory retirement pension or lump-sum equivalent yielding ≥60% of basic pay		Perks type: 4a Perks points: 3
	Free office services		Perks type: 4b Perks points: 3

to basic pay that top officeholders receive into a comparable form – a task that would be beyond the most resourceful tax inspector. The third is the familiar problem of interpersonal comparison of utility of the kind we discussed in Chapter 1.

The related fourth issue is how to deal with perks that are formally available but not used by some or all incumbents of a particular office – for example, many of the perks available to the Japanese Prime Minister, or the choice of Singapore's first two Prime Ministers to live in their own private houses rather than the official residence they are entitled to occupy during office (the same went for Singapore's President at the time of writing). The converse, fifth, issue is that such an analysis may miss far more important informal supplements to (or deductions from) basic pay. For example, Japanese MPs are well known for obtaining such supplements from various sources, including the monetary support that LDP members of the Diet receive from their faction leaders twice a year, while in other states legislators have to pay part of their allowances over to their parties as a 'tax'.

The sixth problem relates to the knotty issue of PPPs mentioned earlier, in that expectations and patterns of elite consumption are far from uniform. For example, the housing accommodation enjoyed by Japan's MPs is at a comfortable middle-class standard for that society, yet their apartments would be considered as cramped rabbit-hutches by those at the top in other societies (such as Australia). The same applies to car usage, for instance, as between elite self-drive cultures like Australia and Singapore and those where nobody of even moderate importance would be ever seen behind the wheel. Similarly, the value of free taxi coupons for private or public purposes is a valuable perk for elites in societies like Japan where taxis are costly, but might be considered more trivial in cases like Singapore or Hong Kong.

Seventh, the value of perks that accrue to officeholders (and their families) for life is particularly hard to assess, and belong more in the territory of actuarial science than political science. The life membership fee of membership organizations is often set at a level somewhere between 9 and 17 times the annual fee, but our more mature readers will appreciate that the value of life membership in anything falls the older we get, so the relative value of perks for life for individuals leaving office will be very different according to how long they have been in office, whether they exit in their 40s, their 60s or their 80s, and whether there are special factors affecting the life expectancy of those who have stepped down from high public office, notably assassination risks. In the face of this conundrum, Table 2.2 gives a notional treble weighting to perks for life as compared with perks while in office. This score probably errs on the high side of such a valuation, but the purpose of this exercise is to not to penetrate to the furthest reaches of actuarial science, only to gain a first indication of the relative 'perks-heaviness' of different types of public office.

Reward transparency in the terms discussed earlier is not fixed for all time, and our cases show that it can go up and down. For example, Korea seems to have moved to substantially higher transparency in 2000, when it made published base salary a much larger proportion of top officeholders' rewards than before, as explained by Pan-Suk Kim in Chapter 7. But Singapore went decisively in the opposite direction when it chose to treat civil servants' individual pay as 'confidential' in the 1990s (and New Zealand moved down a similar path, although general information about top public-service pay in New Zealand is still published). Reward transparency can also vary from one type of office to another. For example, legislators in Hong Kong, Japan and Korea drew a much larger proportion of their total reward in the form of allowances or other supplements to basic pay, than did top civil servants or chief executives in those political systems. In an attempt to take account of these variations, Table 2.3 gives an approximate score for four top public offices across the seven cases in our set both on their 'ladder rankings' in the transparency table (Table 2.1) and on their 'perks points' (Table 2.2).

This analysis is highly approximate, for all the reasons given earlier, but transparency as discussed above matters for our analysis in at least two ways. First, it gives an indication of the sort of rewards 'game' that is being played between top public officeholders and their citizens, to which we return in section on 'RHPOs as a mirror of political life?'. Second, it is important for qualifying the league-table comparisons of base pay with which we began our comparison (Figure 2.1). Given that the reward 'icebergs' appear to be of different shapes (in terms of the relative proportions of their visible, less visible and invisible components), variations in base pay as a multiple of GDP may be very different from the picture we obtain if we factor in additions to the 'base' in the form of supplements, allowances and other add-ons.

A complete picture of total earnings would involve calculating what is left after tax once all supplementary earnings, allowances and other benefits in cash and kind are added to base salary, and those elements would need to be calculated over time to take account of different patterns of lifetime earnings. We can only paint part of that picture here, though all of these elements are discussed in Part II of the book. Our conclusion, summarized in Figure 2.5 for those cases for which data about a basic set of salary supplements are available, is that the relationship between 'iceberg' tips and 'iceberg' bases is indeed variable, over time and between offices as well as between countries. But it should be stressed that the analysis for Figure 2.5 is based on readily available information about cash allowances supplementary to salary – it is not the same as the perks to high-level officials discussed in Tables 2.2 and 2.3.

To illustrate over-time variations, Figure 2.5 gives pre- and post-1999 figures for one of our cases, South Korea, to show that it was moving in the opposite direction from Japan over that period, with Korea rolling up a previous pattern of sprawling allowances into higher base pay, and Japan raising total rewards by the low-transparency route of increasing allowances rather than base pay. Variations among types of office can be seen by comparing the figures for legislators (where total pay was in several cases close to three times base pay) with those for top political executives, where only pre-1999 Korea even approached that multiple. Country variations are also substantial, with pre-1999 Korea substantially ahead of the others in the allowances league, and New Zealand at the bottom, even for legislators. There is no entry for Singapore MPs – as noted earlier, they had no salaries as such, only tax-free electoral allowances that amounted to a modest part-time salary for professionals in Singapore, so with no 'base salaries' the

Table 2.3 Reward transparency for top-level officials: overall scores

		Australia	Japan	China	Korea	New Zealand	Hong Kong	Singapore
Top political executive	Transparency level (T)	4	5	1	5	5	5	2ᵃ
	Perks points (P)	10	2	21	13	9	8	2
Topmost bureaucrat	Transparency level (T)	4	5	—	5	2	5	2
	Perks points (P)	0	4.5	—	0–1	1.4	8–12ᵇ	3
Highest judge	Transparency level (T)	4	3	—	3	4	3	2
	Perks points (P)	4	—	—	1–2	1–5	8–12	2
Member of legislature	Transparency level (T)	3	3	—	4	3	5	5
	Perks points (P)	5	4	—	1–2	3–6	0	0.5
Overall		Fairly high T and medium P	High T and fairly low P	Low T and high P	Fairly high T and variable P	Variable T and fairly low P	High T and high P except for MP/D	Low T and low P

Notes

a After 1995 (same applies to Singapore entries for topmost bureaucrat and highest judge).

b Depending on whether officeholders are on 'agreement terms' or 'pensionable terms' (the same applies to the Hong Kong entry for highest-level judges).

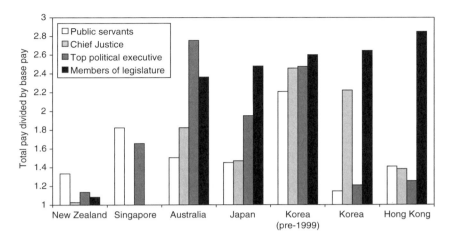

Figure 2.5 Total pay as multiple of base pay, selected public offices, 2000.

multiple is not meaningfully calculable (even readers with rudimentary mathematics will appreciate that an entry that would either have to be nil or infinity shows up the limits of numerical scoring and should be left aside as a special case).

Indeed, Figure 2.5 again brings out some distinctive features about the reward structures of legislators in these political systems. Whereas their base salaries tend to be low, the proportion of total reward that comes in the form of cash allowances tends to be higher than other top public officials. This pattern means that legislators are receiving some of the compensation they have missed elsewhere, but it also means they are receiving a substantial part of their total rewards through less transparent forms, which may in some circumstances appear 'shady' to voters, the media or the public at large. On the face of it, this pattern seems to underline the executive-centred nature of rewards to top public officials in these political systems, although as we shall see in Part II of the book, it is in many cases deliberately chosen by legislators.

Relativities and positional factors

The analysis cannot end here. Another important way of putting the earlier comparisons into perspective is to look at the relationship between rewards at the top and those of others in the society. After all, rewards can be seen in 'positional' as well as absolute terms. 'Positional goods', in Hirsch's (1977) well-known term, denote goods that are valued precisely because they are denied to others (e.g. being better-educated than the average person, or having a bigger house or automobile than your neighbours). You might be a billionaire Nobel prize winner, living in a palace and riding around in a swanky stretch limousine, but if everyone else around you has the same status and material trappings, these achievements can have no positional value. Or, as W. S. Gilbert put it more succinctly (in *Iolanthe*), 'when everyone is somebody, then no-one's anybody'.

Accordingly, from a positional perspective, what matters is not the absolute size of the pay checks going to those in the topmost offices of the state but how they rank relative to others – for example, relative to the rewards of those in different walks of life or further down the pecking order. So, rewards that appeared low in a cross-national league table might still be positionally high if those obtaining such rewards were very much better-off than others in the society. Contrariwise, rewards that look impressive in cross-national perspective may appear less so to top public officeholders if top businessmen and professionals are paid far more or if other people in government are receiving much the same. This is the problem that Jon Quah discusses for Singapore in Chapter 9: the Singaporean Prime Minister may be paid several times what the US President earns, but he is still a small fish compared to the extraordinarily highly paid top professionals and corporate chiefs within Singapore, ranking only in 63rd position of annual income-earners according to tax data. By contrast, Akira Nakamura and Kosaku Dairokuno show that those at the very top of the tree in the Japanese bureaucracy seem to compare quite favourably in the pay stakes with company presidents, especially when bureaucrats' lucrative post-retirement activity is taken into account, though the picture is quite different for middle- and low-level bureaucrats.

Following this line of analysis, there are at least two ways of looking at the positional element of top public officeholders' pay. One concerns relativities within the public sector – how the rewards of those at the top compare with those going to those at the bottom of the public services. The other concerns the relationship between the rewards of those at the top in state offices and those at the top of the private sector.

For the first element, Figure 2.6 compares 'vertical compression' within the public service for our cases (though we had difficulty in securing comparable data for all of them). Vertical compression is a concept often used in studies of reward systems in the public and private sectors. In this case, we are using the concept, to measure the spread of pay within the public sector, and in Figure 2.6 we represent it as the base pay of the topmost ranks in the civil service as a multiple of those at the bottom, for 1980, 1990 and 2000. The first chart takes the 'bottom' as the lowest-paid ranks in the civil service, and the second chart takes the 'bottom' as the entry-level grade for graduates in the public service. As can be seen, there are large variations in the relation of top pay to lower-level pay across our seven political systems. For example, Korea and Japan share a common tradition of public service pay, as mentioned in Chapter 1, but in 1990 top public office-holders in Korea were only paid about three times what entry-level graduates obtained (a substantially more egalitarian system than even that of the People's Republic of China), as against eight or nine times in Japan.

What this analysis shows is that high top-level pay in cross-national perspective does not always go together with low vertical compression (or high salary differentials within the state) or vice versa. As we saw earlier, Hong Kong's top

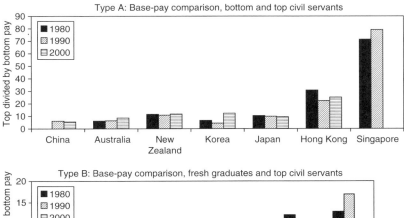

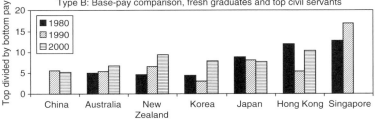

Figure 2.6 Vertical compression.

public officials are lavishly paid in the international perspective and China's leaders are very poorly paid, but the vertical compression of these two systems (taking graduate entrants as the bottom of the pay ladder) was exactly the same in 1990, with the topmost earners receiving less than six times that of the lowest. Similarly, the Australian system has a vertical compression ratio (for graduates) that is not markedly different from that of China, while the formerly egalitarian New Zealand system moved over two decades to a higher vertical compression score (i.e. top salaries as a multiple of entry-level graduate salaries) than that of Japan. At the upper end of the inequality scale, Singapore's top earners were paid 17 times what the entry-level graduates were paid (and nearly 80 times what the lowest ranks in the civil service were paid). The analysis suggests that levels of vertical compression cannot readily be explained by general factors such as 'Asian culture' or even economic system. Something much more system-specific must account for these variations.

As this analysis shows, there is more than one way of measuring vertical compression within a government service, depending on precisely what is taken to be the 'bottom' position in government (in this case, the lowest grades *simpliciter* or entry grades to the professional ranks), and the extent of the spread depends on what is chosen as the lowest rung of the ladder. Moreover, the positions of our seven cases vary from one time period to another – as can be seen, stereotypically 'egalitarian' New Zealand overtook Japan on vertical compression between 1980 and 2000 (by a process explored by Robert Gregory in Chapter 5), and Korea also overtook Japan between 1990 and 2000. But the relative positions of the cases seem to be more sensitive to time period than to which of the two measures of vertical compression is taken.

A final indication of top-level officeholders' relative position concerns not so much how much better off they are than their underlings in the public service as to how they relate to those at the top of the tree in business or the professions. It might be small consolation to Singapore's top public officeholders that they make 17 times or so what the entry-level professionals earn if top private-sector executives or professionals make far more. Such comparisons are hard to make, since systematic published data on this point do not exist for many of our cases, but Table 2.4, taken from the data presented in Part II of the book, presents some indicative comparisons of the pay relativities between top civil servants, chief executives of government-owned companies and chief executives of private companies. It is notable that Japan appeared a relatively 'low discount' country in these terms, ranking much lower than countries like Australia and New Zealand, and in Singapore there was a substantial premium (rather than discount) relative to government companies but a discount relative to top private companies. China – unsurprisingly perhaps – showed relatively low public-sector discount relative to state-owned companies, but a high discount relative to private companies.

We can conclude from this analysis that rewards to top-level officials in these seven cases are a product of politics at least as much as economics (in the sense of GDP per head). The 'iceberg tip' problem (the variable relationship between base pay and total reward) complicates the analysis, but does not remove the 'political deviation' in the relationship between rewards for high public office (RHPOs)

Table 2.4 Public-sector pay discounts: indicative figures for earnings of top executives in state-owned companies and the private business sector relative to top political executive

Base pay of top political executive compared to	Size of public-sector discount[a]			
	Low discount (20% or less)	Medium low discount (21–50%)	Medium discount (51–80%)	High discount (81% or above)
Chief executive positions in state-owned enterprises	Japan (approx. 20%), China (approx. 20%), Singapore (approx. −100%)	Australia (approx. 39%)	Hong Kong (approx. 59%), New Zealand (approx. 60%)	
Chief executive positions in private corporations	Japan (approx. parity)	Australia (approx. 36%)	Singapore (approx. 60%)	China (approx. 100%), New Zealand (approx. 91%)

Note
a Relative gap between base pay of top political executive and executives in state-owned and private-sector companies.

and GDP per head. In most cases, high pay in the international league seems to go with high vertical compression within the state structure, but it does not necessarily mean that high state officeholders are generously rewarded relative to other top professionals in the society.

Less clear, however, are the career incentives for high public officials that are provided by the various 'pay discounts' and different levels of vertical compression. On the former, there may be more at stake than a simple choice between higher earnings in the private sector and the lower but stable rewards working for the government, if top people work in both sectors over their lifetime – an issue to which we return in Chapter 10. Similarly, the effects of high vertical compression may be variable, dependent on the culture and institutional setting. In some conditions high vertical compression may serve as an incentive for hard work, in the hope of a golden future, while in others the poor odds of ever reaching the summit may encourage mobility to other careers.

Causes and consequences of reward patterns for top public officeholders: the modest appplicability of immodest theories

In Chapter 1 we discussed some of the ways that the size and shape of rewards at the top are assumed to matter for good governance, and some of the factors that are assumed to shape rewards to top-level officials. In particular, we referred to the 'immodest theory' that the rewards of top-level leaders might be linked to the performance of the societies they rule. The analogy is with the idea that business leaders' rewards are linked to the profits of the corporations they head.

Economic performance, corruption and rewards to top-level officials

As we noted in Chapter 1, 'immodest theory' has proved to be problematic in the private corporate sector, and its analogy in government is far from straightforward, because the causal mechanisms that might link reward to top-level officials to system performance are various. For example, levels of RHPOs might be associated with economic performance because they affect the quality of individuals who seek and obtain high office and thus shape state capacity for effective policy-making and implementation. We can call this the 'peanuts–monkeys effect', following the well-known (if admittedly 'species-ist') adage that if you pay peanuts you get monkeys. But it is also possible that the prospect of increases in overall economic performance being translated into higher rewards for RHPOs might work like a carrot held in front of a donkey's nose – as an incentive for top state leaders to strive for better state performance and avoid worse performance. We can call this the incentive effect, and as Jon Quah shows in Chapter 9 on Singapore, GDP performance is explicitly linked to bonuses by high state officeholders in that political system. None of the other cases in our set had the same explicit linkage, but it is possible that an implicit incentive effect of the same type might still operate. Again, if we follow the World Bank argument discussed in Chapter 1 it might be that levels of RHPOs are linked to the corruption level in the society, the corruption level affects transaction cost levels, and transaction cost levels affect economic performance. We can call this the transaction cost effect. Or, finally, top state leaders might simply 'tax' the societies they rule in such a way that improvements in economic performance will normally work through to higher RHPOs. We can call this the taxing effect.

It is hard to find a test that discriminates between these three different linkages between pay at the top and economic performance, and particularly between the taxing effect and the incentive effect. Moreover, there are obvious data limitations in such a study. In particular, such cross-national indicators of corruption as are available come mainly in the form of corruption scores or rankings compiled by international organizations such as TI and PERC that are based on the perceptions of international business people and other observers as to the degree of bribery and other forms of corruption they perceive in different societies.[3] These data are problematic both because they are relatively impressionistic and also because any ordinal scale cannot tell us anything about the size of the absolute differences between cases ranked at different points – for example, whether there is only a trivial difference in absolute corruption levels between two cases with adjacent rankings, or whether one case is 10 times more corrupt than the other. Accordingly, we supplemented such rankings by two other conventional indices of overall social corruption, namely the amount of cash in circulation (M1) relative to GDP as revealed by International Monetary Fund (IMF) financial statistics, and the OECD's estimates of the size and growth of the underground economy across its member states. But these measures too have well-known limitations, since indicators like the volume of cash in circulation relative to the size of the economy can relate to variations in level of development or cultural traits rather than corruption alone.

However, we can make a limited assessment of some of the possible effects identified earlier, on the basis of time patterns of top-level officials' pay and economic performance. For the 'peanuts–monkeys' effect to operate, high state office-holders would need to be generously rewarded (to attract the necessary skills and competencies) *before* economic performance could be expected to result. For the incentive effect (and arguably also the taxing effect) to operate, reward levels at the top could be expected to follow economic performance – both in good times and in bad. For the transaction cost effect to operate, reward levels at the top would need to be linked to corruption levels, and corruption levels in turn to economic performance.

Table 2.5 summarizes what could be expected from each of these effects, and gives an account of what we can observe on the basis of our seven cases. What we observe is that the relationship between GDP growth rates and the growth of top-level officials' pay (expressed in base salaries) is quite variable, and even the simplest hypothesis about the relationship between the two elements (that rewards to top-level officials rise when per capita GDP rises and falls when GDP falls) applies to only about two-thirds of our observations. The correspondence between the slopes of the two variables (i.e. how closely related is the extent of

Table 2.5 Three possible linkages between top public pay and economic performance

Linkage	Description	Expected	Observed
Peanuts-monkeys	RHPOs levels are closely related to quality of leadership, which is in turn a casual factor in economic performance	RHPOs levels at t_0 are linked to economic performance (competitivenes and GDP growth) at t_1	Weak rank-order correspondence between (1980–90) top-political executive pay and GDP growth, 1990–2000 (best fit: Australia)
Incentive effect (also taxing effect)	RHPOs levels are linked to economic performance because economic performance feeds into RHPOs levels both positively and negatively	RHPOs levels at t_1 are linked to economic performance at t_0 (positively and negatively, i.e. RHPOs rise when GDP rises and fall when GDP falls)	Weak rank-order correspondence between GDP growth (1980–90 and 1980–2000) and top-political executive pay (best fits: NZ and HK)
Transaction cost effect	Formal RHPOs are linked to economic performance because they are linked to corruption levels, which in turn affect economic performance through their effect on transaction costs	RHPOs levels at t_0 are linked to rankings of perceived corruption levels at t_1, which are in turn linked to economic performance at t_1	Weak rank-order correspondence (i) between (1980–90) top-political executive pay and scores on the aggregate of three corruption indices in 2000 (best fits: Korea and China) and (ii) between 2000 corruption scores and GDP growth 1990–2000 (best fits: Singapore and HK)

change in rewards to top-level officials to change in per capita GDP) is even weaker. Indeed, there is actually a (weak) negative correlation between political executive base pay and GDP growth in our seven political systems over the period 1990–2000.

We get a rather different picture, and one more in line with the 'Singapore theory' of top public pay, when we turn from GDP growth to indicators of international competitiveness as compiled by IMD. Indeed, if we relate chief political executive base pay in our seven political systems to (inverse) international competitiveness scores in 2001, we can observe a high R^2 relationship (0.77 in fact), as shown in the scatterplot of those two items in Figure 2.7. But even this relationship is evidently not a linear one. Readers may recall the idea of 'fantasy football', which can mean a number of things, one of which is the assessment of sport team performance, not according to absolute goal scores but according to the difference between observed goal scores and what would be expected on the theory that the

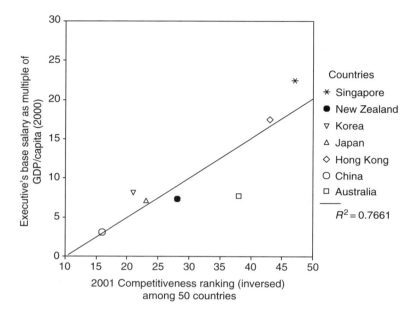

Figure 2.7 Competitiveness, pay of top political executive and fantasy football.

performance of each team is linearly related to the average salaries of its players. In the same way, we can observe from Figure 2.1 that there is substantial scope for aficionados of 'fantasy football' of that type even in the relationship of top public pay to economic competitiveness, since Singapore along with Korea did badly while Australia in particular did well. (And if we do a similar fantasy football analysis for economic growth Singapore is well down the league and China is at the top.)

In this analysis, it would seem that the 'immodest theory' of the consequences of rewards to top-level officials has a rather modest range of application for these cases. It does best for ratings of international economic competitiveness, though even there it leaves plenty of scope for 'fantasy football' analysis. For a range of measures of corruption, the null hypothesis of no association with public rewards of top-level officials seems most plausible. And when it comes to GDP growth, the most commonly used conventional measure of economic performance, there is actually a weak negative association with the base pay of the top-level chief executive for these cases.

Democracy, democratization and rewards to top-level officials

Economic performance and corruption are the items most commonly considered as possible consequences of the type and level of rewards received by those in top state positions. But these rewards might also be linked to political and institutional performance. In particular, corruption is often assumed to affect the performance of political systems, through the way that it can undermine free elections and the rule of law. However, we have found no close correspondence between any of the three conventional corruption indicators (level of cash transactions, OECD shadow economy estimates and TI corruption perception rankings) and the base pay of top-level leaders across our seven political systems, however we do the analysis (i.e. whether we take absolute levels of pay or pay as a multiple of GDP and whatever corruption indicator we take). The assumptions that we discussed in Chapter 1 about the link between corruption and top-level pay cannot easily be justified on the basis of these cases. Raising salaries at the top is probably less likely to deter corruption in high public office (particularly that associated with electoral campaign financing) than are salary increases at the bottom to reduce petty corruption. And when a country is starting from a low base, as in the case of China, a high economic growth rate may be achievable even with relatively high corruption and low bureaucratic capability. Nevertheless, irrespective of any putative link between corruption levels and formal rewards at the top of the state, it is still possible that the leadership qualities these rewards produce might affect the quality of governance.

However, as with the 'taxing effect' we discussed earlier in the context of links between RHPOs and economic performance, the causal direction of any link between the level and type of RHPOs and the nature of the political system is difficult to establish, and can only be assessed by examining change over time. As we noted in Chapter 1, Alexis de Tocqueville posited a relationship between the nature of the political system and rewards to top-level officials in claiming that democracies tend to reward their top leaders more parsimoniously than autocratic states. The implied causal mechanism underlying such an effect is that effective enfranchisement gives the mass of voters (or more strictly, the median voter) the power to punish politicians over the rewards of top-level state office-holders, and that such voters will tend to be unsympathetic to the idea that those who rule them should be paid much more than the ordinary person. As Martin Painter and Robert Gregory show in Chapters 4 and 5, this doctrine was traditionally strongly entrenched in the Australasian settler capitalist countries.

In principle, the cases in our set offer an opportunity to test this 'Tocqueville effect', since they score rather differently on political indicators such as the well-known (if much-debated) 'freedom index' of the world's regimes produced by the international organization Freedom House, and also include numerous cases of democratization and transitions from colonial rule. We can test for the presence of a 'Tocqueville effect' in at least two ways. Perhaps the simplest is to see if there is any association, simple or lagged, between RHPO levels and the scores of our political systems in the Freedom House annual surveys of political rights and civil liberties. The analysis reveals that all of the four cases in our set that were classed as 'free' in the Freedom House index (scores 1 or 2) paid their top political executives a base salary of between 10 and 15 times GDP per capita. The two cases with markedly lower 'freedom' rankings on that index (China and Singapore) fell far outside that range (at 22 and 3, respectively, for 2000) but the Chinese case would fit Tocquevillian expectations if a high estimate was placed on the value of the added perks relative to GDP that form the part of the reward 'iceberg' that is under water.

A second way of examining the Tocqueville effect, better geared to the identification of causal effects, is to look at major regime transitions among the cases in our set and examine the associated changes in RHPOs. Table 2.6 indicates some

Table 2.6 Regime transitions and Tocquevillian effects

Type of case	Specific instance	Expected 'Tocquevillian' effect	Observed
Transition from authoritarian rule	Korea	Depression of top salary levels from high base	Little observable change immediately after the move to a liberal regime after 1987, and in the longer run RHPOs rose rather than fell
Transition from colonial rule	Singapore	Depression of top salary levels from high base	One-off major cuts in early independence period, but superseded by major RHPOs raises 20 years later
	Hong Kong	Depression of top salary levels from high base	Little change, with very minor depression, and later creation of higher-paid elite stratum in the executive
Incremental democratization?	Japan	Depression of top salary levels from (relatively) lower base	Observed changes weakly consistent with hypothesis (RHPOs stagnant or falling except for MPs' pay)
	Australia	Depression of top salary levels from (relatively) lower base	Bifurcation of top pay patterns, with major increases for bureaucrats and relatively depressed/flat reward levels for politicians
	New Zealand	Depression of top salary levels from (relatively) lower base	

of the major cases in our set and the associated observations of what happened to top public officeholders' rewards.

In the light of this analysis, we conclude that if Alexis de Tocqueville were to be spirited back to life to observe these cases, he would need to modify his hypothesis a little to take account of some of the dynamics. He would need to take account of the fact that there are different kinds of autocracies and different kinds of democracies, and that the effect of democracy may not be fixed for all time, given strategic action by the players. The case of China shows that visible rewards at the top may be small relative to GDP in some regimes that score very low on liberal democracy indices of the type used in the Freedom House surveys (though if invisible rewards are added in, it may still fit the Tocqueville hypothesis, as John Burns suggests in Chapter 3). The Korean case shows that a transition from authoritarian rule to democracy does not necessarily bring about a marked reduction in the pay of top officeholders and can even have the opposite effect. Indeed, legislative salaries, in particular, rose substantially in Korea (on what was considered to be a 'point of principle' in establishing parity between legislators and ministers after the end of authoritarian rule), indicating that democratization in that case involved raising rather than bidding down the rewards of the legislators. The case of Singapore shows that a transition from colonial rule to self-government need not involve a once-for-all reduction of RHPOs, particularly if the transition is to a form of democracy that is limited on some of the dimensions considered in the Freedom House index. And the case of New Zealand (and to a lesser extent Australia) shows that in some conditions top bureaucrats can decisively beat the 'Tocqueville effect' in a democracy if they can find a way to break any linkage between their pay and that of the elected politicians. We will consider what modifications a modern Tocqueville might need to make to his hypothesis in the final Chapter 10.

RHPOs as a mirror of political life?

Napoleon Bonaparte once said that the budget is the mirror of political life (because it exposes where the real power to command scarce resources lies). But the same could be said of rewards for high public office, because they expose the relative positions of the rulers and the ruled and the style of governance, particularly when we start to examine the base as well as the tip of the rewards iceberg.

As we have seen, rewards to top-level officials offer one way of assessing stereotypical pictures of countries and political systems. The bureaucratic rulers of the supposedly egalitarian Australiasian states were substantially better paid relative to GDP than their counterparts in the supposedly more hierarchist cultures of Japan and Korea. The rulers of Hong Kong and Singapore both enjoyed pay levels that would be the envy of their counterparts in any developed western country, but Hong Kong's pay structure was much flatter than that of Singapore, and the apparently fabulous wealth of the leaders of both of those systems in cross-national perspective is less impressive when set in the context of international business centres with extraordinarily highly paid professionals and corporate executives. We find little evidence even among this limited set of cases of some general 'Asian way' of rewarding top-level officials, although there are certainly some family resemblances where there are shared traditions, particularly between Japan and Korea and to a lesser extent Hong Kong and Singapore.

In Chapter 1, we introduced the idea of the top rewards 'game' in political systems as the outcome of a set of strategic interactions between rulers and ruled, with the former choosing between open and devious ways of rewarding themselves and the latter choosing between a tolerant/understanding attitude towards the rewards of their rulers, and a cynical or critical attitude.

Readers will recall that such an analysis suggests a 'tragic bias' towards outcomes in which rulers choose to be devious and the ruled choose to be cynical and critical, and the question that then arises is, what it is about institutions and culture that prevents all political systems from drifting into the 'tragic' bottom right-hand cell of Figure 1.1? We shall return to this issue in Chapter 10, but before that we need to probe beyond the general analysis we have pursued here to understand how the top pay game works in each political system, where it has come from and where it seems to be going. That is what the chapters in Part II aim to do. Their role is to look beneath the skin of each of the seven political systems in our study and go beyond what can be said in simple numbers about the relationships between the rulers and the ruled, and the long-term historical dynamics of each of those political systems.

Notes

1 Though, as Jon Quah reports in Chapter 9, Singapore sharply reduced the pay of its top public officeholders subsequently.
2 That means, for example, that Singapore's GDP per head is larger than that of Japan in PPP-adjusted terms, whereas it is lower in unadjusted US$ terms.
3 For details of Transparency International's Corruption Perception Index (a poll of polls) see http://www.transparency.org/documents/cpi/2001/dnld/ methodology.pdf

Part II

The politics behind the numbers

Seven cases

3 Rewarding comrades at the top in China

John P. Burns

Introduction

By international standards, as Chapter 2 showed, China's top leader's have compensated themselves relatively modestly given the rapid growth of the economy in recent years and their responsibilities for managing the affairs of the world's most populous nation. Indeed, in 2001 top leaders received official monetary compensation of as little as RMB 2,200 *yuan* (US$ 268) per month (Ministry of Personnel and Ministry of Finance 2001: 9; see Ding 2001).[1] From the Tocquevillian perspective discussed in Chapter 1, there is something surprising about a country that lacks democratic institutions and yet keeps compensation levels of its top leaders low. How can we explain this curious result?

In common with other developing countries, such as Thailand and Indonesia in Asia, visible rewards at the top in China are relatively modest while invisible rewards are very substantial. Invisible rewards especially in the post-1980 reform era have also included opportunities for corruption. It is argued that since the founding of the People's Republic of China (PRC), top leaders have pursued an income maximizing strategy. Although their cash salaries may appear low by international standards, the leaders' rewards are very generous when they are compared to the average rewards available to China's work force. The gap becomes clearer if invisible rewards are included. Even during periods of intense political conflict such as the Cultural Revolution (1966–76) when wage levels became a political issue, we argue that leaders continued to pursue an income maximizing strategy within the constraints imposed by the political system they themselves had created. We will examine possible alternative explanations such as political–cultural or institutional theories[2] that may seem to explain some periods of recent Chinese history better than our preferred theory. In the end, we reject these alternatives.

The context

The PRC is a unitary state ruled by the Chinese Communist Party (CCP) (Lieberthal 1995). The structure of government is monist, which means all formal power is centralized in the leading organs of the party. Both the legislature [the National People's Congress (NPC) at the national level] and the judiciary are subordinated to the party. In the language of Leninism, the Constitution describes the state as a 'people's democratic dictatorship' and the decision system as 'democratic centralism' (Constitution of the People's Republic of China 1982). Although Chinese citizens enjoy universal suffrage and directly elect delegates to urban district and rural town and township people's congresses, the elections are tightly controlled by the party. Party control is effective enough to prevent what authorities call 'unexpected results' in 99 per cent of cases (Bao 1993: 16–17; *South China Morning Post* 1993; Burns 1999: 591). People's congresses elect executive heads of government, not the voters. Thus, the NPC, itself indirectly elected by provincial people's congresses, elects the President and Vice President of the PRC, the Premier, Vice Premiers, State Councillors of the State Council and the country's top judges (Constitution of the People's Republic of China 1982). In keeping with its monopoly position, the CCP nominates candidates for these positions, none of which have ever been rejected by the NPC. That is, the political system is not a liberal democracy and the legislature lacks the power and autonomy it often enjoys in developed capitalist democracies. Formal political power is organized into a single hierarchy that places the CCP Politburo Standing Committee and its General Secretary (Jiang Zemin[3]) at the top.

The People's Republic is composed of 31 provinces or provincial-level cities (there are four such cities, Beijing, Tianjin, Shanghai and Chongqing). Each province is further subdivided into prefectures or prefectural-level cities (331 in 1999), 2,109 counties or county level cities and 44,800 towns or townships (State Statistical Bureau 2000: 3). In 2001, government employed directly about 5.4 million civil servants[4] (Ministry of Personnel, 25 July 2001), mostly at the local level. By the end of 2000, after a vigorous downsizing campaign, authorities estimated that only 16,000 or so civil servants worked in the central government (*Xinhua* 2000). The civil service is unified stretching from the capital in Beijing to town and township governments throughout the country. Pay policy and pay levels are, accordingly, set in Beijing for the entire country.

Prior to 1993 when civil service reforms were introduced, the CCP managed all government employees as part of the group of administrators, managers and professionals (or cadres) found in all occupation groups throughout the country, a system more appropriate for a centrally planned economy (see Lee 1991: 1–12). Entry to the cadre stratum was generally confined to university graduates, proportionately a small elite in China. Mobility within the group, however, was relatively open. For example, factory managers could become party and government administrators with relative ease. With the introduction of a market economy in the 1980s, cadres became increasingly specialized and various occupation groups began to develop their own incentive structures. By 1987, the party recognized the necessity of a separate management regime for cadres who worked in government agencies (civil servants). Not only did they require special skills, but to effectively regulate a market economy civil servants had to be insulated from or have autonomy from the rest of society. In 1993, for the first time, the CCP clearly identified the boundaries of 'the civil service' and laid down new regulations for its management (Ministry of Personnel 1993). Entry was restricted to those who passed a rigorous entrance exam or went through other procedures. Separate rules governed the training, evaluation, discipline, compensation, promotion and exit of the individuals selected to become 'civil servants'.

Identification of a country's 'top leaders' is bound to be somewhat arbitrary. Here, it is estimated conservatively to include the most senior 2,000 or so officials of the CCP, State Council, Military, the NPC, Judiciary, Procuratorate and provinces at the rank of central ministry, Vice Minister and provincial Vice Governor or equivalent and above (see Tables 3.1 and 3.2). Altogether they constitute only about 0.00016 per cent of the total population, a very select group indeed.

Utility maximizing explanations

During the period 1955–56, after adopting a policy of paying wages to government employees in cash, CCP policy called for high levels of monetary compensation for top leaders relative to average wages in the country as a whole (see Table 3.3). Only in 1955 did the government finally produce cash wage scales for all

Table 3.1 China's 'top leaders'

Rank	Indicative positions	Indicative number
1	CCP Politburo Standing Committee (President and CCP General Secretary; Vice President of the PRC; Premier; NPC Standing Committee Chair; CPPCC Standing Committee Chair; Executive Vice Premier; CCP Central Commission for Discipline Inspection Secretary)	7
2–3	CCP Politburo Members, Alternate Members and Secretaries of CCP Secretariat (Vice Premiers; Central Military Commission Vice Chairmen; NPC Standing Committee Vice Chairmen; CPPCC Standing Committee Vice Chairmen) State Councillors, Central Military Commission Members, President of the Supreme People's Court; President of the Supreme People's Procuratorate; Central Discipline Inspection Commission Deputy Secretaries; CCP Central Department Heads	100+
3–4	State Council Ministers, Provincial CCP Secretaries, Provincial Governors, CCP Central Department Deputy Heads	120+
4–5	State Council Vice Ministers, Provincial CCP Deputy Secretaries, Provincial CCP Party Committee Standing Committee members; Provincial CCP Discipline Committee Secretary; Provincial Deputy Governors	600+

Sources: Ministry of Personnel and Ministry of Finance (1999, 10: 4), CCP Organization Department (1993: 24) and Ding (2001).

Note
This corresponds to Grades 1–5 on the 'Chinese Civil Service Pay Scale, 1999' (see Table 3.2) and *is not complete.*

Table 3.2 Chinese civil service grade structure

Position	Wage grade point														
	1	2	3	4	5	6	7	8	9	10	11	12	13	14	15
President, Vice President, Premier	√														
Vice Premier, State Councillor		√	√												
Minister, Governor			√	√											
Vice Minister, Vice Governor				√	√										
Bureau Chief						√	√								
Deputy Bureau Chief						√	√								
Division Chief							√	√	√						
Deputy Bureau Chief								√	√	√	√	√			
Section Chief, responsible section member									√	√	√	√			
Deputy Section Chief, deputy responsible section member									√	√	√	√	√		
Section member										√	√	√	√	√	
Clerical staff													√	√	√

Source: Adapted from Collection on State Civil Service System (*Zhongguo gongwuyuan zhidu chuanshu*) (1994), Changchun: Jilin Literary Press: 123.

Note
The shaded section identifies the position of 'top leaders' as used in this study.

Table 3.3 Chinese civil service base salaries for selected years, 1955–2001 (unit = *yuan*/month)

	1955	1956	1957	1959	1960	1964	1985	1993	1997	1999	2001
Civil service highest	560	728	655.2	526.5	457.6	468	530	1,210	1,455	1,775	2,271
Civil service lowest	26	32.5	32.5	32.5	32.5	34.5	52	195	215	315	395
Civil service university entrance	NA	54	54	54	54	57	64	218	238	343	426
Ratio of highest to lowest	1:21.5	1:22.4	1:20.2	1:16.2	1:14.1	1:13.6	1:10.2	1:6.2	1:6.8	1:5.6	1:5.7
Ratio of highest to lowest university entrance	NA	1:13.5	1:12.1	1:9.8	1:8.5	1:8.2	1:8.3	1:5.6	1:6.1	1:5.2	1:5.3
National average salary of all 'staff and workers'	43.9	50.1	52	42.7	42.6	48.8	95.7	378.2	539.2	695.5	NA

Sources: *Personnel Management in Contemporary China (Dangdai zhongguo renshi guanli)* Vol. 2 (Beijing: Contemporary China Press, 1994): 89–150; 'Notice of the State Council on Reform of the Wage System for Government Organs and Service Units' (*Guowuyuan guanyu jiguan he shiye danwei gongzuo renyuan gongzi zhidu gaige wentidetongzhi*) (15 November 1993) in Ministry of Personnel (1994: 229); Ministry of Personnel and Ministry of Finance 'Notice on the Question of the 1997 Adjustment of the Wage Standard for Government Organs and Service Units' (*Renshibu caizhengbu guanyu 1997 nian diaozheng jiguan shiye danwei gongzuo renyuan gongzi biaojun deng wentide tongzhi*) in Ministry of Personnel (1998: 305); Ministry of Personnel and Ministry of Finance (1990: 4); Ministry of Personnel and Ministry of Finance (2001): 8–9; State Statistical Bureau (1989: 138); State Statistical Bureau (1999: 158); State Statistical Bureau (2000: 142).

administrative employees who before that time were rewarded mostly in kind. The scales provided for a top salary of RMB 560 *yuan* per month, or about 21.5 times the lowest government salary (Contemporary China Editorial Committee 1994: 91) and almost 13 times the national average urban wage of RMB 43.9 *yuan*. In 1956, when the government moved all public workers on to a cash payment system, the highest wage jumped to RMB 728 *yuan* per month, or about 22.4 times higher than the lowest salary (Contemporary China Editorial Committee 1994: 100) and nearly 15 times the national average urban wage. The national average urban wage at the time was only RMB 50.1 *yuan* per month. Had rural wages been included the gap would have been significantly larger.

Wage decompression in China in the 1950s to some extent resembles the situation in so-called 'high compensation' systems such as Hong Kong.[5] Because of its monopoly position in the political system the CCP faced no pressure from society to reduce base salaries at the top. Moreover, in the 1950s, the party nationalized virtually the entire economy (nationalization was completed in 1958) and replaced market distribution of labour and wages with mandatory central planning. At the time, China's economy was not integrated into the world economy and thus, the country was not influenced by such factors as externally induced inflation. The top leadership made decisions about compensation based on its own values and appear to have maximized their own interests as they laid down a new compensation policy. Undoubtedly they sought to reward themselves for 28 years in the political wilderness.

Not only did the CCP pay relatively high basic salaries by the mid-1950s, but the party continued to develop an elaborate system of mostly invisible rewards-in-kind that had been developed during the Civil War period (1946–49) and the years out of power. Before the CCP came to power, rewards for cadres living in party-controlled base areas, including top officials, were mainly provided in kind. Provisional governments supplied officials with all their necessities at no cost to the individuals, including housing, transportation, food, children's education and so forth. Moreover, after the party came to power in 1949 many officials remained for a time on the reward-in-kind 'supply system'. A cash salary system was only gradually introduced in the 1950s. Beginning in 1951, the government began to calculate pay in terms of 'wage points' (*gongzi fen*) without actually paying wages. Officials were awarded points based on their rank and seniority. The highest position at the time (Chairman of the Central People's Government, held by Mao Zedong) was awarded 2,400 wage points compared to 116 for a district People's Government Assistant at the bottom, a gap of 1 : 20.7. Elaborate tables converted the points into commodities (Contemporary China Editorial Committee 1994: 82–3). Newly hired officials, however, were increasingly paid cash basic salaries. While authorities moved to a cash compensation system they did not abandon the practice of providing free or heavily subsidized goods and services to government officials. As a result, officials continued to obtain free or heavily subsidized housing, transportation, food, medical care and access to special recreational facilities (such as those at the Beidaihe resort on the coast near Beijing).

The system of providing generous non-cash rewards to top leaders continues to this day. As already noted in Chapter 2, China's top leaders have shrouded their extra-base pay in relative secrecy. Little information is published about the specific kinds of non-cash rewards they enjoy. We may assume, however, that they are quite substantial. Like top leaders in many other countries, it is unlikely that China's top leaders have to pay for most goods and services they receive while in office. We should also assume that many top civil servants are able to supplement their incomes from other sources.[6]

These characteristics of the reward system for top leaders are consistent with explanations that focus on utility maximization and the lack of external constraints at the top in non-democratic political systems. We now turn to other possible explanations.

Political–cultural explanations

Possible support for a political–cultural explanation might come from the years of intense elite level conflict during the Cultural Revolution (1966–76) when China's top leaders cut their own base pay and propagated an ideology of egalitarianism. We argue, however, that even in this case leaders continued to maximize their own utility within structural constraints that they themselves had created.

China's political system centralized power in the hands of Mao Zedong who ruled in large part through charisma. In 1956, the CCP under his leadership launched the Hundred Flowers Campaign during which Chinese citizens were encouraged to air their views freely ('Let a Hundred Flowers Bloom and a Hundred Flowers Contend') which many intellectuals did (see MacFarquhar 1974). The Campaign was quickly followed by an anti-rightist campaign to denounce critics of the regime, hundreds of thousands of whom were arrested and imprisoned (Harding 1981: 116–52). Stung by criticism that it was 'removed from the masses' and eager to prove its populist credentials, the CCP leadership took the unusual step of cutting base salaries at the top. In 1957, the top salary was cut by about 10 per cent,[7] compressing the scale somewhat to 1:20.2. The economy in 1956 and 1957 continued to grow, however (see Figure 3.1). We can speculate, then, that the cuts were made primarily for reasons other than economy.

In 1958, the CCP under Mao Zedong launched the disastrous Great Leap Forward. The campaign resulted in staggering economic losses and widespread famine, during which an estimated 28 million people lost their lives (MacFarquhar 1997: 1–8). The campaign also revealed divisions within the elite that resulted in the purge of Minister of Defence Peng Dehuai in 1959 (Harding 1981: 138–44). In 1959 and 1960, the economy contracted substantially (Figure 3.1). In these two years, the CCP cut the salaries of top officials by a further 19.6 and 13 per cent, respectively, so that by 1960 salaries had compressed to 1:14.1[8] (Contemporary China Editorial Committee 1994: 131). In part, the action was prompted by economic considerations. Also important, however, was elite level political infighting.

In the wake of the Great Leap Forward, Mao was eased aside by Liu Shaoqi and Deng Xiaoping who adopted economically rationalist development policies. Remunerative incentives replaced moral exhortation as economic development tools. Resentful of his diminishing influence on public policy especially

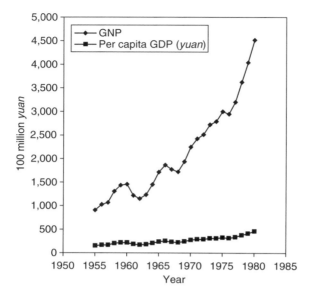

Figure 3.1 Economic growth in China, 1955–80.

in areas that he had traditionally dominated (agriculture and education), Mao fought back.

The Cultural Revolution (1966–76) that followed was dominated by bitter conflict among the political elite (see Harding 1971: 113–64, 1981: 235–328). At issue was the nature of bureaucracy and its relationship to society. Had the bureaucracy become an obstacle to further economic development as Mao suggested in his 'Twenty Manifestations of Bureaucracy'? In his essay he charged that party officials had become authoritarian, and were guilty of 'routinism, elitism, corruption, shirking responsibility, deceit, laziness, talentlessness, formalism, red tape, nepotism, and seeking special privileges' (Joint Publications Research Service 1970: 40–3). Mao and his supporters charged the leadership of the CCP (represented by Liu Shaoqi and Deng Xiaoping) with 'counter revolution'. They had become 'renegades within the Party taking the capitalist road'. Years of bitter infighting ensued as each faction jockeyed for power. The language of the struggle focused on the bureaucracy – was it an elitist institution, seeking special privilege, and out of touch with the people? Maoist radicals argued that it was, and that the inequality stemming from differential wages as well as a differential power distribution (a characteristic of hierarchy) had become the basis of a new ruling class in China (Lee 1991: 122). These views provided the ideological basis for a vicious power struggle within the CCP itself. As one prominent Cultural Revolutionary critic observed of China's officials at the time: 'Once they have secured their spoils, they feel it is time to settle down and feather their cozy nests'[9] (Lee 1991: 122).

In the political conflict, Mao and his supporters emphasized the need for egalitarianism and sharing the hardship of the masses. Obviously, for them to maintain the previous high wage policy was politically impossible in such an environment. In the radical view, officials could only 'serve the masses' if they lessened the distance between themselves and ordinary people. One symbolic way of accomplishing this was to compress basic salaries. Invisible rewards of various kinds, however, continued to be supplied without any cuts.

Part of China's system of providing allowances and subsidies to government officials has perpetuated Cultural Revolution egalitarianism. For example, in addition to the basic salary, civil servants also receive subsidies that are designed to bring their base pay into line with local economic conditions and to provide assistance to needy civil servants. Subsidies are divided into two different categories: general allowances, which include a regional subsidy that is based on the cost of living in an area, and a sectoral subsidy, which is paid to those working in specific areas such as public security (police, courts and procuratorate), audit, and customs. Because the cost of living varies substantially throughout the country, regional subsidies vary accordingly. In July 2000, Ministry of Personnel officials indicated that regional subsidies could be up to 100 per cent of base pay or higher in places like Shanghai that had relatively high costs of living (Interview, Ministry of Personnel, 29 June 2000). Regional subsidies are paid equally to all civil servants regardless of rank.

In addition to general allowances, civil servants are paid a number of specific allowances. Specific allowances include hardship subsidy, seasonal cold or hot temperature subsidy children's education subsidy, medical subsidy, transportation subsidy, housing subsidy, individual insurance subsidy and so forth. Because these subsidies tend to be provided to all civil servants regardless of rank, they narrow even further the gap between the lowest and the highest paid. One official estimated that in the year 2000, the real ratio of highest to lowest paid in the civil service was probably closer to 1 : 3 (Interview, Ministry of Personnel, 29 June 2000). Nationwide, Ministry of Personnel officials estimated that in mid-2000, subsidies of one kind or another (including both general and specific allowances) made up about 40 per cent of total incomes. The rest came from basic salary.

'Top' civil servants do, however, have some advantages, such as in the provision of housing and cars. Until recently, all top civil servants were allocated housing the size of which varied with their official rank[10] and for which they paid only nominal rent. With housing reform, the government has encouraged civil servants to purchase their own homes. According to the current policy of the central government, assistance is provided to civil servants based on their rank to buy their own housing. In Beijing, in mid-2000, civil servants were charged only RMB 1,450 *yuan* per square metre to purchase housing up to their officially permitted size, considerably less than market prices. In mid-2000, housing prices ranged from RMB 4,000 to 9,000 *yuan* per square metre depending on such factors as age, location and floor (Interview, Ministry of Personnel, 6 July 2000). Civil servants were also offered loans at below market interest rates to assist them to purchase these properties. Undoubtedly 'top' civil servants availed themselves of these benefits to purchase their own homes at substantial discounts.

'Top' civil servants were also entitled to the use of official cars. According to the regulations, civil servants of the rank of Minister and above were entitled to a car and driver for their exclusive use. Those ranked below that level (Vice Minister, Bureau Chief and Deputy Chief) used agency pool cars with drivers (Interview, Ministry of Personnel, 6 July 2000). At local levels, a similar system was in operation.

The intense political conflict that motivated China's top leaders to cut their own basic salaries (but not non-cash benefits) during the Cultural Revolution was an outcome of the configuration of institutions and decision making mechanisms that they themselves had established for the country. Throughout the period they determined their own compensation levels and to maintain their power position, felt constrained to cut their base salaries. That is, an interest maximizing strategy offers the best explanation for their behaviour.

Institutional–structural explanations

Since 1980, steps have been taken to institutionalize the system of rewards for civil servants. However, top leaders have exempted themselves from some institutional rules that they have imposed on others and the country has yet to adopt a transparent and regular process for determining rewards at the top. The ubiquity of corruption in China and relatively low detection and conviction rates for the offences indicate that top officials continue to be income maximizers.

From 1978 to 1980, hundreds of thousands of elderly victims of the Cultural Revolution were 're-habilitated' and returned to their old or other official positions. The need for a mandatory retirement system became critical. Although the government had long laid down rules that permitted retirement at a fixed age with a pension, the rules did not require retirement. Establishing a mandatory retirement system was one of the most contentious parts of civil service reform.

In 1980, paramount leader Deng Xiaoping officially endorsed a retirement system. Yet because of intense resistance from his colleagues at the top, introduction of the policy was delayed for two years. Top-level official resistance centred less on the cash amounts to be offered to retirees than on arrangements to continue their access to the perquisites of office, including official documents, housing, medical benefits, cars and special opportunities for their children (Manion 1993: 93). Only after a bitter struggle and protracted negotiations did the party decide to adopt two different systems of retirement for most retirees. Those senior leaders who 'joined the revolution' prior to 1949 (estimated to be about 2.5 million 'veteran revolutionaries') would retire (*lishou*) with full salary and benefits, including access to official documents, housing, medical benefits and cars with drivers. Those who 'joined the revolution' after 1949 would retire (*tuishou*) at age 60 for men and 55 for women with much less generous benefits, such as pensions that amounted to only 60–70 per cent of their pre-retirement salary (Manion 1993). As Manion reports, when bonuses were taken into account, the difference in material compensation between the two groups was clear: the normal retirees received only 57 per cent of what the veterans received (Manion 1993: 63). Once again, the veterans were looking out for themselves.

While they imposed mandatory retirement ages on most of the civil service, China's top leaders exempted themselves from the requirements. In 2001, Jiang Zemin, Li Peng and Zhu Rongji, China's core leadership, all in their mid-70s, continued in official positions. The leader who imposed the new retirement rules, Deng Xiaoping, only resigned his last official post in 1990 at the age of 86! That is, the attempt to institutionalize a new retirement norm, while successful for the civil service as a whole, has been undermined somewhat by the determination of leaders at the top to protect their own interests and maintain their and their family's positions. Thus, interest-maximizing explanations best capture behaviour *at the top*.

The new fixed-tenure rule and China's relatively low level of compensation at the top have encouraged many retirees to look for 'second careers'. In the past top-level retirees were assigned to positions in the nation's legislature, or advisory bodies such as the Chinese People's Political Consultative Committee, or to head government-sponsored associations, societies or not-for-profit organizations. These sinecures, while not especially demanding, would continue to guarantee that they are compensated at or better than the level they had enjoyed during their official career. Increasingly, however, they can look to the market for opportunities. As a result, the party has drafted new regulations that require a sanitation period of three years before a retired official may join an organization in a sector within which he or she has worked while in government (Central Commission for Discipline Inspection 2000). As the economy develops and the labour market matures, authorities will undoubtedly have to give further thought to developing more effective policies to manage the potential conflicts of interests associated with top-level retirees taking up new jobs in the private sector.

Beginning in 1978, the CCP began fundamental structural reform of the economy (see Harding 1987). Accompanying the changes of economic policy in the 1980s was a sea change in the content and relative significance of official ideology. Gone from official party documents were references to egalitarianism and normative incentives. 'To get rich is glorious', proclaimed CCP leaders in a policy that encouraged some to 'get rich first'. The new values undermined the party's egalitarian ideology of the past three decades, and undoubtedly encouraged many officials to look at their new richer non-official neighbours with envy.

China's more open and liberalized economy became vulnerable to new problems, such as inflation and corruption (discussed later). Attempts to address the inflation question were made first in 1985, even before the new civil service system was established with a comprehensive wage reform that included all public sector administrative staff (Contemporary China Editorial Committee 1994: 144–8). The 1985 wage reform revealed that the gap between the highest and lowest paid had shrunk to about 1 : 10.

The party did not lay down separate rules for *civil service* compensation (including those at the top), however, until 1993 when the State Council promulgated the new 'Provisional Regulations on State Civil Servants' (Ministry of Personnel 1993).

Table 3.4 Chinese civil service pay scale, 2001 (unit = *yuan*/month)

Position	Rank, post wage 1	2	3	4	5	6	7	8	9	10	11	12	13	14	Grade	Wage standard	Basic wage
President, Vice President, Premier	480	555	630	705	780	855									1	1,166	230
Vice Premier, State Councillor	400	460	520	580	640	700	760								2	1,030	230
Minister, Provincial Governor	330	380	430	480	530	580	630	680							3 4	903 790	230 230
Vice Minister, Provincial Deputy Governor	270	315	360	405	450	495	540	585	630						5	686	230
Bureau Chief	215	255	295	335	375	415	455	495	535	575					6 7	586 490	230 230
Deputy Bureau Chief	175	210	245	280	315	350	385	420	455	490					8	408	230
Division Chief, County Magistrate	144	174	204	234	264	294	324	354	384	414	444				9	340	230
Deputy Division Chief, Deputy County Magistrate	118	143	168	193	218	243	268	293	318	343	368				10	281	230
Section Head	96	116	136	156	176	196	216	236	256	276	296	316			11 12	231 190	230 230
Deputy Section Head	79	94	109	124	139	154	169	184	199	214	229	244			13	158	230
Section Member	63	75	87	99	111	123	135	147	159	171	183	195	207	219	14	133	230
General Office Personnel	50	60	70	80	90	100	110	120	130	140	150	160	170	180	15	115	230

Source: Adapted from Ministry of Personnel and Ministry of Finance (2001: 9).

Note
Seniority wage – one *yuan* for each year of service.

According to the Regulations civil servants shall be remunerated based on the value of their work (*anlao fenpei*) (Article 64). Pay for civil servants including China's top leaders, is based on elements that reward rank or grade, level of responsibility and seniority (see Table 3.4). The regulations provide that 'a civil servant may also receive a regional allowance or other allowances' (Article 64). For the first time, the rules laid down a system of regular increments and bonuses based on performance (Article 65). The regulations provide that salary levels for civil servants 'shall be commensurate with an employee of a state-owned enterprise (SOE) holding an equivalent position' (Article 66). To ensure that official salaries keep up with (or even exceed) inflation Article 67 states: 'The State shall systematically raise the salary scales of civil servants in accordance with the nation's economic development and increases in the cost of living and price indexes, so that a civil servant's real salary level continually rises.' These rules apply to all civil servants, including those at the top.

There is some evidence, then, that relatively low official salaries are a product of China's economic development. Average Gross National Product (GNP) per capita in China is much lower than in more developed Asian countries such as Japan and Singapore. Indeed, it is the lowest by a long margin of any other country considered in this study.[11] That is, to some extent China rewards its top officials modestly because it cannot afford to do otherwise. Still, in China rewards at the top are increasing as the economy develops, as Figure 3.2 shows.

Attempts to institutionalize the principles have resulted in the promulgation of a new grade/post wage scale for civil servants (Ministry of Personnel and Ministry of Finance 1993) which officials have revised based on surveys of price movements and inflation. In 1993 and 1995 to implement Article 66 of the 'Provisional Regulations', the Ministry of Personnel together with other agencies carried out nationwide pay level surveys that compared the compensation of civil servants to State-Owned Enterprise (SOE) managers. According to the 1993 survey (the 1995 survey was not published), the gap between civil servants and SOE

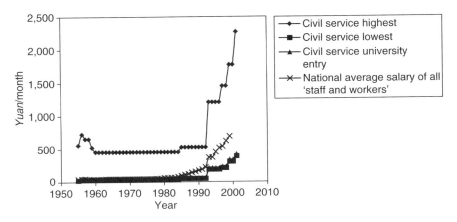

Figure 3.2 Chinese civil service base salaries, 1955–2001.

Table 3.5 Income gap between government officials and SOE managers, 1993

	Total 1	Total 2	Central 1	Central 2	Local 1	Local 2
Total	1.26	1.00	1.31	1.00	1.25	1.00
Vice Minister	1.50	1.00				
Bureau Chief	1.64	1.00	1.48	1.00	1.71	1.00
Deputy Bureau Chief	1.53	1.00	1.48	1.00	1.52	1.00
Division Chief	1.40	1.00	1.41	1.00	1.45	1.00
Deputy Division Chief	1.27	1.00	1.30	1.00	1.25	1.00

Source: State Statistical Bureau (1995: 123–4).

Note
1 = state-owned enterprise; 2 = government agency. The data is based on a comparison of the nominal total income of 71,854 individuals working in state-owned enterprises and 73,040 individuals working in government agencies nationwide.

managers was about 20 per cent nationwide (see Table 3.5). Although the largest gap was found between local bureau chiefs and SOE managers, the gap between officials and SOE managers at Vice Minister level (included among our 'top leaders') was substantial. No data are available for more senior leaders but one can speculate that the gap would have been even larger. Moreover, if the comparison had been made between civil servants and private sector managers, the gap would have been larger still. There is considerable regional variation as well, with poorer provinces such as Anhui reporting little or no gap, while richer provinces such as Guangdong in the South and other developed areas such as Shanghai and Beijing reporting a gap of as much as 100 per cent or more.

As a result of the new wage system, rewards at the top have increased steadily since the mid-1980s. Thus, from 1985 to 2001 top base salaries jumped from RMB 530 *yuan* per month to about RMB 2,271 *yuan* per month, an increase of about 16 per cent per annum at current wage levels. [During the same period real GNP grew at the rate of about 8.7 per cent per annum and real wages of urban employees grew by about 15.5 per cent per annum (State Statistical Bureau 2000: 55).] Given the high rates of inflation China experienced during the late 1980s, one can conclude that official salaries have failed to keep up with the growth of the economy. According to some commentators, further increases can be expected with the top salaries doubling by 2003 (Ding 2001). Even if this materializes, base salaries for China's top leaders would continue to be relatively modest in spite of the new rules and procedures for linking pay to the economy.

Base salaries at the bottom have also increased, so much so that base wages are now severely compressed (see Table 3.3). In 1993, with the introduction of the new civil service system, the gap fell to 1 : 6.2. In the year 2000, officials of the Ministry of Personnel estimated it at 1 : 5.6, and probably considerably more compressed (to say 1 : 3) if allowances and benefits are considered because of the egalitarian way that benefits are distributed (Interview, Ministry of Personnel, 26 June 2000).

According to the 'Individual Income Tax Law' that came into effect in 1994, those earning from RMB 2,000–5,000 *yuan* per month should pay tax of 15 per cent

(CCH Asia Pacific 1999: ¶10–810). No information is available on any special personal income tax privileges for top government officials and indeed the government has required individuals to pay personal income tax only relatively recently. (Individual income tax is charged on all monthly incomes over RMB 500 *yuan* and is deducted monthly from official salaries at source.)

In addition to their official base salaries, top leaders have opportunities to increase their incomes from other, sometimes illegal, sources, including corruption. From the early 1980s to 1995, the number of corruption cases under investigation in China grew from about 20,000–50,000 per year. As King-man Chan points out, from 1987 to 1995, the number of officially defined 'serious' cases of corruption (each involving over RMB 10,000 *yuan*) grew from 13 to 57 per cent during the period (Chan 1999: 311). In 1995, 504 cases involved stakes of more than RMB 1 million *yuan*. By 2001, authorities reported that of the 18,086 cases of bribery they dealt with in 2000–01, 1,335 had involved bribes of more than RMB 1 million *yuan* (*South China Morning Post*, 11 March 2001). Official corruption has had a serious impact on the economy. According to Hu Angang, during the latter half of the 1990s corruption resulted in economic losses of from 13.2 to 16.8 per cent of Gross Domestic Product (GDP), a staggering amount (Hu 2001: 34–58). As was noted in Chapter 2, China ranks lower on the Transparency International's Corruption Perception Index than the other countries included in this study.

Not only is the incidence of corruption in China quite severe, but the chance of being detected and convicted for corruption is also relatively low. According to Hu Angang, from 1993 to 1998 about 42.7 per cent of corruption cases under investigation led to criminal charges and only 6.6 per cent of these led to corrupt officials being sentenced. Hu concludes: 'This means [that] if a person is bribed, there is only a 6.6 percent chance of him being prosecuted. This is a low probability and many people would take the risk' (*South China Morning Post*, 24 March 2001). Although one cannot be sure of the extent to which top officials themselves have been guilty of corruption, authorities reported in December 2000 that during the previous year 21 officials of provincial or ministerial rank were 'disciplined' for corruption offences.[12] Although the penalties for corruption are severe in China, the chances of being caught and prosecuted are apparently relatively low. Officials tolerate low salaries in the reform era because they know they can make up the difference through corruption with relatively little chance of getting caught. Moreover, corruption at the top undoubtedly pays handsome dividends, as witnessed by the case of Cheng Kejie, a senior official who was executed in 2000 (*Xinhua* 2000). Cheng made his money from bribes paid by officials seeking his help with promotions and by ordering SOEs and agencies to sell real estate and commodities at below market prices through his mistress, who remitted the profits to Hong Kong when she had obtained permanent residency. According to the official report, Cheng was able to amass a fortune of tens of millions of *yuan* in a relatively short period of time.

Officials have recognized that low official salaries can contribute to corruption. As Wei Jianxing, Secretary of the Central Discipline Inspection Commission pointed out: 'Because the financial resources of the state are limited, the income of government employees is fairly low. Some government employees are frustrated by the low income and the rather significant disparities in their incomes of state workers in different departments, resulting in a loss of psychological equilibrium, which is an important factor leading to corruption' (Wei 2000). Perhaps recognizing that raising salaries alone will not reduce corruption, officials have rarely discussed this option.[13] Still, when officials raised the salaries of China's judges in 2000, they argued that the steps were necessary 'as part of reforms to ward off corruption' (*Wenhui bao* quoted in *South China Morning Post*, 14 December 2000).

The government has adopted a number of measures to fight corruption at the top that includes increased reporting. From 1995, authorities began to require senior party and government leaders (and their children) at and above county level to report their incomes (*South China Morning Post*, 25 May 1995; 30 September and 1 October 1996; 2 May 1997). In 1997, the Communist Party issued new regulations that required leaders, their spouses and dependent children to report on a wide variety of financial activities to the government. These included information on property transactions, changes to business interests, private trips abroad and 'other important matters that leading cadres themselves deem should be reported' (*New China News Agency*, 24 March 1997 in FBIS-CHI-98, 21 November 1998). The reports are not made public and apparently largely depend on the officials themselves as to what should be included. Although the CCP and the State Council have issued scores of regulations to fight corruption they have been unwilling or unable to take measures such as setting up a powerful, independent agency to fight corruption or strengthening the effectiveness of law enforcement.

The country has successfully imposed new retirement rules and a compensation system on the civil service as a whole, but officials at the top have been able to evade the restrictions. Although the penalties are severe especially for corruption, the changes of being caught are relatively low. Taking bribes to supplement one's income, then, becomes a rational strategy for all officials, including those at the top. One can conclude, then, that an income maximizing explanation is more persuasive.

Consequences

China's relatively low level of compensation for top leaders has had several consequences. First, it has probably contributed to a relatively high rate of corruption. Second, because of the gap between public official and enterprise compensation at all levels, many individuals are probably discouraged from ever pursuing a career in the public service. In a market economy, career choices are made voluntarily. As a result, and because of the relatively closed nature of the bureaucracy, substantial numbers of talented people are probably never considered for positions at the top. Third, wage compression in the system, a product of an ethic that still values egalitarianism to a certain extent, and lack of state financial capacity, have probably undermined motivation and therefore performance in the civil service. A more decompressed compensation system would be better able to motivate officials at the top. Still, officials at this level derive satisfaction from many other sources, such as power and status. Fourth, although transparency about rewards at the top is low in China, citizens continue to adopt a relatively respectful and trusting attitude toward the state. There is evidence, however, that in the reform era they are becoming more cynical and distrusting.

Recruitment and retention

Recruitment and retention of top leaders depends on many factors, only one of which is compensation. In China, in common with other countries in which social values may be characterized as 'pro-state' (Morgan 1996), top government officials enjoy enormous power and prestige especially within the bureaucracy. Status differences are marked and very important. Although difficult to quantify, these rewards undoubtedly compensate to some extent for the relatively modest official rewards the official system now appears to afford. There is no exodus of senior officials from government taking early retirement. If anything, getting rid of incompetent senior bureaucrats appears to be more of a problem. Because of official policies that have favoured the public sector for the past 50 years, the private sector is grossly under-developed. For this reason, there is no pool of talent in the private sector that could be transferred in to staff official posts at the top.

A consequence of China's low official reward system, however, is that young people may not be attracted to join the government. Generally, university graduates join with a basic salary of from RMB 350 to 450 *yuan* per month depending on their educational qualifications. According to the data presented in Table 3.4, however, on entry they will earn at least 20 per cent less than they could in an SOE. Salaries in private and joint venture companies are many times higher again. While the state is not facing recruitment and retention problems at the top presently, such problems are likely in the future.

Performance

The formal system for compensating civil servants, including those at the top, contains elements that reward performance. First, according to the 'Provisional Regulations on Civil Servants', the government may pay cash bonuses to reward excellence (Article 29). The bonuses should be based on the results of annual performance appraisals and may amount to no more than one month's salary per year (Interview, Ministry of Personnel, 29 June 2000). Field work in Hebei province, however, indicates that bonuses of substantially more than that were routinely paid by local governments to among others, tax collectors (Interviews, Hebei province June 2000). Civil servants in Beijing also reported that some government agencies paid bonuses. Generally, only those agencies that earned money through the collection of fees or other income (such as those that managed telecommunications, banking, finance, business and commerce, public security, customs and disaster relief) were able to pay bonuses (Interviews, Ministry of Personnel, 29 June 2000).

The bonus system is undermined, however, by a weak performance appraisal system. According to the 'Provisional Regulations' and the published results of appraisals in local governments, supervisors rate no more than 15 per cent of appraisees as 'outstanding' (*youshou*) (Interview, Ministry of Personnel, 29 June 2000). Authorities rate all of the rest (85 per cent) as 'competent' (*chengzhi*), and rarely use the other two categories ['basically competent' (*jiben chengzhi*) or 'incompetent' (*bu chengzhi*)]. That is, virtually all employees receive some kind of performance reward, including, one may presume, those at the top.

Ministry of Personnel officials have also argued that the 14 steps of the responsibility wage scale are meant to reward performance and that the civil service grade structure, ranging from section member to premier, is also performance based (Interview, Ministry of Personnel, 29 June 2000). Generally, top officials are rewarded primarily through promotion. Given the weaknesses of the appraisal system, not surprisingly, officials fall back on other factors, such as seniority when making appointments. Indeed, the government has laid down strict age and years of service requirements for each post. The extent to which performance rather than factors such as personal relations (*guanxi*) is critical for the posting of top leaders is unknown. Anecdotal accounts indicate that seniority and personal relations are important.

In addition to rewards, performance at the top is also managed through punishments, including dismissals. In recent years, the central government has dismissed many 'top' leaders for failing to perform to the required standard.[14]

Citizen attitudes: trust

The case of China indicates that factors other than democratic institutions may have kept reward levels relatively low for top public officials. These include a relatively low level of economic development and an ideology of egalitarianism. According to one view, lower level rewards also tend to be associated with more open reward strategies and trusting and respectful citizens (Hood and Peters 1994: 9). Conversely, higher rewards levels are consistent with more cynical citizen attitudes and more secretive or 'devious' rewards strategies. A utility maximizing analysis predicts that most countries will move toward this outcome (Hood and Peters 1994: 10–11).

We have argued that citizen attitudes in China are relatively 'pro-State' in the sense that citizens expect and approve of the state playing a major role in the economy. While we have no data on the extent to which citizens trust government, survey data on citizen expectation of equal treatment by government do exist and may be used as a surrogate for trust (Nathan and Shi 1993). According to a nationwide random sample survey carried out in the early 1990s, more than half (57 per cent) of Chinese respondents expected equal treatment from their government, a relatively high result (Nathan and Shi 1993: 109). Similar results were also found in Germany and Italy (in contrast to the USA and the UK where 83 per cent of respondents expected equal treatment). Based on these results, we may classify Chinese citizens as relatively respectful and trusting of government – that is, government is relatively legitimate in China.

Officials in China have pursued a relatively secretive or 'devious' strategy for managing rewards at the top. In keeping with the country's non-democratic political system, most government processes are not open to public scrutiny. Contrary to the prediction, however, official reward levels are relatively low. How can we explain this puzzle?

One possibility is to factor in the relatively high incidence of corruption. If we include corruption (the ultimate 'secret' reward strategy) then the real reward structure may be much higher than reported. That the CCP has had to draft so many rules and regulations to prevent spouses and family members from exploiting a top leader's official position is an indication that this kind of behavior is a serious problem (see Wei 2000). Given also the relatively low prosecution rate, many officials and their families probably expect that high public office will make them rich in spite of the relatively low official reward structure.

Insofar as corruption continues to be a serious problem in China, one can expect public trust in government to be undermined. There is some evidence that this is happening. Official surveys of citizen opinion carried out in the 1990s by the Academy of Social Sciences, for example, routinely place corruption among the most serious problems facing the country. One can expect, then that more cynical and disrespectful attitudes will develop and that the case of China will move (has already moved?) in the predicted direction. Devious strategies accompanied by cynicism may be accompanied by less visible and higher rewards. Table 3.3 also records substantial increases in relative terms of base salary for officials at the top since 1993. The rate of increase for those at the top is much higher than for other civil servants.

Conclusions

The case of China demonstrates that unrestrained by democratic institutions leaders at the top will attempt to maximize their own incomes. When they first established official pay scales in the 1950s, the gap between top salaries and the average pay of 'staff and workers' in China was relatively large. Elite conflicts in the 1960s and the 1970s encouraged top leaders to cut their own base salary as a strategy to stay in power. The institutions that they themselves had established imposed this constraint upon them. In the reform era, when the policy of 'becoming rich is good' became official mantra, top leaders have used a variety of strategies, legal and illegal, to maximize their incomes. Opportunities for corruption have played an important role.

The significance of the China case is that it reminds one that one should classify top leaders' rewards levels according to internal conditions. What may appear low by Hong Kong or Singapore standards, may be high according to internal standards. The China case also demonstrates that incentives may operate to increase or to cut salaries even without the pressure of a democratic electorate.

Finally, the China case illustrates the importance of attempting to understand as best we can as outsiders the contours of the vast invisible rewards component for leaders at the top especially in developing countries.

Notes

1 In 2001, RMB 1 *yuan* = US$ 0.12.
2 See Hood in Hood and Peters (1994: 49–69) for an example of these explanations applied to the UK.
3 Jiang Zemin is also concurrently President of the PRC.
4 Since 1993, the Chinese government has defined 'civil servant' as an administrator, professional or manager who works for a government agency. This definition excludes all manual workers who work for government agencies. Moreover, authorities define 'government agency' so as to exclude most health, education and social service providers. If these providers are included, they add another 29.57 million people to the total number of 'public employees' (Interview, Ministry of Personnel, 6 June 2000).
5 In 1997, for example, the highest civil service salary was about HK$ 216,000 per month compared to the average monthly salaries of from HK$ 8,000 to 11,000 in various occupation groups for a gap of from 1 : 18 to 1 : 27. See *Hong Kong – A New Era. A Review of 1997* (1998). Hong Kong: Printing Department
6 These include honoraria or fees for publications. Although civil servants are now prohibited from themselves running businesses, they may make investments from which they could earn income. Family members also may run businesses. In addition to the legal methods of supplementing their incomes, of course, many top officials have accepted money from illegal sources.
7 Salaries for the top 1–5 grades of the 30-point scale were cut by 10 per cent, while Grades 6–8 were cut by 6 per cent and grades 9–10 were cut by 3 per cent. No cuts were made to grades 11–30. See Contemporary China Editorial Committee (1994: 130).
8 In 1959, grades 1–3 were merged and paid at the Grade 3 rate. In 1960, cuts were made as follows: 12 per cent for grades 1–3; 10 per cent for Grade 4; 8 per cent for Grade 5; 6 per cent for Grade 6; 4 per cent for Grade 7; 2 per cent for Grade 8; and 1 per cent for grades 9–17 (Contemporary China Editorial Committee 1994: 131).
9 From 'Gang of Four' leader Zhang Chunchao, who was arrested and imprisoned in 1976.
10 For the officially approved housing standards by bureaucratic rank see Miao (2000: 12).
11 GNP per capita in 1999 for China was US$ 750, compared to 32,280 (Japan), 30,060 (Singapore), 23,670 (Hong Kong), 20,300 (Australia) and 7,970 (South Korea). See World Bank (1999), (*http://www.worldbank.org/data/countrydata*).
12 See 'Wei Jianxing Calls for Greater Intensity for Fight Against Corruption,' *Xinhua* (New China News Agency), 25 December 2000 in FBIS-CHI-2000-1225, 25 December 2000. The article identifies the following 'top' leaders as having been corrupt: Cheng Kejie, former Vice Chairman of the National People's Congress Standing Committee; Hu Changqing, former Vice Governor of Jiangxi Province; Qin Changdian, former Vice Chairman of the Chongqing Municipal People's Congress Standing Committee; and Wang Shihui, former Vice Chairman of the Chongqing Municipal Committee of the Chinese People's Political Consultative Conference. To these should be added former Beijing Mayor and Politburo member, Chen Xitong and Beijing Vice Mayor Wang Baoshan. The Beijing case allegedly involved bribes and

embezzlement of more than US$ 18 billion. See also *Wenhui bao* (Hong Kong), 15 September 1997 for a discussion of the Beijing cases.

13 See, for example, 'Central and State Organs Attach Importance to Work of Fighting Corruption by Grasping at the Source: More than 100 Departments Work Out "Implementation Methods"' (2000) Xinhua 24 December in FBIS-CHI-2000-1224, 24 December 2000 and many other similar reports.

14 For examples of relatively senior leaders being dismissed for poor performance see cases from Shaanxi, Hebei and Jiangxi provinces in *South China Morning Post* (Hong Kong) 18 May, 19 June and 20 June 2001.

4 Rorts, perks and fat cats
Rewards for high public office in Australia

Martin Painter

Popular hostility to politician 'fat cats'

Few issues in Australia arouse the ire of the public more than politicians' pay and allowances. Most scandals in Australian public life stem from relatively petty abuses of the perks of office, or 'rorts' as Australians describe them. An example is the case of a prominent minister who let his government-provided phone charge card fall into the hands of his son, whence it ended up being used by others. The minister voluntarily repaid an amount in excess of A$ 50,000. Such an incident is immediate headline material, and prompts letters to the editor and irate calls to talk-back radio hosts. As a result of such intense scrutiny and public hostility, the issue of pay and rewards is treated with kid gloves by governments – who would rather sweep it under the carpet – and opportunistically by oppositions, who find it hard to resist the temptation to side with popular sentiment. One strategy of governments in the face of this sentiment has been to seek to depoliticize the issue, albeit with mixed success, as discussed later.

A widespread view that politicians are only 'in it for themselves' is part of a growing cynicism and alienation towards politics and politicians. Opinion pollsters Roy Morgan Research conduct a regular poll on the standing of various occupations in the Australian community. In October 2000, only 11 per cent of the population gave federal members of parliament a rating of 'high' or 'very high' for 'ethics and honesty'. The highest rated occupation was nursing (88 per cent) and the lowest was selling used cars (3 per cent). The rating for politicians dipped to 7 per cent in 1998. Since 1976, when the first survey was conducted, their rating has steadily declined – the average for the first five surveys (1976–84) was 18 per cent, while for the most recent five (1996–2000) it was down to 11 per cent (Morgan, Roy and Associates 2000).

Data from the Australian and World Values Surveys show a similar trend in public attitudes. When asked in 1983 'How much confidence do you have in the federal government?', respondents were far more positive than when asked the same question in 1995. The percentage that responded 'a great deal' or 'quite a lot' fell from 55.3 to 26.1, a decline of 29.2 percentage points. The legal system fared little better with a decline from 60.5 to 34.7 (down 25.8), although the public service declined less sharply, from 46.7 to 38.9 (down 9.4). The armed forces had a stable positive rating by this measure of around 66 per cent, as did the police at close to 80 per cent (Papadakis 1999).

Some of this disillusionment with government and politics is reflected in growing support for minor parties and independents, which regularly shows up in opinion polls at close to 20 per cent. The Australian Democrats, who hold several seats in the Senate, have campaigned on the slogan 'Keep the Bastards Honest', with a sharp focus on rorts and perks. More recently, the One Nation Party of Pauline Hanson has gone further, with 'Kick the Bastards Out'. The marginalized and the under classes (particularly in non-metropolitan Australia) have targeted their representatives' relatively comfortable life styles as a symbol of politicians' seeming indifference to the injustices they feel, and have let fly. It is ironic, then, that the comparative analysis in Chapter 2 shows that Australian politicians are not extravagantly paid compared with other countries. The 'feeding frenzy' is never satisfied.

Public servants are not such obvious targets, but public discussions of their pay reveal signs of an egalitarian sentiment. In the case of top public servants, the attempt to match burgeoning private-sector rewards is treated with scepticism. There is a salacious fascination with the search for the 'highest paid public servant in Australia'. But the search for who really tops the league sheds little clear light, as corporations such as Telstra (Australia's telecom, which is listed on the stock exchange but owned 51 per cent by the Commonwealth) are hard to categorize as 'public' or 'private'. In New South Wales (NSW), the highest paid public officer is the Chief Executive Officer (CEO) of North Power, a government owned company which proudly claims to be the 'state's largest rural retailer of electricity'. He earned A\$ 425,000 plus performance bonuses of A\$ 177,000 in 1999–2000 (about six times the salary of a backbench MP).

Over the last few years, controversy over performance bonuses has crystallized resentments towards public service 'fat cats'. In 2000, the NSW Labor Government decided to terminate performance bonuses for top public servants. The decision came in response to an Auditor-General's critical comment about a lack of transparency. He subsequently came out in defence of incentive payments, hoping the Government had not acted on the mistaken view that he opposed them. The Treasurer described the bonus system as 'modern American crap … a bit like getting a star or a smiley stamp on your homework' (*Sydney Morning Herald*, 31 August 2000). Was this a case of politicians (who had not benefited so generously from the quest for private sector comparability) getting a bit of their own back?

The politics of rewards for high public office is complex, controversial and expresses paradoxes and tensions that are deeply rooted in Australian popular beliefs and political culture. In that context, this chapter explores in more detail the manner in which the process of determining pay and rewards for high public office is managed; tries to explain the outcomes; and explores some of the possible consequences. The bulk of the analysis focuses on the Commonwealth (national) level.

Trends in levels of reward

Chapter 2 compared levels of and changes in a set of Australian rewards for high public office (RHPOs) with the other political systems that are examined in this book, and more details of these rewards will be given later. Chapter 2 also looked at relativities between top public-sector rewards, Gross Domestic Product

(GDP) per head and top private-sector or professional rewards to the extent that relevant data are available. In the case of Australia, the gap between most HPO salaries and average earnings has grown. In 1980, the High Court Chief Justice was paid a salary 5.2 times average earnings; by 2000 the ratio was 6.6. In the same period, the ratio between private-sector CEOs and average earnings grew from 6.3 to 10.4 while for the Prime Minister there was a widening of the gap from 4.6 to 6.2. The increasingly inegalitarian distribution of rewards is even more marked if we take account of data for Total Remuneration Packages (TRPs) rather than base salary alone. A Department Secretary's TRP in 1980 was 5.3 times average earnings, but by 2000 the ratio had grown to 8. Meanwhile, the wage of the entry-level clerical position in the public service remained frozen at a ratio of just over half the average earnings throughout this period.

As applies to most of the other political systems in this study, the reward pattern for legislators is different from that applying to executive government. There seems to have been more restraint on rewards for members of the legislature than for HPOs in the executive and judiciary. Backbench MPs earned just over two and a half times average weekly earnings in 1981, and 2.9 times average weekly earnings in 2000, and as Chapter 2 showed, MPs are paid relatively modest salaries. They were paid an annual salary of about US$ 55,000 in 2001, and the figure includes an electoral allowance that is notionally for office expenses but paid regardless of whether any expenses are incurred.

Some puzzles are posed by the Australian reward patterns shown in Chapter 2. If there is an egalitarian sentiment, why have members of the executive, but not ordinary politicians, managed to escape its restraints? What kind of system of setting rewards sees increases in senior public servant's salaries outstripping those of politicians? Why have senior public servants' salaries so rapidly outgrown those of their subordinates? Before exploring these (and other) questions we need to clarify the data. Perhaps gaps in the data on TRPs (particularly for politicians) conceal the real situation. With a view to shedding light, we turn next to a fuller description of the range of types of reward available to higher public officials in Australia.

Types of reward

Judges and bureaucrats

High Court Judges have the most straightforward remuneration package. They earn a salary, are entitled to travel allowance, and are provided with a government car with private license (registration number) plates instead of the normal plates applying to government cars. A Canberra-based High Court Judge is entitled to an allowance of A$ 20,000 if resident in Canberra. Judges enjoy a non-contributory superannuation scheme – that is, they receive a fully funded government pension for life following retirement to which they make no contributions out of their salaries – which, to a Federal Court Judge with 10 years service, could be equated with an annual employer superannuation contribution of A$ 168,714 (November 1993).[1] Taking this into account, the total remuneration including long leave and other benefits for such a Federal Court Judge was A\$ 348,674, of which the salary component was A\$ 147,995. If she or he served for 20 years, the total annual remuneration estimated by this method would be A\$ 233,238 (Remuneration Tribunal 1994: xii–xiii).

Department secretaries (heads of government departments) until recently were remunerated on the basis of a salary plus a modest fixed allowance, which was taxed unless receipts for work-related expenses were presented. They had a contributory pension fund with an employee as well as employer component. Certain other benefits were provided. The highest-paid department head in 1993 earned A\$ 134,440 in base salary, plus an additional A\$ 52,793 in benefits, comprising A\$ 30,921 for superannuation contributions, A\$ 8,000 for a private plated car, A\$ 1,000 for parking, A\$ 5,000 for spouse travel, A\$ 600 for 'leave loading', A\$ 165 for domestic telephone bills, A\$ 3,361 for long service leave and A\$ 4,000 in fringe benefit tax payment.[2]

In 1999, the benefits, in addition to base salary, were wrapped together in a total package, which could be taken in various combinations of salary and benefits (so long as benefits did not exceed 50 per cent of the total) (Remuneration Tribunal 1999; see also Nethercote 1999). A 20 per cent loading was provided for those on fixed-term contracts rather than permanent tenure. Contract employment was now the norm, but incumbents with existing tenure rights could retain them at a cost of a 20 per cent lower salary. The package also included performance pay provisions for the first time. The Senior Executive Service (SES) (the 1,400 or so top civil servants in the Commonwealth government bureaucracy, excluding departmental heads, who are a separate corps) had begun to receive some of their rewards in this type of package in 1989, and after 1996 they enjoyed extra flexibility in negotiating packages, including taking such items as fitness club membership in lieu of salary.

The base salary of the highest-paid department heads as of March 2000 was A\$ 225,000, but the total remuneration, including benefits, was A\$ 305,000. Performance bonuses are in addition to these amounts. The reward for 'superior performance' is 10 per cent of total remuneration, and for 'outstanding performance' 15 per cent. If outstanding performance is achieved, the total remuneration including other benefits would be A\$ 350,750, or 35 per cent higher than the base salary (information on actual bonuses awarded to individuals is confidential). Also, there is a provision for compensation for 'early loss of office', that is, dismissal before the term of a contract expires.

A corresponding pattern applies to members of the SES, as noted earlier. In 2000, the average base salary of an SES Band-3 officer (the highest band) was A\$ 145,764, while the average total remuneration including performance bonuses was A\$ 210,644.[3] Fringe benefits tax (under which such components of a remuneration package are taxed at the highest marginal rate) applies to packaged benefits, and is taken into account in calculating the value in terms of remuneration. Tax changes in recent years have eliminated most of the tax advantages of packaging, but there remains some tax advantage from packaging superannuation payments and cars.

Politicians

Expanding on the analysis in Chapter 2, Table 4.1 lists the various entitlements of politicians, ranging from salary to funding for staff and offices.[4] The benefits and allowances paid to each MP in addition to base salary are nowhere consolidated or reported as a total remuneration amount. A recent audit report estimated the total cost of all entitlements in Table 4.1 (excluding superannuation) to be approximately A$ 350 million in 1999–2000, of which just in excess of A$ 23 million was salaries (ANAO 2001). This figure includes expenditure on maintaining politicians' staff and offices in Parliament and in their electorates, and the expenses incurred by ministers in the conduct of their executive duties.

As Table 4.1 shows, many entitlements are uncapped, leading to wide variations in payments to individuals. For example, the cost to a minister's department of providing ministerial non-salary goods and services ranged from A$ 47,000 to 267,000 per minister.[5] Twenty-nine parliamentarians made no use of their statutory entitlement to distribute free Australian flags to constituents while, among those that did, the cost ranged from A$ 28 to 16,880. In the case of personalized stationery, newsletters and printing, expenditure ranged from A$ 1,294 to 219,004 in 1999–2000. There is little to prevent this expenditure being a direct subsidy to a political party, as distinct from a contribution to an MP's constituency expenses. Some of the main entitlements are described in more detail later.

Superannuation is another much disputed perk for politicians in Australia. The current parliamentary superannuation scheme dates from 1948 (with many subsequent amendments). MPs' contributions are 11.5 per cent of salary for the first 18 years of parliamentary service. After this the contribution rate falls to 5.75 per cent.

Parliamentarians become eligible for the full pension after serving three terms, and it becomes payable immediately upon leaving office, regardless of age. Seventy per cent of MPs, since the scheme was introduced, have qualified for the full pension. At the 1993 and 1996 elections, five MPs who left office were aged less than 40, and they received pensions of between A$ 40,000 and 52,000 per annum (Senate Select Committee on Superannuation 1997). The pension varies between 50 and 75 per cent of the full salary, depending on length of service. For those serving less than three terms, a generous lump sum payment is made. The amount is higher if the retirement is involuntary (equivalent to 233 per cent of personal contributions to the scheme). In response to persistent public criticism of the scheme, the Government in June 2001 introduced amendments. Existing MPs would retain their current entitlements, but newly elected members would be restricted from collecting a pension until they reached the age of 55. The Bill was heavily criticized by Independents and the Australian Democrats for not going far enough in reducing benefits (*Sydney Morning Herald*, 3 July 2001).

All parliamentarians receive an electorate allowance that ranges from A$ 27,300 to 39,600, depending on the size of constituency. If the full amount is not expended on electorate expenses, it is taxed at the marginal rate. Allowable expenses are numerous, and include donations, presentations, subscriptions, home computer and other equipment, professional library, home office, additional secretarial

Table 4.1 Politicians' entitlements in Australia

Uncapped	Dollar limit	Occurrences limit	Content limit
Travelling allowance	Salary	Travelling allowance (within electorate)	Staff
Scheduled travel	Superannuation	Travel for party/parliamentary committees	Office accommodation
Travel by special purpose aircraft	Electorate allowance	Non-official spouse and dependant travel	Office equipment
Car transport	Charter transport	Retirement travel (post-1994 rules)	Office supplies
Private vehicle allowance	Postage and other delivery services	Newspapers and periodicals	Privately plated vehicles
Telephone services	Overseas study trips		Photographic services
Personalized stationery and other printing	Spouse and dependant travel		Constituents request program (including flags)
Retirement travel (pre-1994 rules)			Overseas delegations travel
All ministerial non-salary entitlements			

Source: ANAO [2001: 72 (adapted)].

Notes
Uncapped entitlements can only be accessed in terms of relevant legislation and regulations, but without overall financial limit in a given year.
Dollar limit capped entitlements are subject to a financial cap in a given year.
Occurrences limited entitlements are restricted by the number of occurrences in a year.
Content limited entitlements are goods and services subject to rules about content and form.

assistance beyond that already provided (there is no no-nepotism rule and payment of a spouse for this purpose is allowable), accommodation and meals while travelling in the electorate, and other travel expenses in addition to those otherwise provided for. Moreover, some of the costs of home telephone and fax services are paid for, and MPs have a telephone services charge card. Up to A$ 22,000 is available for use on mail, courier and other delivery services for 'legitimate' electoral and parliamentary business. This provision supposedly excludes party business, and once parliament is dissolved and an election called, claims cannot be made.

In addition, distance is an Australian obsession, and compensation for the costs of overcoming it are a major source of additional allowances and benefits. Parliamentarians are entitled to first-class travel between their 'principal place of residence' and the seat of parliament, Canberra, and for travel on parliamentary business, such as committee work and national party conferences. Living away from home allowances are payable, based on schedules distinguishing between ordinary members or senators, parliamentary officers and ministers, for all travel on parliamentary business. This allowance is also payable to parliamentarians while in Canberra during sittings, if their principal place of residence is elsewhere.

Abuse of travel allowances is a major source of scandals. In 1997, it brought to an end the career of several ministers (one of whom was the Minister for Transport) in a series of events dubbed 'Travelgate'. Most of the rorts in this area arise from claiming allowances that are not, strictly speaking, allowable (e.g. among the Minister for Transport's transgressions was to use government chartered flights to visit his sick father). Most victims blame their staff for keeping poor records, or plead careless accounting. An Audit Office report (ANAO 1997) also found lax administration by the Department of Administrative Services (Travelgate also claimed the scalp of that Department's Minister for an attempted cover-up). The latest audit report found a number of continuing deficiencies in the manner of reporting and accounting for travel expenses. The system relies on self-reporting through Travel Declaration Forms, but there is no legal obligation in the regulations that they be submitted, and there are frequently gaps and errors in the information. The Department of Finance does not follow-up rigorously in cases where they suspect an error in a claim (e.g. by demanding receipts) (ANAO 2001: 145–6, 153).

MPs may be provided with an Australian-made private plated car at government expense. The terms and conditions are the same as those applying to the SES, including a personal contribution out of salary. The government meets all running and maintenance costs, and the car is available for private use. Government or hire-car transport is made available for local trips when an MP is on parliamentary business. A spouse receives free travel to any approved function at which the MP is officiating, and is entitled to up to nine return trips to Canberra per annum, dependants up to three. Spouse and dependant travel claims by MPs ranged from zero to A$ 40,935 in 1999–2000. This figure reflects an underlying problem with many capped entitlements: the procedures do not allow for efficient monitoring to ensure caps are not exceeded. In some cases, but not all, the Department of Finance seeks recovery. Members representing electorates of

10,000 square kilometres or more, and all Senators except those from the ACT, are provided a special allowance for chartered transport within their electorate. The amounts allowed range from A$ 11,500 to 51,300.

After three years of service, a senator or member is entitled to an amount equivalent to a round-the-world first-class air ticket to undertake an 'overseas study tour'. Further, such funded trips are available in the life of each Parliament. The amount can be used to contribute towards the travel of a spouse and accommodation costs. MPs must justify the purpose of the trip, and submit a report upon returning. An ordinary member who serves in seven parliaments or for 20 years (whichever comes first) is entitled to travel free within Australia for up to 25 return trips a year until death, other than for business purposes. This is known as the 'life gold pass', and is a much prized perk. Ministers qualify after only one year. On such travel, a spouse can accompany the retired MP without cost. Widows and widowers get a year's grace following death of the retired member. Retired members who do not qualify for the gold pass are entitled to free travel for periods of between six months and five years, depending on the length of parliamentary service. This benefit has been explained away as 'an appropriate public recognition of public service (at) minor cost' (Remuneration Tribunal 1992: 27) and it is not taxed. As with MP's travel claims, administration relies on self-reporting and enforcement is weak. The Department of Finance makes some effort to recover expenditures that should not have been incurred. As of July 2001, recoveries were in progress in relation to 43 retired MPs (ANAO 2001: 176).

Going beyond the various cash allowances and related perks, non-salary tangible rewards of office can be considerable for politicians, especially for Ministers and the Prime Minister. Such rewards range from subsidized restaurants and other facilities in Parliament House to the perks of official entertainment. The Prime Minister and his family traditionally occupy 'The Lodge' in Canberra (at government expense) – a relatively modest suburban residence – and each new incumbent and spouse invariably call in the interior decorator. At the time of writing, the current Prime Minister has gone one better: he and his family have taken up residence in Kirribilli House in Sydney, a nineteenth century mansion on Sydney Harbour opposite the Opera House. This property was conventionally at the disposal of the Prime Minister and other ministers, but also (in the past) was used for housing visiting dignitaries and for social functions. The refurbishments to accommodate the tastes of the Howard family have brought a predictable response from the media.

There is no institutionalized system that guarantees additional income-earning opportunities during or after a high-level judicial, political or public service career, as applies to Japan and to a lesser extent Korea, as described in this volume. In addition, rules prohibiting 'second jobs' while in office are closely observed. The major Australian political parties by and large insist on their parliamentarians being full-time politicians, attending to their constituency or undertaking party work. Judicial officers are severely discouraged from seeking or taking some kinds of further work upon retirement, for fear that it would compromise their judgment in anticipation of such employment. However, they frequently pick up various *ad hoc* quasi-judicial assignments in their golden years, such as appointments to head government inquiries.

In the case of public servants, there are few restrictions or inhibitions on post-retirement employment. The Commonwealth superannuation scheme is relatively generous to those taking early retirement, and senior ex-public servants are commonly observed pursuing second careers as lobbyists and consultants. This is a growing trend. Department heads (for example) in the 1980s and 1990s spent on average somewhat less time in the job and left at a younger age than their predecessors (Weller and Wood 1999: 23). The growing range of linkages with the private sector, as a result of outsourcing and various forms of 'partnering', has widened opportunities for launching a lucrative late career move on the basis of high-level public service experience. With the growth of contract employment, the expectation of such a transition is growing, and is increasingly viewed as normal.

However, there is no institutionalized equivalent to the Japanese 'descent from heaven' for retiring public servants. Part-time appointments to various tribunals and boards are common, but rewards are modest. For the more significant of such positions, they have to compete with the Government's partisan friends and allies. This affords retiring politicians some lucrative prospects, but they are none too reliable. For the ordinary backbencher, involuntary loss of office before retirement age can come at considerable cost. There are many anecdotes offering testament to the struggles of reestablishing a career outside politics, and they receive frequent airing in defence of the generosity of the superannuation scheme. Ex-ministers upon retirement find more openings, whether they be government posts or opportunities in the private sector. If the former, however, tenure is subject to the vagaries of partisan fortune, as incoming governments customarily clean out the stables and install their own friends.

The politics of rewards

The arrangements for determining rewards for high public office are complex and have varied over time, but there has been a strong preference for the independent tribunal in order to take some of the political heat out of the issue. The political strategy has not worked. The independent Remuneration Tribunal has frequently recommended pay rises for politicians which governments and oppositions have found it politic to oppose, because they appeared too generous to a cynical public. At the same time, politicians compensated themselves in other ways, thereby digging themselves deeper into difficulties. They enhanced the range and size of less-visible allowances and maintained a generous superannuation scheme. Meanwhile, top public servants are beginning to break free of the shackles of these institutional and political constraints through taking advantage of the newly sanctioned norms of commercialization in the public sector, and receiving greater private-sector parity.

Given Australia's political culture, institutional traditions and political arrangements, these outcomes might be explained employing a combination of rational choice, institutional and cultural theories (see Hood and Peters 1994). As a game between a sceptical and hostile public on the one hand, and a political class keen to maximize its income on the other, the outcome – relatively low pay accompanied by attempts to shift compensation to more opaque, less accountable forms of income – is broadly the predicted one. The result is a classic vicious circle – insisting on low pay encourages politicians to look for devious ways of alternative compensation, which brings disrepute down on their heads, further increasing the public's resistance to pay increases.

Institutional explanations can also aid in understanding some of the observed patterns. Such explanations give primacy to how rules and norms constrain and facilitate certain patterns of outcomes. For example, the Australian tradition of quasi-judicial wage arbitration, operating through the means of a remuneration tribunal, help us understand some of the traditional linkages and relativities between different RHPOs. The recent shift towards deregulation of wage setting, and a greater role for the market, has created a different set of institutional restraints and opportunities, with resulting changes in these relativities. Top bureaucrats, for example, have found their hands strengthened by deregulation in the labour market and have struck better deals.

Finally, a cultural explanation would look first at the role of changing sentiments and ideas, and would predict less regularity in the effects of institutions, or of any rational calculus adopted by groups and individuals struggling for advantage. For example, the beginnings of the 'break-out' in senior executives' pay (including such things as performance bonuses) might be seen as part of a cultural shift, in which a society has become increasingly ambivalent about its egalitarian traditions and more individualistic in its sentiments, thereby helping to legitimize increasing levels of income inequality. There may also have been a decline in the notion of 'service' as a reward in itself. Cultural ambivalence is evident, moreover, in the extent of the public backlash against these changes, and the way they further restrain the salaries of those who are singled out for blame – namely, politicians. Cultural approaches might help understand anomalies, fluctuations and U-turns.

The analysis here explores each of these types of explanation through describing aspects of the processes and the outcomes of recent decisions about RHPOs. This approach inevitably focuses on institutions as the 'sites' of such processes and decisions, but such a focus does not entail pre-figuring a bias towards an institutionalist explanation, in the sense outlined earlier.

Institutional arrangements

Many matters concerning the remuneration and allowances of higher public officials are under the jurisdiction of the Remuneration Tribunal, established in 1973. Before that date, politicians' pay was determined directly by parliament, frequently with the assistance of specially appointed quasi-judicial inquiries. The express aim in 1973 was to de-politicise the process. This turned out to be far from the result. In the case of politicians' allowances and other entitlements, the situation is complicated by the fact that some entitlements – for example, politicians' superannuation – fall outside the tribunal's jurisdiction. Over matters within its jurisdiction, the tribunal in some cases determines, in others it recommends. Over time, its powers have been varied as governments have chosen one or another strategy to manage the politics of pay.

The tribunal has followed a number of principles that derive from what it sees as objective criteria and fair and reasonable standards. These include grounds familiar to all wage-fixing tribunals in Australia, namely relativities, inequities and work value. For example, the tribunal has tried with mixed success to maintain relativities within the public sector, such as the tradition that High Court Judges are the highest-paid public officers in the land. The tribunal has also had regard to the size of gaps between ranks, for example, the distance between department secretaries' remuneration and that of officers in the SES. The tribunal has also paid some attention to comparability with private-sector pay levels. In the late 1980s, for example, it reported on the difficulties in recruiting senior judges, as levels of remuneration in private legal practice far outstripped their pay. In the 1990s it paid growing attention to the lag in departmental secretaries' pay behind that of CEOs in the private sector.

Politics and the tribunal

Although the existence of the tribunal provides an ostensibly non-political, impartial basis for pay determination, the situation is more complex. The government of the day remains the main actor in the process. Its role and influence are expressed in a number of ways. First, it can amend the tribunal's legislation to alter its powers or to ensure that it has regard to particular matters. Second, it makes regular submissions to the tribunal expressing government policy, and the responsible minister engages in more regular and detailed communication. Third, its various powers over determinations and recommendations – either the potential to disallow a determination, or the refusal to enact necessary legislation where the tribunal only has powers of recommendation – provide it with both influence and authority should it wish to deploy them. As a consequence, not only does the government occasionally determine matters unilaterally, the tribunal also sometimes complies with its stated policy positions. In many such cases, it has done so while stating its disapproval.

For example, the 1983 Hawke Labor Government in one of its first major decisions signed an Accord with the trade unions, involving agreement to a set of principles to rein in wage rises in return for other policy concessions. The Accord, which included agreement on centralized wage-fixing principles and procedures, remained a centrepiece of successive Labor Governments' economic policies. The application to the work of the tribunal of the Accord's main principles was achieved by an amendment to its act in 1984. But the tribunal argued strongly that special circumstances should continue to apply to the remuneration of higher public officials, and during the second half of the 1980s came into repeated collision with the government. One cause of such conflict was of the government's own making. In 1988, it announced the removal of a number of offices from the jurisdiction of the tribunal, namely those of the chief executives of major government business enterprises. In the process of commercializing these bodies, the government allowed their Boards the power to hire and fire CEOs on terms and conditions that they saw fit, in line with commercial practices. As a token gesture, the tribunal had to be 'consulted'. Not surprisingly, these remuneration packages increased substantially, taking them beyond the levels currently applying to judges and top public servants under the tribunal's jurisdiction.[6]

The tribunal's 1988 review of MPs' pay recommended increases above and beyond the national wage case (which, under the Accord, was the supposed benchmark for all pay rises). Reviews of pay for other public officials also resulted in recommendations for increases. The government, intent on setting an example of wage restraint, refused to implement the recommendations and persuaded (more precisely, bullied) the tribunal to delay its determinations (Remuneration Tribunal 1990: 6–7). The result was to freeze the pay of judges, politicians and department secretaries (aside from the national wage case rises). The tribunal protested vigorously and continued to advocate increases. In 1990, the government lost patience and effectively took the power of determination of politicians' pay out of the tribunal's hands. It legislated to provide for a phased increase of MP's salaries up to the top level of SES Band 1 (the lowest). Once salaries reached this level, subsequent adjustment of parliamentary salaries would follow any adjustments made to SES salaries.[7] The tribunal retained jurisdiction over review and recommendation of most MPs' allowances, along with ministers' remuneration.

In sum, the change was designed to remove the annoyance of the tribunal's criticisms of the government, while at the same time instituting a new, routine mechanism for pay increases – that is, an alternative form of depoliticization. But in 1998, the tribunal's role of recommending increases had to be restored, because the existing automatic adjustor had became inoperable in 1996. Under the Workplaces Relations Act of that year, SES members were required to enter into individual contracts with their employer. As a result, there is no standard ladder of SES salaries. The tribunal in 1999 recommended a 'reference salary' for MP's pay at a point just below that of the lowest-paid Commonwealth CEO under its jurisdiction (the effect was to grant MPs a 9.95 per cent increase).[8] This, along with another recommendation to adjust MP's salaries annually in line with average weekly earnings, was accepted by the government. The tribunal's role as the buffer between the Parliament and the public was restored, but only so long as the Parliament continues to accept the tribunal's recommendations and the automatic increases.

Decisions about non-salary allowances and entitlements have also exhibited only a weak form of depoliticization. In the case of allowances under the tribunal's purview (the principal ones being the electorate allowance, communications and travel) the decisions are publicly announced, but the process of arriving at them is far from transparent. Most of the allowances originate in government or parliamentary initiatives. A former member of the tribunal gave his view of the process:

> … typically this is what would happen: a politician or party would make a submission to add a phone card (for example) to the politician's arsenal

of perks; the Remuneration Tribunal would conclude the request was resonable but must be protected from abuse; strict guidelines on the use of the phone card are debated, drafted, re-debated and re-drafted; the tribunal's determination is then issued.

(*Sydney Morning Herald*, 2 November 2000)

Some entitlements arise indirectly and enter via the back door. For example, as a consequence of tying the salaries of MPs to those of the SES after 1990, the more favourable terms under which SES officers received motor vehicles flowed on to MPs. In 1998, the tribunal attempted to consolidate and review all the entitlements, but the result was mainly to codify and refine those already existing.

Not only with allowances, but also in the case of superannuation, the argument has been made that they compensate for the 'loss of earnings' that can arise from being an MP rather than engaging in a professional or business career. A 1997 Senate inquiry into MP's superannuation failed to produce a firm recommendation – despite strong evidence that the scheme was in need of major reform – largely because backbenchers objected strongly to having such entitlements removed, at the same time as their salaries were being restrained. One of the arguments advanced in favour of the decision by the government to accept the recommended 1999 pay rise was to take the pressure off demands for cutting back on such benefits.

Managerialism and the market

One of the paradoxes of recent pay trends among HPOs is that the public service has fared better than politicians, at a time when public-sector reforms have sought to increase the level of political control and to subordinate more effectively the public service to the government of the day. But public servants, it would seem, while accepting a new set of less secure and more subservient arrangements in relations with the political executive, have exacted a price in their system of rewards (McAllister and Painter 2000). One of the reasons for this growth in effective bargaining power lies in the consequences of marketization of various public-sector practices.

The bulk of public servants traditionally had their pay set not by the Remuneration Tribunal but by collective bargaining in the framework of the arbitration and conciliation system. Recent changes in industrial-relations policy have seen most aspects of the traditional system disbanded in the name of labour market deregulation, and this has affected the way public-service rewards are determined. Public-sector reforms have also affected many aspects of conditions of employment. The establishment of the SES in the 1980s was one such change that in turn brought about new conditions for determining rewards. In 1989, the government reached agreement on a series of measures to allow remuneration for members of the SES along lines more familiar to executives in the private sector. Increases in base salary were approved, along with a system of incentive payments, or performance bonuses. Further changes in 1996, in line with new industrial relations rules encouraging wider use of individual contracts, brought the system even closer to that of private-sector executives, with SES members now required to negotiate individual remuneration packages with their department heads.

One result of these developments, as mentioned earlier, has been to end standardization of senior HPO rewards. Another, related outcome has been a growing gap between the highest and the lowest within a category or band. Between 1996 and 1999, the range between the minimum and maximum salary in Band 1 grew from A\$ 13,892 to 44,660; in Band 3, the range grew from A\$ 26,643 to 65,797. A comparison of the results of this survey with other data showed that the gap between remuneration for public- and private-sector executives was much higher at the upper levels of the SES than the lower, and that state government SES members in the higher reaches also earned more than their Commonwealth counterparts – on average about 10 per cent (Mercer Cullen Egan Dell 2000b). One can draw the inference that these gaps increased the bargaining power of those at higher levels in the Commonwealth SES. The combination of contract employment and individual wage bargaining work in the favour of those with the scarcest skills who, almost by definition, are those at the top. The result is an increasingly inegalitarian system of rewards.

The other source of variability, apart from the differences in individual contracts, is the existence of performance bonuses. Since 1996, there has been no restraint in the SES on the level of annual bonuses payable as the result of meeting the terms of a contract. The majority (84 per cent) of agencies reported paying bonuses, and 58 per cent of officers in the survey reported receiving them. The average maximum payable was 10 per cent. The highest actually paid was 38 per cent of base salary, while the average in Band 1 was 5.5 per cent (A\$ 5,921) and in Band 3, 6 per cent (A\$ 10,864), indicating that the performance bonus system was being used as a selective rather than an across the board reward mechanism (Mercer Cullen Egan Dell 2000a). At the same time, a portion of the available bonus has become a normal expectation. While measures of individual performance have been instituted, some part of the bonus in most cases rests on meeting 'normal' (average) expectations of competency and output.

The restructuring of department secretaries' remuneration by the tribunal in 1999 was also a step towards marketization. The Howard Conservative Government elected in 1996 made several new appointments to the tribunal from the private sector, making it more amenable to such developments. The significant increases that emerged in the 1999 pay rise were a combination of increases in base salary over two years of 10 and 12 per cent respectively, a 20 per cent loading on base salary for relinquishment of tenure, and performance bonuses. The opportunity to engage in packaging was an additional benefit. The increases were in part prompted by the spectre of individually bargained SES officers' rewards catching up with those of their bosses, and also by the disparities between remuneration for Commonwealth, compared with state government, department heads. The tribunal was at pains to point out that the aim was not to achieve parity with the private sector, but the growing gap – caused in part by the deliberate government restraints of the previous decade – was nevertheless a consideration.

These changes were part of a wider movement that saw the public sector in Australia swept up in the new public-management movement. In the SES, employment by contract and performance pay were key parts of these reforms. The ideas underlying them ran counter to many of the principles by which public service remuneration had traditionally been determined. In particular, they challenged the expectation that public servants would perform effectively under an incentive regime that relied on a self-imposed sense of public duty, a calling for public office, and the promise of a decent, secure retirement after long service at a relatively modest salary. The tribunal remained somewhat ambivalent about the new trends in the face of the unlocking of public enterprise CEOs from the parities of other public-sector pay scales, the emergence of the SES and the new measures for department secretaries. This ambivalence was echoed in the face of other changes, as their own cherished principles of work value and equity were being overtaken by the forces of supply and demand. The tribunal was mindful of the budget restraint and noted community sentiment when recommending the changes to department secretary rewards: '… the community expects that the remuneration paid to public sector chief executives will be below that paid in the market place' (quoted in Nethercote 1999).

Opposition and scepticism about some of these new remuneration practices was evident in the wider community and in the parliament. The views of the NSW Labor Government have already been noted. The Senate Standing Committee on Finance and Public Administration, like the tribunal, drew attention to the interests of the taxpayer and the issue of rising costs in sounding a warning against some of the trends (Senate Finance and Public Administration Reference Committee 2000). In several reports the Committee has opposed performance pay in the public service, on the grounds that 'performance' cannot be accurately measured, and that 'outstanding' public service by an individual can better be rewarded by Public Service Awards and other schemes of recognition. They noted with disapproval the tendency to provide bonus payments for what was merely 'competent' performance and, in particular, the secrecy with which the whole process was surrounded.

An additional source of scepticism and opposition has come from the ranks of those left behind. The union movement opposed the deregulation of the labour market because they foresaw that one possible consequence would be a growing level of income inequality. They were right. The growing differentials are seen starkly within the ranks of the public service itself. Between 1980 and 2000, the ratio between the salary of the highest-paid Department Secretary and the entry-level clerical grade has grown from 6.3 to 8.6. In fact, nearly all of this increase has occurred since 1995. If we take the TRP as the relevant figure, the ratio has grown from close to 9 to 13. In other words, the gap between the top and bottom has grown one and half times, most of it in recent years.

Overall, the effect of marketization in employment and remuneration practices has been to give senior public servants greater bargaining power. The reservations and tensions reflected in the statements of the tribunal and of backbench MPs reflect an ambivalence in the outcome, and possibly a lack of intentionality.

At the same time, the probability is that politicians see in this situation an opportunity to embark on a catch-up, an element of which was reflected in the 1999 tribunal decision on politicians' pay.

Ministers – executives or politicians?

The Remuneration Tribunal recommends the additional remuneration to be paid to all Parliamentary Office-holders, Parliamentary Secretaries and Ministers. The Prime Minister receives an additional salary of 160 per cent of his basic MP's salary (an additional amount of A$ 144,000 in 2000). Cabinet Ministers receive a 75 per cent additional salary and the Leader of the Opposition receives an additional 85 per cent. The Howard Government in 1996 implemented a two-tier pay structure for ministers, resulting in a reduction in pay for non-Cabinet ministers of A$ 10,000. Aside from this, the relativities between the salaries of ministers and the Prime Minister have not changed significantly.

As the data on the Prime Minister's pay suggested in Chapter 2, members of the political executive seem to have benefited recently from the pressures exerted by private-sector pay increases, even if ordinary MPs have not. The trend seems to have begun in the Australian states, where there was a stronger tendency to mould the roles of Premier and of Ministers along private-sector lines. In the late 1980s and during the 1990s, reforming premiers such as Nick Greiner in NSW and Jeff Kennett in Victoria deliberately promulgated the notion that 'running the state is like running a business'. Both public service and ministerial rewards in these states overtook those of the Commonwealth. This, as much as the private-sector comparison, caught the eye of the tribunal, and was one of the reasons it was prepared to recommend a large increase in remuneration for ministers (as well as department secretaries) in the late 1990s.

But the Remuneration Tribunal has not recommended that members of the political executive should have their salaries set to match those of private-sector corporate executives, nor is there any longer much excitement over relativities with chief executives of public enterprises, which have 'flown the coop'. Cabinet ministers earn considerably less than the TRP of their department heads and, as we saw earlier, a lot less than the chief executive of a NSW rural electricity utility.

Conclusions

The Remuneration Tribunal has acknowledged the expectation of the Australian public that politicians will receive a relatively modest salary, and has pointed to some of the dilemmas this presents:

> The Australian egalitarian tradition would argue for remuneration levels of parliamentarians not too far distant from those of the general community that they represent .... In order to attract talented people to the role of

Members with a sufficient commitment to their work, their remuneration need not match, but must at least be adequate in comparison with, the rewards to those requiring comparable abilities in the community at large .... The egalitarian approach is inconsistent with a context in which pay differentials are widening in the labour market.

(Remuneration Tribunal 1995: 64–6)

In the face of the evidence of widening differentials in the past two decades, the egalitarian sentiment would seem not to be dead. Politicians and, to a lesser extent, top public servants, are subjected to increasing levels of resentment. One interpretation might be that politicians are being singled out for presiding over the growth in inequality, by not being allowed to be among the main beneficiaries. But even this does not surround them with any aura of virtue. Ever-growing cynicism mounts in response to the stratagems they adopt to protect their living standards and life styles in the face of salary restraint. They have clung to their perks and, in the eyes of many, increasingly rorted them. The monetary value of these additional benefits and allowances is not always publicized, for good reason: their opaqueness is what allows some MPs to continue to exploit them.

Meanwhile, the salaries of top public servants and, to a lesser extent, members of the political executive, seem recently to have escaped any egalitarian restraint. Top public servants have supposedly entered the brave new world of the market, where they live and die by their wits. Contracts and performance pay bring higher levels of risk, and greater potential rewards for success. But they, too, face dilemmas rooted in cultural ambivalence. The notion that a career in public service is a 'higher calling' for a chosen elite is foreign to Australia, and the belief that it reflects democratic aspirations lingers (Painter 1990). The state and its servants are there to soften the edges of harsh economic realities, not to reflect them. Hence, there is deep suspicion of market-driven executive salaries, packaged perks and performance bonuses. They seem to bring extra rewards for no tangible results. There is a strong suspicion that what is occurring is corrupting, and against the public interest. Cynicism also accompanies the spectacle of ex-public servants who have completed their contracts and taken out their early retirement superannuation, and have gone to work for the very private corporations that they were formerly regulating.

But to argue that both politicians' and public servants' remuneration systems are in some senses 'corrupting' is, in the Australian context, a statement about a clash of cultures rather than an objective judgement on the propensity for corrupt behaviour, or on the overall level of systemic corruption in public administration. Australia ranks 13th – between Switzerland and the USA – among nations included in the world-wide Transparency International Corruption Index. The angst is about norms of public service and public duty as intrinsic activities, rather than about objective consequences. Much of it is about appearances – a hope for a glimmer of sincerity rather than opportunism, and empathy rather than antagonism. The logic of the prevailing structures of incentives seems to be driving events towards the more dismal of these scenarios.

Notes

1 This amount was actuarially calculated, based on the level of employer contribution to the Commonwealth public-service superannuation scheme.

2 These benefits as of 1993 were revealed as a result of a Remuneration Tribunal inquiry in 1994, but otherwise were not published as part of a total reward package until 1999.

3 The most common items available for packaging include: financial counselling fees, disability or income protection insurance premiums, self-education expenses, work-related travel expenses, personal computers, briefcases, calculators and electronic diaries, computer software, professional development, contributions to a private super-annuation fund, motor vehicle leased for private use, fees and subscriptions to professional associations, mobile phones and health insurance premiums.

4 Appointments of office staff are within the gift of each MP, and may include party supporters, friends or family.

5 These figures represent the average cost of each of the several ministers making up a portfolio.

6 In the Australian states, it had long been accepted that the heads of the larger public enterprises enjoyed higher rewards than department heads, which was a reflection in part of the high status in Australian administrative traditions of specialist, professional as distinct from generalist, administrative work (Painter 1987: 38; 45–9).

7 In 1994, in a schedule tucked away in an Industrial Relations Legislation Amendment Act dealing mainly with the coal industry, MPs' salaries were in future to be tied to Band 2 of the SES (Healy and Winter 2000).

8 The base salary of MPs in 2000 was roughly equivalent to the average Band 1 SES base salary.

5 New Zealand – the end of egalitarianism?

Robert Gregory

> But when everybody does have bread, as is certainly the case in New Zealand, what is to be done about cake? Either cake must be abolished altogether on the ground that it is undemocratic, or else some cake must be given to everyone, and then nobody can be allowed to receive more than a crumb. Under either alternative only one thing is certain: cake will not be enjoyed.
>
> (Lipson 1948: 490–1)

Introduction

New Zealand's rewards for high public office (RHPOs) are generally low in comparison with the remuneration paid to its top business executives, and, as Chapter 2 showed, they are very much lower than those for governmental officials in some of the other countries included in this study, notably Singapore and Hong Kong. But the state sector reforms of the late 1980s and the 1990s, incorporating New Public Management (NPM) ideas, have been associated with significant pay rises for top state bureaucrats, resulting in major changes in RHPOs relativities.

These reforms were a component of much wider, radical, public policy changes, which have had a major impact on the country's strong egalitarian tradition. By 2000, public attitudes towards the size and scope of remuneration packages payable to high public officeholders were torn between a commitment to traditional egalitarianism and a need to come to terms with the imperatives of an increasingly dominant market culture, in both the private and state sectors. This angst has been exacerbated by growing socio-economic inequality, on the one hand, and on the other by the emergence of an apparently privileged managerial elite whose relatively high levels of remuneration are not obviously a function of either executive competence or improved national economic performance.

The New Zealand story of RHPOs change over the past 20 years has to be seen as a contrast between two distinct historical periods. The first embodies the years up to the late 1980s, before the state sector reconstruction brought about by the State Sector Act 1988 and the Public Finance Act 1989. The second period runs from then till the end of the millennium. An understanding of what has occurred as a consequence of the changes in the late 1980s is best provided by responses to the following questions. First, why in an egalitarian culture have politicians stayed on relatively modest remuneration levels while bureaucrats have secured substantial pay rises? Second, why in an advanced democracy, which has made 'transparency' a catchword of state sector reforms, have RHPOs become more opaque, politicians' perks and allowances more controversial, and public trust more tenuous? Third, why in a country with low RHPOs have levels of state sector corruption also been very low, and what effect have increasing remuneration levels had, if any, on issues of corruption in government administration?

An explanation redolent of the rational choice school of politics is offered in answer to the first question. Reduced transparency in the case of rewards for top bureaucrats can be explained by the introduction of contractual appointments in place of the unified permanent career service, while the opacity and controversial nature of parliamentary allowances and entitlements is a function of long-standing egalitarian pressures. Contractualism and sharply rising levels of pay for top bureaucratic officials have probably had negative effects on levels of public trust, and have invited some reconsideration of the meaning of 'corruption' in the New Zealand context.

Institutionalized politicians and marketized bureaucrats

Changing fortunes

The most dramatic change in RHPOs patterns in New Zealand has been in the relativity between top public servants and members of the political executive. Between 1982 and 2000, the pay of New Zealand's top department official, the Secretary to the Treasury, rose by a massive 463 per cent. This rise compares with 247 per cent for the Chief Justice, 169 per cent for the Prime Minister, and 165 per cent for cabinet ministers and MPs. Whereas in 1982 the Prime Minister received 24 per cent more than the Secretary, by 2000 the relationship had been dramatically reversed, with the Secretary receiving 59 per cent more than the country's top politician. Years before the state sector reforms, many departmental permanent heads were paid well above the basic salary rate for cabinet ministers. In 1982, a minister's base salary was 22.5 per cent lower than the Treasury Secretary's pay. By 2000, however, it was 62.7 per cent lower. Moreover, by then not only were almost all departmental chief executives receiving substantially more than cabinet ministers' base salary plus allowances, but about half of them were being paid more than the Prime Minister's base salary plus allowances.[1]

However, there has been considerable 'horizontal decompression' in both public and private sector pay. In 1988, the State Sector Act brought base pay for departmental chief executives up to levels approaching the base rates applying in the top private sector positions. But in the face of huge increases in pay for private executives, in 1997 the government abandoned its previous policy of directly linking the remuneration of departmental chief executives to that of their private sector counterparts. The latter's pay had risen in real terms by about 130 per cent in the previous several years, compared to the 10 per cent real term rise for top public servants.

Nor has it been possible for the government to ensure parity between the remuneration for departmental chief executives and for the heads of some other state agencies. While the Secretary to the Treasury is New Zealand's highest paid public servant, the chief executive of New Zealand Post, the largest state-owned enterprise, is the highest paid state official, with a salary package in 2000 that was 55 per cent more than that received by the head of the Treasury. The Governor of the Reserve Bank of New Zealand, the country's central bank, in 2000 received 24 per cent more than the Secretary to the Treasury, and 123 per cent more than the Prime Minister's base salary.

Seizing opportunities

These changes occurred in fulfillment of the intentions of the State Sector Act 1988. The multifaceted dimensions of New Zealand state sector reform have been much elaborated and examined elsewhere (Boston *et al.* 1996; Scott 2001). Suffice it to stress here that they sought to replace, in virtually one fell swoop, an institutionalized structure of procedurally driven bureaucracy with a system driven more by competitive-market imperatives focused on the achievement of specifiable results. This shift constituted an attack on the cultural roots of the unified career service, expressed in the complex apparatus of appointments and appeals and state sector wage-setting that had been in existence for many decades. Roberts (1987: 86) aptly described the system as it was shortly before the reforms:

> New Zealand, in deference to a deep egalitarian impulse, has always rejected the creation of an elite group analogous to the French or British higher civil service ... the system ideally provides a classified structure of specific positions to which anyone from any department with appropriate qualifications may aspire, knowing that appointments will be made in the light of a possible need to justify their fairness and objectivity to an appeal tribunal.

The reforms abolished permanent tenure, which was replaced by a system of fixed-term contractual appointments of organizational chief executives and their senior staff. The State Services Commission (SSC) was now responsible for the appointment of departmental chief executives only, and for the terms and conditions of their contracts, including remuneration. Chief executives in turn were responsible for the appointment and remuneration (within central guidelines) of staff in their own organizations.

The sharp increase in the remuneration for Public Service chief executives compensated for the loss of permanent tenure, and for the greater political risk that has been transferred to officials under the generally more 'decoupled' relationship between ministers and the bureaucracy. It was also justified by the perceived need to achieve greater parity between their pay and that of their counterparts in the private sector, and to make the Public Service much more competitive in the general marketplace of executive talent, following the abolition of the closed career service.

The State Sector Act 1988 rendered passé the notion of a 'public service discount'. The remuneration payable to the topmost Public Service chief executives jumped overnight somewhere between 38.5 and 64.5 per cent in the case of the Secretary to the Treasury, and between 12.5 and 38.5 per cent for the State Services Commissioner. The precise increases are not publicly known as the actual salaries being paid in 1988 have not been disclosed. Previously, chief executives had received little in addition to a base salary, which had been published each year. After 1988 they were able to negotiate remuneration packages, including base salary together with income for a car, expenses, memberships fees, superannuation and a performance incentive payment (PIP). The latter is effectively an annual bonus, originally payable at a rate of up to 10 per cent of base salary to a maximum of NZ$ 10,000. In 1995, the maximum was removed, and in 1998 up to 15 per cent of the total remuneration package became payable as a PIP.

The rudiments of a pay for performance regime had been introduced in the mid-1980s by the Higher Salaries Commission (HSC), but the State Sector Act 1988 allowed it to be institutionalized and extended down through the organizational ranks. Management theory was seen to support a closer alignment between individual performance and reward. It was also believed that performance pay would help in the retention of skilled staff, and that it was necessary to slow the growth-rate of the Public Service wage bill by removing automatic increments.

Paying the politicians: shades of de Tocqueville?

The critical institutional change was that the authority to set pay levels for top public servants was taken out of the hands of the independent statutory body earlier established for this and other purposes, the HSC, and transferred to the SSC, though the Commissioner's own remuneration continued to be set by the HSC. This move paved the way for a sharp change in pay relativity as between top bureaucrats and cabinet ministers.

Historically, New Zealand is one country in this study that on the face of it confirms de Tocqueville's general thesis, discussed in Chapter 1, about downward democratic pressures on pay levels for top state officials. The epigraph to this chapter captures the egalitarian spirit which, together with democratic scrutiny of governmental pay levels, has created problems for those who would have preferred to see much higher pay for these positions. In New Zealand, politicians and bureaucrats, and even from time to time the judiciary, have been 'fair game' whenever there has been any public suggestion that their remuneration or perquisites should be increased. For example, adverse public attention led Parliament to cancel, for those MPs elected for the first time in 1999, the subsidized travel expenses that are still available to MPs elected before that year (and their spouses), even after they have left Parliament. The House also agreed to bulk public funding of Parliamentary parties and tighter scrutiny of spending by MPs. In addition, as in Australia as discussed by Martin Painter in this volume, there has been political controversy over 'gold plated' superannuation and retirement provisions for the many former MPs who have served a minimum of nine years in Parliament and who are aged 50 or over.

Until 1974, Parliament had been responsible for setting its own remuneration rates, including allowances (both for MPs and cabinet ministers). But in that year the Labour Government placed this authority in the hands of the HSC, which it had just set up. The Commission was charged with determining remuneration rates not only for the legislature, and for the judiciary, but also for a wide range of state sector employees, including leading local government officers. Determinations made by the HSC are mandatory.

At this time, New Zealand was moving into a much more turbulent economic and political era than it had experienced during the generally buoyant decades of the 1950s and 1960s. Stagflation was biting, full employment was rapidly being eroded, the sustainability of the welfare state was beginning to be more widely questioned, and neo-Keynesian approaches to economic policymaking were being increasingly challenged.

The egalitarian ethos, together with political sensitivities over inflationary pressures, had always exerted strong restraints on the levels of remuneration paid to members of the legislature. As the HSC commented in 1981:

> A basic problem in fixing parliamentary salaries is that it seems to be commonly held here and elsewhere that Members of Parliament should live under a continuing self-denying ordinance as an example to the country at large. Indeed, Parliamentarians themselves had tended to foster this attitude by declining or delaying increases in salaries and allowances recommended in the past by former Royal Commissions.
>
> (HSC 1981: 16)

In the years since the establishment of the HSC, the salaries and allowances payable to MPs and cabinet ministers have continued to arouse periodic political controversies. In 2000, the Minister of Finance expressed the view that the HSC had 'an impossible job', and that if it brought MPs salaries into line with those paid with 'comparable positions', particularly in the private sector, the increase would be so large that 'we'd probably have to put an electric fence around Parliament to protect us from public outrage'. He believed salary increases for MPs and cabinet ministers' should be linked to increments in the average wage.[2]

For its part, the HSC has held that the level of Parliamentary salaries has been 'significantly below comparable levels for positions with the same degree of responsibility, complexity, and workload', that the position has worsened in respect of 'the more senior positions in the House', and that '[I]t seemed incongruous for some Ministers to be paid significantly less than the departmental heads who report to them'. Further, 'any reduction in salaries in relative terms could only increase the risk of lowering the standard of governance in New Zealand' (HSC 1999: 13). In 2000, it found itself in an even more difficult position. Although Parliamentary salaries were 'significantly below' the levels for comparable positions with the same degree of responsibility, complexity and workload, and although it wanted to 'fairly reward' Parliamentarians, the Commission was 'all too keenly aware of the desire for restraint'.[3]

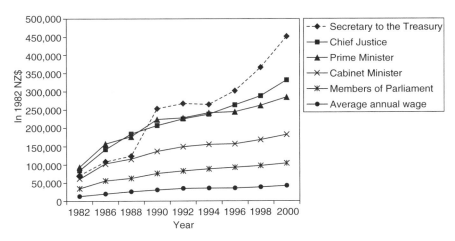

Figure 5.1 New Zealand remuneration levels, 1982–2000.

As indicated in Figure 5.1, during the period 1982–2000 there was no dramatic change in the relationship between New Zealand's average wage and the remuneration paid to the Prime Minister, Cabinet Ministers, MPs and the top judicial officer. The average wage has continued to represent about 13–15 per cent of the Prime Minister's income (base salary plus allowances as set by the HSC), about 20–23 per cent of a Cabinet Minister's, between 37 and 46 per cent of a backbench MP's, and about 13–15 per cent of the remuneration for the Chief Justice.

However, when compared with the average New Zealand wage, current Public Service chief executives are now far better off than were permanent heads under the pre-1988 regime. Whereas in 1982, the average New Zealand worker's income represented about 18.5 per cent of the pay of the Secretary to the Treasury, by 1990 the figure had dropped to 12 per cent, and by 2000 it was 9.4 per cent. General public sector workers had to be content with annual salary increases of 2 or 3 per cent; and under industrial legislation New Zealand workers in general had lost penal rates for work at nights and the weekends, access to employer-supported pension schemes and special allowances. According to the Minister of State Services in the centre–left coalition that took office after the 1999 election, there was an 'enormous gap' between the salary increases granted to departmental chief executives and those for 'ordinary New Zealanders'.[4]

Would top bureaucrats have received even higher increases if they had remained under the jurisdiction of the HSC? Almost certainly not, given the evidence. The market rationale which dominated the 1988 reforms had been invoked earlier by the HSC, but much less vigorously. The Commission had sought to make the pay for top public servants more comparable to that received by leading private sector executives. Between 1982 and 1986, under the HSC's jurisdiction the rate for the Secretary to the Treasury rose by 53 per cent in real terms, while that for the Prime Minister increased by 68 per cent; for cabinet ministers, 69 per cent; and for MPs, 61 per cent. Throughout, the Commission was obviously concerned to maintain traditional relativities between cabinet ministers and their top departmental advisers.

As shown in Figure 5.1, however, when pay-fixing for top officials was transferred to the State Services Commissioner from 1988, the Secretary's remuneration increased in real terms by a massive 266 per cent up until 2000. This increase far outstripped the 61 per cent rise determined by the HSC for the Prime Minister, and the 57 and 65 per cent increases, respectively, for cabinet ministers and MPs, during the same period. The increase for the Chief Justice during this time was about 80 per cent. Although not represented in Figure 5.1, the remuneration levels for the second- and third-ranked Public Service bureaucrats have also risen sharply above those payable to other principals during the 1990s. By 1992, the combined average remuneration for these two levels had come to exceed, by 9 per cent, the pay for the Prime Minister. By 2000, the differential had increased to 25 per cent.

It is also worth noting that the remuneration for the State Services Commissioner, which continues to be set by the HSC, was less than that paid to the three highest chief executive positions (ranked by remuneration levels), in four of the five years between 1996 and 2000.[5]

The parliamentary 'iceberg'

In 2001, a report by the Controller and Auditor-General was strongly critical of the lack of transparency surrounding the setting of salaries, allowances and entitlements for MPs (Controller and Auditor-General 2001). His investigation had been inspired by public controversy over the range of MPs' allowances and entitlements that had accrued over the years, even though, as shown in Chapter 2, the cash allowances were not large in comparative perspective. The report indicated that constituency MPs were able to earn about 50 per cent more than their base salary by way of allowances and entitlements, and the MPs elected through the party list system 23 per cent more. Cabinet ministers could receive up to 15 per cent more. Moreover, significant amounts of supra-salary income paid to MPs under the system of parliamentary rules effectively avoided taxation. The report recommended that a total and fully transparent remuneration package should be paid to legislators to overcome these shortcomings and that the HSC should be the body solely responsible for setting all parliamentary payments (rather than the existing complex system which includes parliamentary agencies).

Base salaries probably do not constitute a small tip of a huge iceberg in the sense discussed in Chapter 1, and the total parliamentary income received by MPs and ministers is best seen as something of an inverted iceberg. The largest proportion, the base salary, is visible, while smaller, but very substantial, allowances and entitlements are far less so.

A case of rational individual utility maximization?

How can the relativity change between top bureaucrats and politicians best be explained? No plausible explanation can ignore the 'economics-as-politics' assumption of self-interested utility maximization on the part of leading bureaucrats who were among the main architects of the reforms. As Goldfinch (1998, 2000) has shown, the main economic and governmental reforms of the period were all promoted by a small, cohesive, policy elite, probably of no more than about two dozen people, and operating under the imprimatur of the fourth Labour Government. The group was able to take advantage of what Kingdon (1984) has called a 'window of opportunity' to push their agenda by taking advantage of the dominant position then enjoyed by the political executive vis-à-vis the legislature at what was a critical juncture in New Zealand's history (Aberbach and Christensen 2001). They adopted a determined political method (called 'crashing through'), which virtually obliterated overnight the restraining potential of cultural and institutional factors.

Members of this policy elite subscribed largely to public choice theoretical interpretations of political and bureaucratic behaviour, though publicly (and perhaps paradoxically) they would assert that the changes they were pushing were in the public interest. But members of this group gained in material terms far more than they lost as a consequence of their legislative programme. Certainly, this is true of two of the most influential participants in the group, the Secretary to the Treasury himself, Graham Scott and the then Deputy Governor of the Reserve Bank, Rod Deane. Clearly, the top public servant gained substantial pay increases, arguably far more than would have been granted under the HSC's jurisdiction. Scott was appointed to the top Treasury job in the early years of the reform process, in a sudden deposing of the former incumbent who had been in the job during most of the nine-year term in office of the previous government of Prime Minister Robert Muldoon. Scott resigned from the Public Service in 1993 and established his own international consulting agency, travelling widely to advocate the benefits of New Zealand's pioneering version of NPM and economic reform. For his part, Deane, after taking over for a short time as State Services Commissioner (the better to advance implementation of the state sector reforms), soon became chief executive of one of the largest state owned enterprises created by the changes (Electricorp). He became chief executive, and later chairman, of the country's largest listed company, Telecom New Zealand Ltd (formerly a state-owned enterprise, since privatized), becoming New Zealand's highest paid executive on nearly 2 million New Zealand dollars per year. He has also been appointed to a part-time university professorship.

Thus, career paths have been changing. Under the pre-reform regime it was virtually unheard of for any permanent head of a government department to take early retirement (generally, before the age of 60 or before completion of 40 years service) in order to take up a top full-time position in the private sector. An important factor precluding such movement was the non-portability of a generous government superannuation scheme, to which most belonged. However, the demise of the unified career service has opened up public sector career paths that are now far more varied, fluid and individually opportunistic (although perhaps less so in the Public Service than in the wider state sector). In 1997, the then Secretary to the Treasury, still in his early 40s, resigned to take up a position in the private sector and has since become the head of one of the region's largest trading banks. ('It was a chance to live my professional life twice, as it were'.[6])

While a number of executives from private business moved into the state sector in the period after the reforms, very few came into the Public Service as such. Most took up positions in crown entities and state-owned enterprises, probably because of the higher rates of remuneration payable in many of those organizations.

Remuneration controversies in New Zealand have not been confined to the public sector. The blurring of the distinction between 'public' and 'private' management, and a growing belief in the perceived virtues of generic management, have been largely consistent with Sampson's (1995) analysis of the emergence of a new breed of corporate chief executive. These are the people, in both the public and private sectors, who are willing and able to take 'tough decisions' in an era of intense global corporate competition. According to Frank and Cook (1995), they operate in a 'winner take all market', and have collectively enjoyed massive pay increases.

In New Zealand, issues surrounding the pay for top business executives have generated considerable negative attention, over massive exit payments, and huge in-kind payments, with the size of remuneration packages bearing little if any relationship to the performance of the executives' companies. Some recent academic studies in New Zealand have shown no evidence of any positive relationship between executive pay and organizational performance, nor between executive pay and governance and ownership structures (Andjelkovic *et al.* 2000; Elayan *et al.* 2000). Rather, pay is more closely aligned with factors such as company size, use of leverage and business risk. This evidence supports the immodesty of the 'immodest theory' challenged years earlier by Broom and Cushing (1977), as discussed in Chapter 1.

The changes that occurred in the 1980s constituted New Zealand's third, not first, experience of comprehensive state sector reorganisation. But the previous two instances, in 1912 and 1962 (see Henderson 1990), resulted from manifestly independent investigations conducted by royal commissions of inquiry, rather than from the concentrated power of a policy elite acting with little concern for public consultation and debate. Given their desire to seize a political opportunity for radical reform, the dominant policy elite of the 1980s would not have been overly enamoured of the prospect of another lengthily comprehensive royal commission on the subject.

A social cost of a strategy whereby policy designers are seen to benefit directly from the outcomes of their designs is likely to be diminished public trust in policymaking processes.

Less transparency, less trust and increasing inequality

At least on the face of it, an attenuation of New Zealand's egalitarian practices, a shift to norms of competitive individualism and the adoption of contractualist bureaucratic appointments, have contributed to a marked shift from cell one to cell two (with growing impetus towards cell four) of the 'top rewards game' that was depicted in Chapter 1 (Table 1.1). That is, up until the1980s RHPOs were largely visible (with the possible exception of parliamentary allowances and entitlements), and the public was less cynical and more respectful of officeholders than was the case during the last 15 years of the twentieth century, when rewards became much higher and less transparent.

Visibility

Reward visibility has undoubtedly been reduced under the managerialist regime instituted as part of the state sector reforms. Under the former system the precise salaries of *all* Public Service permanent staff were published in what was colloquially known, in racehorse-breeding parlance, as 'The Studbook' (a register published by the SSC). The advent of the State Sector Act 1988 brought the end of this publication. Instead, only the pay of departmental chief executives is now published, in the annual report of the State Services Commissioner, but with limited and changing degrees of visibility. In 1989–90, the information was published in NZ$ 30,000 bands, but since then the totals have been presented in NZ$ 10,000 bands. From 1998, detailed figures on the make-up of individual packages were not provided (e.g. the proportions of base salary and benefits in kind, the types of benefits in kind, and the percentage earned by way of performance incentive payments). The impact of non-disclosure is exacerbated by the fact that sums paid each year to chief executives as performance-based rewards can be substantial in both relative and absolute terms. In some cases the money involved could be well above the average annual New Zealand wage.

The contractual arrangements under which Public Service chief executives operate are underpinned by the philosophy that their total remuneration should be linked to their performance. However, because it has been officially deemed that citizens and taxpayers are not entitled to know how much each chief executive earns in full detail, this is tantamount to clothing in secrecy the SSC's assessment of their annual performance, given the very rare occurrence of non-renewal of a chief executive's contract.[7] (Nor is the performance assessment process itself publicly transparent.)

The increased opacity is officially justified on the grounds that details are the rightful business of the contracting parties only, and that release of this information in NZ$ 10,000 bands strikes a balance between the public's right to know and the individual executive's entitlement to privacy. However, this policy can be breached arbitrarily when political circumstances demand, as they did in 1999, when the controversial performance of the chief executive of the country's largest department led the State Services Commissioner to publicly disclose that the official would be denied any performance payment for the year.[8]

Since 1997, New Zealand companies have been obliged by law to publicly disclose the cash and non-cash compensation of all executives earning more than NZ$ 100,000 per year. Previously, they were not legally required to disclose any such information. This requirement also covers the growing range of (non-departmental) state sector agencies known collectively as crown entities, including state-owned enterprises, whose remuneration packages, including severance pay, have generated the most public controversy in recent years. The pay for the top executives of these agencies is set by their controlling boards (appointed by the government), and in most cases has not been subject to approval by the State Services Commissioner.

The pay for performance scheme has been used to provide payments to staff in some public agencies, in lieu of salary increases in cases where their base salaries have dropped below market levels. In 2000–01, this practice was the subject of further political controversy, with sections of the news media headlining a 'bonus bonanza' for public servants. One department's staff received an average bonus for the year 2000 of NZ$ 5,685 each. The publicity impelled the Prime Minister to direct an SSC inquiry into the practice, which in her words did not constitute 'the open transparent system you'd want to see'. She was reportedly 'dismayed at the widespread allocation of perks to public servants'.[9]

Similar issues of visibility have surrounded the remuneration for MPs, culminating in the Controller and Auditor-General's 2001 report referred to earlier. The Official Information Act has been used by politicians, journalists and researchers in their quest for data on 'golden handshakes' paid to a number of state sector executives under the contractualist regime, but the Act does not apply to the Parliamentary Service, which administers backbench MPs' salaries and allowances and some entitlements, so it has been virtually impossible for citizens to find out exactly how much any MP receives in any particular year. As one metropolitan newspaper commented, 'What the system needs is a bright light shed upon it. Transparency has been a catchcry of the current and previous governments as embarrassing details of State sector salaries and payoffs have come to light. But transparent is precisely what MPs' perks are not'.[10]

Legitimacy

During the past 15 years or so New Zealanders, like citizens of many other western democracies, have become more cynical and less trusting towards politicians and political institutions generally. In 1998, a nation-wide survey posed the question: 'Would you say that this country is run by a few big interests looking out for themselves or that it is run for the benefit of all the people?' Seventy per cent of respondents agreed with the former proposition, a result that was 16 per cent higher than that produced by a similar survey conducted nine years earlier. The survey also showed 'a picture of a high degree of cynicism about the functioning of democracy', with 'relatively few people' believing that central government is responsive to the public (Perry and Webster 1999: 44, 92). In addition, the survey found that the 'degree of confidence' in a variety of public institutions had dropped markedly since 1985. Twenty-nine per cent of respondents had 'a great deal' or 'quite a lot' of confidence in the Public Service, a decline of 19 per cent from 1985. A survey of New Zealanders conducted by Massey University in 1997 showed that 44 per cent disagreed or strongly disagreed that, 'most public servants can be trusted to do what is best for the country', while 24 per cent agreed or strongly agreed (Massey University 1997).[11]

Generally negative attitudes towards parliamentarians were also reflected in the result of a Citizen's Initiated Referendum held at the time of the 1999 general election. A total of 81.5 per cent of the valid votes were in favour of the proposition that the number of MPs be reduced from 120 to 99 (Boston *et al.* 2000). This public mood helps to explain the HSC's reluctance to raise MPs' base salaries to the levels it would apparently prefer, and the consequent tendency for parliamentarians' real income to be boosted by means of a complex range of only partially transparent allowances and entitlements.

The end of egalitarianism?

According to one prominent commentator, New Zealand's neo-liberal policy reforms of the 1980s and early 1990s heralded 'The Decade of Greed'. In his view:

> It may be true that greed had never been such a prominent part of the philosophy of public policy – at least since the nineteenth century. Perhaps New Zealand was ruled by the "gimme" generation – or more precisely the "gimme" part of a generation – but there had always been self-interest driving individual actions. In the past, at least in public rhetoric, and often in public action, that selfishness had usually been moderated by the public interest.
>
> (Easton 1997: 249)

Some of the most prominent public controversies in New Zealand during the past few years have involved governmental appointees who appeared to be in a win-win situation, when the only way they could be removed from their jobs was by paying them large 'golden handshakes'. In one instance, it appeared that a controversial departmental chief executive had been kept on mainly because it would have been too politically costly to have paid her out of her contract. Further, huge public controversy surrounded a breach of contract payout of around NZ\$ 6 million to a New Zealand television newsreader sacked by TVNZ, a state-owned enterprise.

The New Zealand experience indicates that a sort of 'contractualist game' may be played in 'remuneration shaping' ways that add further texture to public choice interpretations of bureaucratic behaviour. A national newspaper editorialized:

> What is needed now is a rigorous return to some core public service values. These include: a wish to serve the public good rather than to accumulate private wealth; a commitment to frugality and accountability in the spending of taxpayers' money; loyalty to the people's elected representatives and respect for the voters who put them there. These are not the dominant values of private business. They are the principles which should guide officials in a democracy.
>
> (*Sunday Star-Times*, 18 July 1999)

Such controversy, surrounding both the public and private sectors, has been played out against a background of New Zealand's continuing economic difficulties. Broadly, New Zealand was ranked fourth on the Organization for Economic Cooperation and Development's (OECD's) Gross Domestic Product (GDP) per capita index in 1960 but by the late 1990s it was ranking around 20th place. After an economic contraction from 1985 to 1992 there was a strong cyclical recovery in the mid-1990s. However, this has not been sustained (see Roper 1997; Dalziel and Lattimore 1999). In 1990 New Zealand's GDP per capita was US$ 13,000, reaching US$ 14,000 by 1999, and projected to be US$ 16,000 by 2010. By comparison, with a population roughly the same as New Zealand's, Singapore had a GDP per capita in 1990 of US$ 14,000, reaching US$ 28,000 in 1999, and predicted to be US$ 63,000 by 2010.[12] Ireland, a country of comparable population size, which has also adopted similar reforms but with a more proactive role by government in attracting 'greenfield' business investment, has since the mid-1980s increased the value of its share market from about NZ$ 2 billion to 155 billion, compared with New Zealand's increase from NZ$ 19 billion to 45 billion.[13]

New Zealand's inflation levels have been kept low (0–3.0 per cent) during the last few years, under the tutelage of the Reserve Bank, and unemployment had declined by 2001 to 5.6 per cent, the lowest figure since 1988. However, during the 1990s New Zealand experienced what is arguably the largest growth in income inequality in the western world, which has fractured the older egalitarian ethos (Hills 1995; Podder and Chatterjee 1998; Stephens 2000).[14]

The New Zealand experience suggests that public concern over dramatic increases in the levels of remuneration to top executives in *both* the public and private sectors is likely to be the focus of much more critical attention when the economy as a whole is seen not to be doing well, and when there is a growing disparity in income distribution.

A Massey University survey found in 1999 that 75 per cent of respondents thought income differences in New Zealand were too large. Only 30 per cent believed that large differences in income were necessary for the country's prosperity, while 60 per cent saw New Zealand as a society like a pyramid, with a small elite at the top and most at the bottom. Most respondents preferred 'a more egalitarian society', and most thought cabinet ministers deserved NZ$ 80,000 per year rather than the NZ$ 120,000 they were perceived to be earning (Massey University 2000).[15]

Thus, in New Zealand egalitarian norms remain deeply rooted. Politicians, in particular, operate under a well-understood expectation to demonstrate life-styles that are not greatly distinguishable from those which are characteristic of the public at large. And although personal security provisions are rather more separating than they were a couple of decades ago, members of the political executive from the Prime Minister down fully understand that the motor vehicle to which they are each entitled for private use, unlike the cars they use for official business, does not come with a taxpayer-funded chauffeur.

Maximizing remuneration and minimizing corruption

Corruption, if understood as the use of public office for private gain through acts such as bribery and fraud, has never been a problem within New Zealand's governmental organizations. The very low levels of corruption, in this core sense, can be explained by a number of factors.

The egalitarian culture has been a major influence. Income disparities in New Zealand through most of the twentieth century were not large. Most of the British settlers who arrived in New Zealand in the previous century wanted nothing to do with the class system that dominated social relations in their country of origin. Socio-economic disparities did not become cemented as social barriers. The prevailing view was that 'Jack is as good as his master', regardless of occupational position or relative income. Racial tensions were latent, to surface more explicitly in the later twentieth century, but until then New Zealand was a relatively well integrated, intimate, type of society, characterized by high levels of what Putnam *et al.* (1993) and others have termed 'social capital'. By and large people could trust one another, since any serious offence against the law left the transgressor with an acute awareness of social shame and opprobrium. Crime rates were low by international standards. Few citizens felt any need to lock their back doors at night.

On top of all this, for a considerable period during the century New Zealand citizens enjoyed one of the highest standards of living in the world, on the back of exports of primary products to secure (mainly British) markets. From the middle of the century, New Zealand's rapidly developing welfare state was a primary source of *secure* employment for many thousands of citizens. While various forms of veniality were common in some of these state organizations – for example, the pilfering of materials for private use – the unified career service which shaped the long-term employment expectations of state servants usually imbued them with a strong sense of ethical probity. This in turn was buttressed by a rigid system of bureaucratic controls, which was a major safeguard against any temptation to indulge in corrupt activity (and which were later to be seen by state sector reformers as being a part of the problem of governmental inefficiency). As one commentator observed in the 1950s, the New Zealand public servant 'is subject to more extensive controls than most private citizens: he is more likely to be caught if he commits an indiscretion: his career may suffer even if there is only a suspicion of unsatisfactory conduct' (Polaschek 1958: 283).

In short, and unlike the case of China in this study, where visible RHPOs are also low but where corruption is rife, New Zealand's low levels of governmental corruption are directly associated with a strong culture of compliance in both the public and private sectors, based on formal, rules-centred controls.

In Chapter 2, we explored comparative ratings of our cases on Transparency International's Corruption Perceptions Index and noted that New Zealand was consistently ranked as one of the 'cleanest' countries in Transparency International's (TI's) surveys. Generally speaking, the long-standing culture of a non-corrupt state sector remains intact.

Nevertheless, since the state sector reform, the situation has become less certain. There has been an attenuation of some of those important social factors outlined above, which have previously worked to minimize corruption. New Zealanders are less trusting of their neighbours; back doors are now seldom left unlocked. More specifically, a high profile case like that of a former Controller and Auditor-General, none other, who in the mid-1990s was imprisoned after conviction on fraud charges, provided some pause for reflection, but does not necessarily indicate a major trend. However, in 2001 an important watchdog group noted that, 'The relative absence of corruption whether pecuniary or in other forms, in the New Zealand state sector is frequently commented on. Nonetheless, there have been recent reported incidents of corruption that underline the need to be vigilant...' (State Sector Standards Board 2001: 10).[16] In 2000, the State Services Commissioner himself devoted the leading section of his annual report to a discussion of corruption in the public sector. Although the tenor of his argument was one of public reassurance about the incidence of corruption in New Zealand, he nevertheless offered the blunt warning that, 'Any public servant who is discovered behaving corruptly can expect to be prosecuted' (State Services Commission 2000: 6).

Public perceptions of what constitutes corruption might be changing. While corrupt practice in the harder sense of the term remains rare, there is a wider public view of illegitimate (though legal) expenditure of taxpayers' money in ways that are judged profligate, unwarranted and out of kilter with the country's formerly strong egalitarian ethos. In 1998, a public survey asked a question from the World Values Survey: 'How widespread do you think bribe-taking and corruption is in this country?' Just on 13 per cent of respondents believed that 'almost no public officials are engaged in it', while 52 per cent thought that 'a few public officials are engaged in it'. About 25 per cent said they did not know (Perry and Webster 1999: 45).[17] These figures seem somewhat surprising in light of the country's tradition of corruption-free government.

Some other aspects of the state sector reforms have reinforced public distrust and cynicism. There has been a huge increase in the amount of policy advice contracted out to private consultants, many of whom had been formerly in-house public servants. During the 1990s, largely piecemeal and by no means complete information on the multi-million dollar sums of money paid for this advice has been generated by news media investigations under the Official Information Act and by Parliamentary questions. No full publicly accessible ledger exists. The fact that the information is not published as a matter of course, and often has to be extracted from reluctant providers who invoke appeals to its 'commercial sensitivity', raises further questions about the claim that the reforms have enhanced governmental 'transparency'.

Conclusion: a culture in transition

The move to transform the New Zealand state sector along private sector lines has tended to threaten the culture of public trusteeship that has for many decades underpinned the country's system of governmental administration. The Public Service ethos has become more uncertain with the increasing emphasis on market values and norms, which sit uneasily with the country's traditional egalitarian culture.

These and other post-1988 changes in relative RHPOs levels, and in the associated behavioural patterns of government officials, are much more apparent when gauged against national – or at most, Antipodean – rather than international benchmarks. For example, when compared with Singapore or Hong Kong, New Zealand Public Service remuneration levels remain low, with real top pay rates that are greatly inferior to those applying in the two Asian jurisdictions. And any evidence of increased corruption in New Zealand's case is insignificant when compared with the endemic malfeasance characteristic of countries like China and Thailand. Moreover, in comparison with other countries in this study, New Zealand remains essentially an egalitarian ('self-drive') society, even if it is becoming less so.

The first years of the new millennium will be crucial in determining the longer-term outcome of the transition from egalitarian to market culture in the levels, structure and scope of New Zealand's RHPOs. Further political controversy surrounding state sector remuneration may continue to erode public confidence in governmental administration, and could adversely affect the quality of public sector recruitment. Alternatively, it may serve as a springboard for policy changes which seek a new balance between egalitarian values and market imperatives.

Acknowledgements

The author gratefully acknowledges the work done by research assistant, Mark Thornton, in providing data for this project, the generous cooperation of the Higher Salaries Commission, and the information provided by the Parliamentary Service. The usual disclaimer applies.

Notes

1 In New Zealand, the state sector encompasses all agencies that are owned and operated by the state. The Public Service embodies departments under direct ministerial control.
2 *The Dominion*, 17 November 2000.
3 *The Dominion*, 17 November 2000.
4 *The Dominion*, 6 and 13 October 2000.
5 The years in question are 1996, 1998, 1999 and 2000.
6 *The Sunday Star-Times*, 12 August 2001. This was Murray Horn, who is also the author of an important academic work in the economics-as-politics school (Horn 1995).
7 Between 1988 and early 2001, no departmental chief executive had his/her contract terminated before its expiry, for poor performance. On only one occasion did a chief executive fail to have her contract renewed on expiry. However, some contracts were re-negotiated on expiry for shorter terms than the chief executives preferred.
8 An appeal by the author to the Ombudsmen, against the policy applying to the Public Service, and requesting full disclosure of the actual pay received by departmental chief executives, with itemized components of the total package, was unsuccessful.

9 *The Dominion*, 19 and 27 January 2001.
10 *The Evening Post*, editorial, 26 February 2001.
11 The survey was a part of a Cologne-based International Social Survey Programme (ISSP).
12 Data source – Standard and Poors; McKinsey (quoted in *The Dominion*, 17 February 2001).
13 From Radio New Zealand interview of 7 October 2000, with Brian Gaynor, economist and columnist for the *New Zealand Herald*.
14 In New Zealand, during the period 1985–86 to 1995–96 the Gini coefficient (probably the most widely used measure of inequality) rose from 0.394 to 0.471, according to figures from Statistics New Zealand on actual household market income. The usual values for family or household income lie in the range 0.25–0.45. For a detailed analysis of this issue see the Treasury working paper by O'Dea (2000: 23–32).
15 This survey was also part of the ISSP programme.
16 The Board was established by the government the preceding year, to clarify the government's expectations of the state sector, and to report annually on the state sector ethos.
17 No comparative figures are given.

6 Japan's pattern of rewards for high public office

A cultural perspective

Akira Nakamura and Kosaku Dairokuno

Introduction

This chapter aims to use rewards for high public office (RHPOs) as a window for assessing both the degree and quality of Japan's democracy in comparative perspective. It briefly explores both the 'vertical' and 'horizontal' dimensions of RHPOs that were identified and discussed in Chapters 1 and 2. That is, it compares rewards at the top with those lower down the income scale and it compares the rewards of top public officeholders with their private-sector counterparts.

Although the chapter follows the general comparative agenda laid out at the outset, the Japanese case reveals some important cultural dimensions of the topic. As we shall see, Japan's RHPOs are culturally distinctive in several ways. What counts as an act of corruption is one of the cases in point. Corruption, any act that violates prescribed laws and regulations, comprises two different dimensions, the legal and the moral. In both the political and administrative arenas, it often involves people in high social or governmental positions. It commonly entails financial transactions: untraceable cash changing hands behind the scenes has become one of the most frequently exposed types of corruption internationally. High incidences of money politics have also been a problem in Asia in general, and in Japan, China and South Korea in particular. This type of corruption is perhaps one of the primary reasons why Transparency International[1] (TI) does not rank these East Asian countries well in the category of clean politics, as we saw in Chapter 2.

The moral dimension of corruption involves behaviour that infringes a perceived ethical standard to which persons in respected public positions are supposed to adhere. Frequently, cases of this nature comprise sex scandals, particularly in some Western democracies. For example, until US President Bill Clinton publicly tarnished the image (with his impeachment in 1998 over the statements he had made about his relationships with a young intern) not only had the American President been the head of government, but had also been the champion of moral standards in his country. Private lapses and extra-marital affairs were far from unknown, but American Presidents, in their public persona at least, had long been considered the very embodiment of ethics and morals in the US. Such characteristics may apply to the leaders of some other democracies, and a departure from those standards may be considered as a kind of corruption, insofar as

Clinton appeared to have degraded the Presidency as an honoured institution by his relationship with a female subordinate as revealed in the impeachment proceedings.

Indeed, any study of corruption must consider rather complex characteristics. The definition of corruption is neither universal nor absolute: it is relative and, as often as not, culturally bound. An act regarded as unethical in one country is not necessarily corrupt in another. The example in which former US President Clinton was involved (a sexual relationship with a young intern on his staff) can serve to demonstrate this point. Had Clinton been a government leader in Japan, he would have resigned long before his misdemeanours could have been disclosed. Fearing public humiliation, any Japanese leader would resign if he were even suspected of wrongdoing. For most Japanese, it is simply beyond comprehension that former President Clinton tried everything he possibly could to thwart public criticism and to remain in power. It is simply un-*samurai* conduct that a Japanese would avoid at any cost. In Japan, leaving one's post without rebutting criticisms or making excuses is considered ideal behaviour for a person in a position of significant status.

For example, during the late 1990s, a highly popular comedian-turned-governor, Yokoyama Knock, ran Osaka Prefecture. He was first elected to this position in 1995, then re-elected four years later with resounding public support. However, during the gubernatorial election of 1999, he was said to have sexually harassed a female campaign worker. Originally, he claimed innocence, but was eventually cornered by the media, and pleaded 'no contest' when the issue went to court. Many voters, taking this legal tactic as an admission of guilt, turned a cold shoulder on this once popular governor. In the wake of mounting public criticism, in line with the traditional norms of the country, Yokoyama decided to step down from his post a few months later – a move that facilitated the election of Japan's second female governor in 1999.

This example illustrates how the Japanese will not tolerate a sex scandal. However, they appear much more lenient if an issue involves money. To non-Japanese, for instance, a scandal involving former Prime Minister Tanaka Kakuei probably remains incomprehensible. Tanaka was Prime Minister of Japan from 1972 to the end of 1974. While in office, he was implicated in one of the worst political scandals in the nation's history, charged with taking bribes from Lockheed Aircraft. Although indicted, he was re-elected with overwhelming majorities in several elections and remained prominent in Japanese politics until his death in 1993. Even now, Tanaka still commands a great deal of respect from both fellow politicians and his hometown constituency.

One reason why Tanaka remains in high esteem is intrinsic to the Japanese cultural perception of what an ideal leader should be. The majority of Tanaka's followers do not regard his conduct as a serious crime. In their opinion, certainly, Tanaka took the bribes; however, they argue that he did not use them for his personal benefit. Instead, his supporters contend, he dispensed all the bribe monies to his followers for their various political activities. In the view of his allies, Tanaka was a 'caring man', who epitomized the role model of a Japanese leader, because

Table 6.1 A four-part categorization of RHPOs

Formality of reward	Tangibility of reward	
	Tangible	Symbolic
Formal	Quadrant 1	Quadrant 3
Informal	Quadrant 2	Quadrant 4

he tried the best he could to look after his supporters. Paternalism, a key factor in Japanese political behaviour, is revered and respected, unlike in the West where it is often associated with corruption (Rothacher 1993: 102–22).

As these examples indicate, corruption must be examined within the contexts of culture and tradition. It is more complex and less straightforward than it is often perceived to be in Western democracies. A study of the issue must take cultural heritages and traditional legacies into consideration. To define the intricate nature of the problem, it must be categorized in a manner that takes cultural differences and traditions into consideration.

Against such a background, this chapter examines Japanese RHPOs in the post Second World War period using a four-part categorization comprising intangible and more tangible rewards in one dimension, and formal and informal rewards in the other. This four-part categorization was foreshadowed in Chapter 1 and is depicted in Table 6.1.

Formal and tangible rewards (Quadrant 1)

Elected officeholders

Quadrant 1 in Table 6.1 connotes tangible rewards that HPOs receive for their services. In Japan most tangible RHPOs are formal and legal. Ordinarily, they do not raise any intricate issues of corruption. Japan's national legislators present a typical case in point.

In Japan, information about the compensation paid to the country's political, administrative and business leaders is accessible to the public, especially in the case of lawmakers. Beginning in 1984, members of Japan's cabinet began voluntarily to disclose their personal fortunes, a practice that started in the aftermath of one of the worst scandals in the country's history, the Lockheed Affair in the 1970s, that has already been mentioned.

The disclosure was eventually extended to include all elected members at different levels of government, and in 1992, the national legislature passed a law to that effect. The statute requires the elected members of all levels of government to reveal their personal wealth within 100 days of taking office. It also obliges lawmakers to make public their annual incomes in April of each year.

During the Hashimoto administration (1996–98), ministers averaged JY 100 million, or US$ 950,000 as personal assets. Corresponding data for fiscal 1998 indicated that the average personal wealth of the members of the Obuchi

Cabinet stood at JY 266.5 million, or US$ 2,530,000. At least in terms of personal affluence, the ministers in the Obuchi cabinet looked better off than those in the Hashimoto administration.[2]

Each national legislator in Japan receives an income from the government. In fiscal year 2000, it amounted to JY 16.5 million (US$ 157,000) per annum. Further, the lawmakers receive three bonuses per year, totaling approximately 3.5 months of their basic income, or JY 4.8 million (US$ 45,800). The government also covers the postal and communication costs of each legislator up to JY 12 million (US$ 114,000) per year. It further provides research funds on a monthly basis, amounting to JY 650,000 (US$ 6,200) a month, or JY 7,800,000 (US$ 74,300) per annum.

Japanese national lawmakers have free access to all modes of transportation, riding the country's famous bullet trains without charge, and flying free to and from domestic destinations of their choice. While in Tokyo, legislators have free access to all local public transportation such as bus or subway. Further, on top of these allowances, the government provides housing at a modest fee to each legislator. Housing being exorbitantly expensive in Tokyo, this benefit is one of the major rewards for members of the national legislature. The combined annual total of these benefits, excluding travel grants, come close to JY 41 million or US$ 391,000.

Although these varied forms of remuneration for legislators look substantial from the perspective of the public at large, the lawmakers themselves contend that they are not sufficient, often claiming that the major portion of the funds goes to cover the salaries of their staff members. By law, public funds supply three support staff for each legislator; but in practice legislators maintain, on average, 10 additional secretaries in either Tokyo or their home constituencies. Many Diet members hold that these extra employees are essential for their legislative work. The cost for these extra staff members is at least JY 20 million monthly; so that according to the legislators, the financial rewards they receive from the government are simply not enough. However, these lawmakers do not usually realize that the various remunerations they receive help incumbents to remain in office. Newcomers to Japanese politics, to whom these allowances are unavailable, are usually forced to mount strenuous campaigns if they are to oust current officeholders.

Non-elected officeholders

In Japan, the National Personnel Authority, created after the Second World War, plays a major role in deciding formal rewards to non-elected public officials. Each year, it recommends to the Cabinet the level of rewards to be paid for bureaucrats, usually at a level that is commensurate with the average salary for their private counterparts. The Government and the Diet usually follow its recommendation. Further, the promotion of public officials above the level of section chief in each ministry has to be approved by the Authority, and retiring public officials have to get the Authority's approval, when they try to get positions in the private sector over which their public positions have direct control in the last five years. The

Authority has been successful in keeping the rewards for public officials more or less representative of the whole society, and in preventing high public officials from becoming the sort of privileged stratum that they constituted in the prewar period (Nishimura 1999).

RHPOs since the Second World War have been unimpressive, compared to those in the pre Second World War period.[3] However, that does not mean that non-elected HPOs in Japan are underpaid. Given that the average yearly income (including bonuses) of workers in the private sector was JY 7,236,000 in 1999, Japanese high public officeholders in central government are relatively well paid, as is shown in Tables 6.2 and 6.3. This conclusion becomes clearer when one looks at the distribution of income in Japan.

Table 6.4 shows that in the late 1990s, the percentage of people who earned more than JY 20,000,000 (US$ 188,679) per annum was only 0.4 per cent of a salaried labour force of almost 45 million, but most of the high public officeholders officials listed in Tables 6.2 and 6.3, elected or career, were paid more than JY 20 million per year. In this sense, RHPOs in contemporary Japan appear by no means low, since these officeholders are in the highest strata in terms of income. Even comparing the RHPOs with the average income for presidents of private companies, does not change the conclusion much. According to a 1997 survey, the average monthly income for company presidents was JY 1.9 million (US$ 18,396) with a bonus of JY 6.4 million (US$ 61,037) a year, bringing the total annual salary to JY 30.1 million (US$ 283,962). The total figure is almost equivalent to the yearly income of cabinet ministers (Wage Management Institute 1997). On this evidence, too, high public officials are relatively well paid in Japan.

Table 6.2 Annual salaries for major positions in the special service category (April 1999), unit: JY

Position	'Basic'[a]	Bonus	Total
Prime Minister	30,965,760	9,676,800	40,642,560
Speakers of Both Houses	30,965,760	9,676,800	40,642,560
Supreme Court Chief Justice	30,965,760	8,524,800	39,490,560
Supreme Court Justice	22,606,080	6,307,500	28,913,580
Cabinet Ministers	22,606,080	7,064,400	29,670,480
Chief Cabinet Secretary	22,606,080	7,064,400	29,670,480
President of the National Personnel Authority	22,606,080	7,064,400	29,670,480
Chief Secretary of Cabinet Legislation Bureau	21,638,400	6,762,000	28,400,400
Member of the House of Representatives[b]	18,480,000	5,755,000	24,235,000
Member of the House of Councillors[b]	18,480,000	5,755,000	24,235,000

Source: Ministry of Finance (2000), *Public Officials Remuneration Data Book*.

Notes
a These figures include the monthly salary adjustment.
b Each Diet member receives the postal and communication allowance of 1 million yen per month. An additional 650 thousand yen per member are paid monthly to the parliamentary party to which each member belongs. Travel expenses for public activities are almost fully covered.

Table 6.3 Annual salaries for designated positions in the regular service category (April 1999), unit: JY[a]

Position	Basic	Bonus	Total
President (Tokyo and Kyoto University)	16,500,000	6,806,250	23,306,250
Administrative Vice-Minister of each ministry	16,152,000	6,662,700	22,814,700
Director-General of National Police Agency	16,152,000	6,662,700	22,814,700
President Hokkaido, Tohoku, Nagoya, Osaka and Kyusyu University	16,152,000	6,662,700	22,814,700
Superintendent General of Metropolitan Police	15,228,000	6,281,550	21,509,550
President of 'Old 10' University (Chiba, Hitotsu-bashi, etc.)	15,228,000	6,281,550	21,509,550
Director-General of Administrative Agencies	14,220,000	5,865,750	20,085,750
Deputy Minister of each ministry	14,220,000	5,865,750	20,085,750
Deputy Vice-Minister of each ministry	12,300,000	5,073,750	17,373,750
Director-General of Bureau within ministries	12,300,000	5,073,750	17,373,750

Source: Ministry of Finance (2000), *Public Officials Remuneration Data Book.*

Note
a Various allowances are not included.

Table 6.4 Distribution of annual income among salaried employees, unit: 10,000 yen

Income bracket	Number (thousand)	Composition (%)
Less than 100	3,294	7.2
100–200	4,639	10.2
200–300	6,783	14.9
300–400	8,118	17.9
400–500	6,587	14.5
500–600	4,796	10.6
600–700	3,485	7.7
700–800	2,428	5.3
800–900	1,647	3.6
900–1,000	1,103	2.4
1,000–1,500	1,995	4.4
1,500–2,000	394	0.9
More than 2,000	177	0.4
Total	44,896	100

Source: Ministry of Labour (1997), *Wages in the Private Sector.*

In contrast to the rewards of top public officeholders, the average salary for rank-and-file public employees was lower than the one for workers in the private sector (see Table 6.5). And data concerning salaries for entry-level jobs in the private and public sector (Table 6.6) indicate that in all the educational categories

Table 6.5 Comparison of salary between the private and public
sector (April 1999), unit: JY

	Yearly (average)	Bonus/total (%)	Experience (years)
Private	7,236,000	36.1	17.1
Public	6,566,400	29.2	17.5

Source: Ministry of Finance (2000), *Public Officials Remuneration Data Book*;
National Tax Bureau (2000), *Salary in the Private Sector*.

Table 6.6 Monthly salary for entry-level jobs in the private and
public sector, unit: JY

	Private	Private (less than 500) employees	Public
College	192,391	188,967	187,583
Junior college	161,412	164,447	173,398
High school	153,168	151,007	148,320

Source: Ministry of Labour (1997), *Wage in the Private Sector*; Ministry of
Finance (2000), *Public Officials Remuneration Data Book*.

except junior college graduates, the average salary was higher in the private sector. The implication is that even prospective senior bureaucrats, who have passed
the highly competitive National Public Officials Examination Category I, had to
start their career with a relatively low salary.

The entry-level monthly salary for these career bureaucrats was JY 184,200
(US$ 1,738), almost US$ 100 less than the corresponding average monthly salary
for college graduates in large private companies. In many cases, the difference in
entry-level salary between career bureaucrats and managerial track employees in
large private companies was much larger (the difference ranged from US$ 500 to
1,000). This situation did not change unless career bureaucrats were promoted to
positions above the section chief, which usually took at least 15 years. In other
words, even high-flying career bureaucrats were relatively underpaid when compared to their private counterparts, when they were still young. However, once
they were promoted to positions above the section chief and to the topmost positions
depicted in Table 6.3 they came to be paid relatively well even in comparison with
their counterparts in the private sector.[4]

Although by definition they comprise a small portion of public officials, these
HPOs in the central government have been rewarded relatively well in the postwar period. And those in the topmost positions have been treated particularly
generously at the time of their retirement. In the post-Second World War career
system, the very structure of rewards for high public officials – relatively low
salary in the first 15 years or so, relatively well-paid salary beyond the section
chief, and well paid post-retirement employment opportunities based on the last
position they held – has given prospective senior bureaucrats a strong incentive to
work hard to reach higher positions. This point can be illustrated by the size of

Table 6.7 Comparison of retirement lump-sum grants, unit: JY

	Amount (average)	*How many months of basic salary*	*Experience (years)*
Private[a]	28,710,000	45.3	30
Public[b]			
Administrative Vice-Minister	55,522,500	41.25	30
Director General of Agencies	48,881,250	41.25	30
Councillors	48,881,250	41.25	30
Deputy Minister of Ministries	42,281,250	41.25	30

Source: Ministry of Finance (2000), *Public Officials Remuneration Data Book*; Ministry of Labour (1997), *Wage and Working Hours.*

Notes
a Figures in 1997.
b Figures in 1999.

the lump sum severance fee that Japan's high-ranking bureaucrats would usually receive at the time of their retirement as is shown in Table 6.7.

Tangible and informal rewards (Quadrant 2)

Turning to the bottom left-hand quadrant of the reward categorization in Table 6.1 (informal and tangible), it is important to note from the outset that the giving of gifts is a custom long embedded in Japanese culture. Ordinarily, people give a gift to their superiors in mid-summer and again at the end of the year, as a token of appreciation for being looked after. This common cultural custom has spilled over into the political arena and has frequently become a cause of corruption. In Japan's political milieu, the demarcation line between legal and illegal gift giving is extremely subtle and hard to draw, as the following case illustrates.

Chief executives of local governments bring special local products as souvenirs to the Finance Ministry when they come to Tokyo to negotiate subsidy hikes with the central government. For instance, the Governor of Fukui Prefecture, where crabs are a delicacy, will probably take this product with him when he meets a Vice Minister of the agency. This is an old and deep-rooted tradition, as often as not regarded as a social lubricant to smooth negotiations. The problem with this practice has been that the cost of the gifts probably comes from the public coffers of the prefectural government, so that taxpayers in the Fukui region pay for souvenirs that go directly to bureaucrats in the Finance Ministry.

The high incidence of gift giving in both private and public organizations is one of the tangible but non-institutionalized rewards that remain significant in the Japanese political environment. Although the practice is frequent and widespread, it is also informal, and thus difficult to measure. However, the following examples should shed some light on the nature of this covert system of rewards given to the country's politicians.

From their vantage point in society, politicians are frequently in receipt of different sorts of information, some of which they may be able to cash in for monetary advantage. In the late 1980s, a great political scandal occurred in Japan, involving a private firm, *Recruit Cosmos*. This company published various journals featuring job placements and housing rentals. Although it was the leading firm in its field, it wanted to strengthen its position in the industry.

The president of the enterprise sought to establish close and amicable relationships with the elite of Japan, and decided to give its pre-market stock to leading members of politics, administration and academics. The firm's stock was about to be floated on the Tokyo stock exchange, and as soon as the stock was floated those Japanese leaders who had received the shares sold them and made substantial profits. The list of recipients of the *Recruit* stock was, even for a Japanese electorate accustomed to scandal, mind-boggling. Incumbent as well as former Prime Ministers such as Nakasone, Takeshita and Miyazawa were involved, while Vice Ministers of the Labour and the Education Ministries were also implicated.

It was a case of insider trading *par excellence*. More than 20 politicians and several leading bureaucrats were charged with malfeasance and graft for their conduct. Subsequently, several politicians resigned, as did some bureaucrats and academics. Although insider trading on the grand scale of *Recruit Cosmos* is rare, it is considered that this scandal may merely indicate the tip of the iceberg. Conservative party members, particularly privy to receiving to various kinds of information, must be circumspect and discreet, to avoid another serious scandal (Rothacher 1993: 102–22; Curtis 1999: 73–8).

High-level bureaucrats enjoy distinctive forms of informal tangible rewards. Of approximately 800,000 national public officials, and an additional 4.2 million local government officials, about 4,000 are defined as the 'elite corps' in Japanese bureaucracy. These privileged few central government officials, who form the nucleus of the country's governmental structure, are typically labelled as bureaucrats – *Kanryo* – in Japan.[5] However, in contrast to the situation in some other democracies, in Japan the term *Kanryo*, or bureaucrat, does not necessarily have a pejorative implication. Within Japan's strong Mandarin tradition, the elite central bureaucrats attract public respect, or even awe. They are normally graduates of the most vigorous university, the University of Tokyo, and have passed the most competitive civil service examinations in the country. Members of this high-flying elite corps are therefore nicknamed 'Bullet Trains', because their promotion in the central government is so fast. In contrast, lower-ranking public officials are classified as 'Local Trains'.

Elite bureaucrats in Japan retire early. On average, they voluntarily leave their careers at the age of 55, which is not compulsory, but is a long-standing practice unique to Japan's leading public officials. Once retired, these elite bureaucrats usually have three options. They may run for public office, usually under the banner of the LDP. In the 2000 House of Representatives election, former elite bureaucrats took 86 seats, or 18 per cent of the 480 seats contested. As with the Singapore politician-bureaucrats described by Jon Quah in Chapter 9, these bureaucrats remain one of the important reservoirs from which politicians emerge (*Asahi Shimbun*, 26 June 2000, evening edition).

Some of the retiring elite bureaucrats choose a second option: they move to the private sector. As mentioned in Chapter 1 and several other chapters, this practice is generally referred to as the 'descent from heaven'. Although a number of regulations exist to prevent this practice, loopholes abound. To avoid conflict of interest, the law forbids a bureaucrat to take a position in a private firm for at least two years, if the company in question has come under his direct jurisdiction for the five years immediately before his retirement.

The only way for the bureaucrat to get around this provision is to submit a petition to the National Personnel Agency. However, this obstacle is less formidable than it might appear, because the Agency rarely turns down these petitions. The reason? The National Personnel Agency itself needs places in the private sector for its retiring bureaucrats. As much as any other central organization, the National Personnel Agency has much at stake in keeping the present system alive. In 1996, 134 elite bureaucrats were approved to move to the private sector. Of those, 22 took executive positions in different private firms. In 1998, 88 national bureaucrats sought jobs in the private sector, a decrease of 30 from the previous year and a substantial fall from the 200-plus cases a year in the late 1980s and early 1990s. The declining number of 'descents from heaven' reflects growing public criticism of the practice.

For many years, the Finance Ministry always topped the list; however, due to several disclosures of malfeasance, the number of cases from the Finance Ministry has been reduced. Recently, the Telecommunication Ministry has increased the numbers of former bureaucrats who seek post-retirement employment in the private sector. Table 6.8 gives the number and distribution of 'descents from heaven' in the early 1990s for the Ministry of Finance and the Ministry of Construction.

The third option for retiring bureaucrats is to seek employment in semi-public organizations. In Japan, the central government has created a large number of 'special purpose public corporations', to facilitate the implementation and operation of public policy. An example is the Japan Highway Public Corporation, which was created in 1956 as an operating arm of the Ministry of Construction. Similarly, the Employment Promotion Corporation was created in 1961 as an

Table 6.8 'Descents from heaven', 1990–93, in two selected ministries

Positions after retirement			
Ministry of Finance			
Bank	Non-profit organization	Unknown	Total
161	60	226[a]	440
Ministry of Construction			
General Contractor	Non-profit Organization	Gov. Est. Organization	Total
204	177	49	430

Source: Tsutumi, Kazuma (1997) Kanryo Amakudari Hakusho (Descent from Heaven White Paper), Tokyo, Iwanami.

Note
a Most of the retirees eventually find their way to banks and non-profit organizations.

extension of the Labour Ministry to assist displaced coalmine workers seeking re-employment. By 1995, 92 of these public corporations existed at the central level and they often generate unique and difficult problems. The case of the Japan Highway Public Corporation can be used to illustrate this issue.

The Corporation has developed a large number of subsidiaries, which are constituted as private corporations, and hence are not legally bound by government regulations. In 1995, there were 67 of these subsidiaries, including the Highway Service Incorporation and Rest Area Services. These private firms have more than 171 restaurants, 311 convenience stores and 193 gas stations in rest areas along the toll roads operated by the Japan Highway Public Corporation. In fiscal year 1995, these 67 subsidiaries with more than 26,000 employees made net sales of JY 545 billion. They have proved to be highly profitable.

These thriving firms provide the next employment stop for retiring bureaucrats. In the case of the Japan Highway Public Corporation, the subsidiaries take large numbers of retiring public officials from the parent organization, as well as from the Construction Ministry. These former public officials usually become executives, if not presidents, of the subordinate corporations. In many cases, they transfer from one subsidiary to another, to make room for a new group of departing bureaucrats from the parent organizations. This practice, generally referred to as 'migrant birds', usually results in substantial severance pay for each transferring ex-official (Inose 1997).

In one case, a Vice-Minister in the National Land Development Ministry netted JY 55 million (US$ 423,000) in severance pay when he left office to become Chairman of the Board of the Japan Highway Public Corporation. Eventually, he vacated this post and moved to the Highway Facilities Association, collecting another JY 39 million (US$ 300,000) along the way as severance pay from the Highway Public Corporation. Four years later, he stepped down from his post in Highway Facilities, receiving an additional JY 26 million (US$ 200,000) for these short four years of service in the Association (*Asahi Shimbun*, 14 March 1997).

One of the problems in Japanese central bureaucracy is that both the 'Descent from Heaven' and 'Migrant Birds' practices have become a widespread and entrenched part of public management. These tactics, exclusive to high-ranking public officials, are now so consolidated that few public officials question their legitimacy; most central bureaucrats appear to nonchalantly take these privileges for granted. It is no wonder that Japan is frequently described as a 'heaven for public officials'. However, there has been mounting public disapproval of the practice of 'descent from heaven'. The criticism is especially strong among housewives and female voters, who increasingly show disapproval of the country's bureaucrats at election times.

Formal and informal symbolic rewards (Quadrants 3 and 4)

In this section, the right-hand quadrants of the rewards categorization in Table 6.1 are treated together, because both of those quadrants involve the symbolic dimension. They are hard to assess, because they often call for tricky cultural and historical assessment. Nonetheless, various forms of symbolic rewards are extremely important in Japan. They often become the seedbed of corruption in the country's political context. A discussion of symbolic rewards in Japan requires a word of explanation about the status and power of elected and non-elected public officials. Three specific reasons make these public officials highly significant in Japan and form the social backdrop for the various symbolic rewards that the country's HPOs receive.

As already noted, the country has a long history of popular respect for the role of government officials, which conversely tends to degrade the private sector (i.e. business and commerce) as inferior. An historical saying states that 'public is revered, while private is despised' (*Kanson Minpi*). The origin of this social view dates back to the pre-modern period known as the *Edo* era (1603–1867), an age of rigid social stratification. At the apex sat the ruling *samurai* class (the public officials of that time), while merchants were at the lower end of the community scale.

Although Japanese society is no longer feudal, nor as structured, this traditional outlook subtly continues even now. The business community in Japan, however viable and global, is not on par with the government, especially in terms of societal leadership. It is expected to stay subservient and to follow the lead of public authorities even in matters of economic activity. Traditionally, most Japanese governments have been uninfluenced by business management ideas, at least to the same extent as many other Organization for Economic Cooperation and Development (OECD) countries, such as New Zealand, described by Robert Gregory in the previous chapter. This attitude reflects the 'public revered and private despised' tradition which is ingrained in Japanese political and administrative culture.

The country's legislators at different levels of government enjoy the fruit of this entrenched political culture in different ways as well. In Japanese politics, one of the more bizarre symbolic rewards is a pin in a lapel. It is generally referred to as a 'Badge'. All Japanese lawmakers at the national levels want this pin. The pin is rather cheap, costing about JY 5000 (US$ 47); however, it has a significant symbolic value, as it identifies the wearer as an elected member of the national legislature. It is a sign of power and prestige and, as often as not, becomes an instrument of political corruption.

In Japan, local legislators try to copy the customs and traditions of the central legislature: community lawmakers usually have a replicated copy of this pin on their lapels. With the pin, these locals look the same as their national counterparts. Wearing the pin, they are both mentally satisfied and psychologically content with their achievements as members of community government. The Japanese public has an ambivalent perspective on the power of the pin. Many urban voters resent it, perceiving that it symbolizes the legislators' arrogant and domineering attitudes towards the electorate.

Conversely, rural voters often view the pin as a symbol commanding respect, or even reverence. For the less sophisticated rural electorate, the local legislators, wearing replicas of the national pin on their lapels, appear powerful and authoritative, and command servitude. In these small communities, these local lawmakers are known as *Sensei*, an honourable term meaning 'teacher'; thus, this simple, cheap pin symbolically represents power, prestige and dignity. Subsequently, many voters and business people come to these holders of symbolic formal political power to ask for different favours and various preferential treatments.

In addition to the formal symbolic rewards, Japanese social traditions grant informal symbolic rewards to both national legislators and elite bureaucrats. The whole concept can perhaps be summarized as social protocol. Wedding receptions provide a good example: in Japan, wedding receptions are usually held in commercial hotels, and are important family events celebrated as formal social occasions.

Quite often, a politician is invited as a friend of the father of the bride or groom. The politician is expected to sit in the centre of the room, where he can be seen, and to give the first toast or speech on behalf of the newlyweds. In other types of social gatherings also, elected members are treated as prestigious figures, and according to social protocol, make speeches observing the occasion. Often two or more politicians come to the same party: Japanese social etiquette gives priority to the elder, so that a seniority system takes the difficulty out of intricate situations. When politicians and bureaucrats attend the same function, protocol usually calls for politicians to take precedence.

The critical point to be emphasized here is that both elected and non-elected members of the country usually command a great deal of public respect. They likewise generate significant political influence. Frequently, however, these HPOs unfortunately misuse their symbolic powers of various kinds for personal advantages. A high incidence of abuses often results in a series of political scandals in Japan.

Conclusions

As Chapter 1 in this volume has noted, rewards for high public office have traditionally been one of the major concerns in political science and public administration. Indeed, as Hood and Peters (1994: 2) put it in an earlier publication, 'Spinoza sought to link RHPOs to performance. Hegel in the 1820s stressed the importance of adequate pay to lift the public service above narrow sectional concerns. Bentham placed pay and reward at the center of his utilitarian philosophy of government, paying particular attention to honorific service and methods of keeping public salaries as low as possible. Tocqueville feared that extension of the franchise would lower formal RHPOs to the point where only wealthy people could afford to be HPOs, thus effectively transforming democracy back into an aristocracy.'

All of those classical concerns with RHPOs implicitly share the assumption that the level and structure of RHPOs can make a difference in politics and public administration. For Spinoza, it was a fear that HPOs would increase rewards regardless of their performance. For Hegel, it was the low level of RHPOs that mattered, for it might lead to corruption. Bentham expressed a traditional concern over the cost of public administration. Tocqueville spotted a paradox that an increasing level of democracy would not necessarily guarantee equality of opportunity for those aspiring to high public office. Overall, these classical arguments imply that the performance, integrity, efficiency and representativeness of HPOs are major determinants of good public service, and that these determinants are likely to be influenced by the level and structure of RHPOs.

From this perspective, corruption can be considered as a consequence of the level of RHPOs. In fact, as was noted in Chaper 1, The World Bank Report on *The East Asian Miracle* in 1993 (World Bank 1993: 175) claimed that corruption was closely related to levels of rewards at the top-level. Further, as we saw in Chapter 2, Singapore and Hong Kong have been known in Asia as cases where high RHPOs coincide with low level of corruption, whereas China, Vietnam, Pakistan and Indonesia, where RHPOs are low, are perceived to be highly corrupt.

At a glance, the World Bank hypothesis seems very convincing, for it is logically reasonable to assume that underpaid HPOs would be more susceptible to the temptation of corruption, other things being equal. However, as this volume shows, there are numerous cases that do not fit this received theory. In Chapters 4 and 5, we have already noted that in Australia and New Zealand relatively low RHPOs go together with comparatively low corruption scores on TI corruption indicators. The Japanese case discussed in this chapter indicates the opposite pattern, with relatively high RHPOs going with significant levels of corruption. These cases suggest that there are other intervening factors than the level of RHPOs, which may affect the incidence of corruption.[6] The editors return to this issue in Chapter 10, but this chapter has aimed to explore some of those intervening factors that apply to the Japanese case, particularly the nature of the state, its dominant values or ideology and its political heritage.

Notes

1 Transparency International ranks Japan 25th, South Korea 50th, China 58th and Thailand 68th in its annual ranking of International Corruption Perceptions Index. See *www.tranparency.de/documents/cpi/index.html*.
2 These figures come from a computerized data system, *Data Paru 2000*. Shogakukan Publisher prepares it as a part of its computerized Bookshelf, Version 2.0.
3 As we saw in Chapter 2, Japanese top public rewards are also unimpressive when compared to the RHPOs in Singapore. For instance, at the time of writing, the annual salary for the Prime Minister in Japan is US$ 383,420 as opposed to US$ 1,293,333 in Singapore.
4 Positions above the section chief comprise 11.8 per cent (2,326) of the total number of career bureaucrats (19,763) who have passed the National Public Officials Examination Category I and have served various agencies. The total number of designated positions (1,722) comprises only 0.2 per cent of the total number of public officials in the regular service category (810,701). See *http://www.jinji.admix.go.jp/hakusho/f-hakush.htm*.
5 Rothacher (1993: 125–79) provides an interesting general account of bureaucracy in Japan.
6 Leslie Palmier, for instance, identified opportunities for corruption and policing along with the level of rewards as three major causes of corruption in Asia, by saying that 'At one extreme, with few opportunities, good salaries, and effective policing, corruption will be minimal, at the other, with many opportunities, poor salaries, and weak policing, it will be considerable.' See Palmier (1985: 272).

7 The politics of rewards for high public office in Korea

Pan-Suk Kim

Introduction

Korea is a key case in this study for several reasons. First, Korea is the main example of democratization in the seven political systems included in this book and, therefore, offers an opportunity to explore the effects of democratization on rewards for high public office. Beginning in the late 1980s, the Korean government moved away from the authoritarian practices of the Park and Chun regimes toward a more open and democratic regime. In addition, the economic development that Korea has experienced in the period after the Korean War has to a significant degree been state-led, so rewards for high public office may be more closely related to economic performance than in some other systems, especially non-Asian countries. The question of the role of government in leading the economy became more important when, like many countries in Asia, Korea had to confront a significant economic crisis and consequently had to make decisions about rewards for high public officials in the face of declining resources. This economic downturn was one of the reasons for undertaking significant human resource management reforms, with these management reforms seen as a means to enhance economic competitiveness (Kim 2000a,b; Kim *et al.* 2001).

The question of rewards for high public office is also linked to several other questions about the nature of the public personnel system in Korea. One is the reform of an extremely traditional system of personnel management within government as a whole. The Korean government had long used a seniority-based wage and promotion system. The seniority-based wage system means that an employee's wages rise in proportion to the length of his or her service and age. Moreover, promotions based on an assessment of short-term performances are generally avoided in Korea because most commentators believe that such practices might disturb the team feeling among employees and lower the overall morale of workers. This culture of reward posed substantial obstacles to the development of performance-based pay systems for senior officials. So, the Kim Dae-Jung Administration decided to include pay reform as one of its 100 key reform measures in 1998. Accordingly, the Civil Service Commission is attempting to change gradually from the seniority-based wage system to a system based on job performance, competency and commitment.

Further, each Korean government employee's remuneration is composed of two elements: base pay and allowances. These allowances have become an increasingly important component of remuneration since Japanese colonial rule.[1] Part of the reliance on allowances stems from the fact that base pay scales are officially published and reported annually in major newspapers, resulting in great attention from the public and the press. So, government has had a tendency to create new allowances instead of increasing the base pay. Under the current law as of 2001, there are 49 kinds of allowances including welfare expenses, which arguably should be curtailed and integrated with the base pay in the near future. In the face of demands for greater democratic transparency, large-scale reliance on allowances to reward officials becomes less tenable, especially for elected officials.

The reliance of the existing pay system on allowances is indicated by the budget for civil servant pay. In 2000, this budget was 14.3 billion dollars and amounted to 18 per cent of the annual expenditure budget. According to a recent report from the Civil Service Commission (2000), the elements of the pay budget consist of the basic salary (45 per cent) and allowances (55 per cent) including welfare expenses, indicating that allowances have been overdeveloped over time in Korea and distort the pay structure. Up to the changes made in 2000 and depicted in Figure 2.5, a rule of thumb to estimate a top Korean civil servant's total pay was to double his or her base salary. This rule of thumb still applies to lower-level civil servants but not to those at the top.

Allowances have been an additional remuneration to public employees that is paid separately according to the position and living conditions of individuals and such information is often not well relayed to the public. The number of allowances is decreasing as part of pay-reform measures initiated by the Civil Service Commission: 56 in 1999, 48 in 2000 and 43 in 2001. Among several allowances, special allowances are major targets for readjustment. The welfare expenses that are paid to civil servants include meal payments, grade-support payments, household-support payments, commutation payments, traditional holiday bonuses and non-vacation payments.

Rewards for the highest public officials in government also have depended heavily on allowances and other non-salary compensation. For example, the amount of the 'expense accounts' (*pangong-bee*) for government leaders including agency heads, the Prime Minister and the President is substantially higher and generally unknown to the public. (Such accounts certainly amount to more than the officeholders' base salaries, but the exact multiple is not known.) Since the late 1980s, various Non-Governmental Organizations (NGOs) began to emerge when Korea gained more political stability and democracy, and in line with the 'Tocquevillian' expectations discussed in Chapters 1 and 2, they criticized such practices openly.[2] For example, the Citizens' Coalition for Economic Justice (2000), a leading public-interest watchdog that was at the heart of the civil movement in Korea from the late 1980s released a report in 2000 on the use of expense accounts by the State-Owned Enterprises (SOEs).[3] According to this report, some SOE chief executives had an expense account that was more than their total pay. Up until a few years ago, such information on expense accounts was not available for public scrutiny. This practice has been used in Korean society for several decades and it is hard to eliminate suddenly. Such funds have been used for dignity maintenance (*poomwi-yoozi*) including contributions for various activities such as support for employees, task promotion and coordination, contribution for wedding and funeral ceremonies of employees and supporters, and other political and social activities of government executives. Therefore, it is fair to say that rewards for high public office (RHPOs) have two faces: a low level of base salary but a high level of the expense accounts for additional rewards.

Variations and the different faces of RHPOs in Korea

The Korean central government has a centralized, uniform system for compensation of public employees. The Civil Service Commission, in collaboration with the Ministry of Planning and Budget, attempts to set the wage level of the civil service on par with the private sector (Kim 2000a). Also, the Korean government is trying to open the public employment market and encourage mobility, particularly at Grade 3 or higher levels, between the public and private sectors.[4] However, it seems likely that the public sector will not attract a sufficient number of highly talented professionals for the time being because government pay will probably continue to lag behind that of the private sector.

Responding to a number of factors, pay for public employees in Korea has changed significantly over the past several decades. Except for the base of each job category, there are no significant differences in pay changes among different types of high-profile officeholders. As shown in Chapter 2, all pay curves move together without much variation. When government decides to increase the pay rate by a certain percentage, it increases salaries by the same rate in all job categories in the public service. However, there are some interesting deviations from the pattern.

First, members (representatives) of the National Assembly were paid at the Deputy-Minister level during the 1970s and 1980s, but they achieved pay parity with Ministers from 1989. This change, which is without parallel in any of the other political systems considered in this book, was of major symbolic importance in the process of democratization, establishing the status of members of the National Assembly as equivalent to the leading members of the political executive. Under an authoritarian leader like President Park Chung Hee, members of the National Assembly had a very limited role in politics. But as the degree of democracy and political stability increased, the role of the legislature has been strengthened and higher monetary rewards have been provided to the members of the National Assembly, in contrast to Tocquevillian expectations. Chapter 2 pointed out that the political systems included in this study tend not to reward legislators well, but this is a clear case of the increasing compensation for that group of officeholders.

Second, senior judges were paid amounts equivalent to the Minister-level throughout this time and the Chief Justice received a salary similar to that of the

Prime Minister. The rewards and privileges for the Chief Justice and the other justices are related to an idea that legal professionals should be rewarded as much as possible to maintain the rule of law within the government.[5]

Third, the salaries of the Prime Minister and the President have been increasing rather rapidly, as shown in Chapter 2. From 1999 (as seen in Chapter 2, Figure 2.5), the government began to use a yearly stipend system that rolled together pay and a number of allowances to reward its higher-level civil servants,[6] and the same practice was adopted for the President and the Prime Minister. Among the yearly stipends for high public officers, the yearly stipend of the President and the Prime Minister have increased more than the others. This fact probably reflects the Korean government's efforts to enhance the transparency of RHPOs because of political scandals with campaign funds in the past, and increasing attention from civic groups, the press and NGOs at present to rewards. Thus, the total levels of rewards may not have increased so rapidly, but the amount being given to these top executives is now more public and more visible.

Finally, despite the economic problems in Asia in general and Korea in particular, salaries for high public office in Korea continue to increase, especially for the officials at the very top of government. As we saw in Chapter 2, the rewards for holding office in Korea by no means approach those in Singapore or Hong Kong, but they are continuing to increase. Some of the changes reflect a shift from allowances to the annual stipend, but it is notable that even in a period of economic uncertainty the Korean government has been able to increase the publicly visible component of rewards to officials. These increases reflect either substantial political courage or an understanding of the rewards game presented in Chapter 1. That is, the government appears to understand that being more open about the rewards being given to public officials may in the end increase their legitimacy.

Factors determining changes in rewards to top-level officials

Decisions about pay levels are influenced by several factors, such as the dominant political philosophy, market and job evaluations. Government can lead, match or lag behind what other employers offer employees. Historically, public servants in many societies were expected to make financial sacrifices in exchange for job security and the opportunity to serve the citizenry – the public service 'discount' discussed in Chapter 2. Pay systems reflect not only law and policy but also explicit or implicit comparisons of similar jobs in different organizations based on salary surveys (external competition), comparisons of job content within an agency employing job evaluation techniques (internal consistency) and comparisons among employees in the same job category in the same organization using seniority, merit, skill or group pay (individual contribution). Culture, prestige, job security and other advantages of public employment would lead to lower pay compared to the private sector. This chapter cannot deal with all the factors influencing rewards for top public office, in Korea, but focuses on four key factors – politics, economics, culture and institutions.

Political factors

Compensation is affected by political factors such as regime stability and the timing of presidential elections. Historically, government pay was viewed as a stalking horse for instigating consequent increases of consumer prices and pay in the private sector. So, the government tried to control pay as much as it could, and when it did increase public-sector pay it tended to do so by minimal increases in the base-salary component which is most open to public scrutiny, accompanied by creation of new allowances or substantially increasing the amount of existing allowances which are not openly available for the general public. As a result, the number of allowances increased significantly,[7] distorting the overall reward system for those in public office.

In addition, the evidence shows that the previous authoritarian governments raised government pay substantially during their political campaigns to acquire political support from government employees. President Park was assassinated in 1979 and the political situation became highly unstable. Prime Minister Choi Gya Ha then assumed the presidency. In 1981, a military junta led by of Chun Doo Hwan took over the presidency through an indirect system based on a presidential Electoral College. The regime faced serious opposition from a broad range of people and President Chun removed numerous government workers who were not loyal to his regime. At the same time, in 1983, he raised the government pay scale significantly to get more support from civil servants for his presidency. Also, it is interesting to observe the effect of presidential election years in 1987, 1992 and 1997, as shown in Figure 7.1. Figure 7.1 suggests that presidential elections tended to produce increases in government pay.[8]

Economic factors

Government pay is also affected by economic factors. According to a 2000 study (Kim and Bae 2000), economic conditions such as increases in nominal Gross National Product and increases in government revenue were very important in shaping changes in government pay before 1986.[9] Historically, government pay was affected significantly by an equity factor (matching the rate of pay increases in the private sector) and by changing patterns of labour relations. During the late

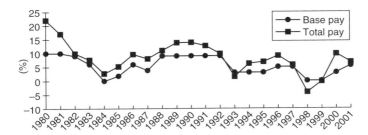

Figure 7.1 Rate of change in government pay.

1980s, labour disputes in the private sector were very serious. As a result, overall private sector wage levels increased substantially since the late 1980s, and this increase also affected the pattern of public-sector pay, as shown in Chapter 2.

In many political systems rewards for high public office are, at least to some degree, driven from below. Lower echelon public employees form unions and place an upward pressure on the entire pay structure, especially to maintain the relatively higher rewards for senior civil servants. This is not the case in Korea, given limitations on the rights of labour to organize. Union membership is only available for some public-sector workers, namely those who work in the postal service, railroad service, national medical institutions and public schools. Even these workers have a limited scale of rights of organization, collective bargaining and collective action. Only in 1999 did the Korean government allow the lowest-level civil servants to organize the Workplace Association of Government Employees (WAGE), and even then WAGE was not strictly a labour union and as of early 2001, only 15–16 per cent of civil servants at Grade 6 and lower belonged to it.[10] Thus, it is fair to say that pressure from unions has not hitherto been a significant determinant of government pay in Korea, although that may well change in the future.

Socio-cultural factors

Confucianism is not usually interpreted as encouraging high monetary reward for 'gentlemen',[11] in spite of the views of Singapore's Goh Chok Tong as discussed by Jon Quah in Chapter 9. According to 2:12 in the Original Analects, Confucius said, 'the gentleman is not used as an implement'. This also implies that the 'gentleman' is not a specialist, but needs scope for generality, as contrasted with standard bureaucratic limitations of functions and responsibilities (Brooks and Brooks 1998: 111). Following the Confucian tradition, in common with Japan, Korea has valued the generalist over the specialist throughout its history. Even today, the Korean civil service is based on a generalist approach, and rewards to encourage specialist skills have not been common in the Korean tradition. Also, a clean-handed official (*chung-baek-ri*) has traditionally been regarded as the ideal government worker, and the term connotes 'uprightness and integrity'. Such values have been heavily emphasized socially in the civil service to cultivate a culture of 'good bureaucrats'. For example, bureaucrats and political leaders who owned a luxurious foreign car were criticized openly and prosecuted in the 1960s and 1970s. Such practices are deeply rooted in an older egalitarian tradition in Korean society.

Historically, the value of high prestige attracted talented individuals into the civil service. Confucian thought, with its veneration of scholars and preoccupation with written tests, especially civil service exams, remains a powerful force in Korea (along with Singapore, Hong Kong, Japan, Taiwan and China; Republic of Singapore 1994). Passing the entrance exam or winning a competitive civil service promotion was akin to being inducted into the hall of fame and it signals to the public that an individual is special. So, talented persons were eager to become civil servants, although the salary was not attractive. As these social and political systems are more influenced by managerial ideas and the need to attract and retain high-quality personnel in government, the influence of these traditional values may decline, but are likely to remain at least a small part of the equation of pay determination.

Institutional factors

Up to now, the Korean government has had a highly centralized pay structure.[12] Government pay changes are determined by a complex process involving a mix of semi-independent players, executive government and the legislature. First, the Civil Service Commission recommends pay increases or an adjustment plan in government (before 1999, the Ministry of Government Administration and Home Affairs did it) and sends it to the Ministry of Government Administration and Home Affairs (MOGAHA). Second, the MOGAHA drafts a bill for pay increase or adjustment. Third, MOGAHA sends a draft to the Adjustment Committee for Government Pay in the Prime Minister's Office and the Adjustment Committee for Government Pay discusses its plan and makes adjustments for pay increases. Fourth, MOGAHA consults with the Ministry of Planning and Budget, the ruling party, the Prime Minister and the President. Fifth, the Cabinet members discuss the overall plan and decide on it in the Cabinet Council Meeting. Sixth, the President makes a decision whether or not to approve it. Seventh, the National Assembly reviews financial allocation and approves the budget.

The current wage level of civil servants is low compared to Japan, Singapore and Hong Kong, as we saw in Chapter 2 (Figure 2.1) and also compared to private-sector salaries in Korea. To improve this situation, the Korean government should pursue a 'generous policy for both the lower and the upper' (*ha-hoo, sang-hoo*), but it has maintained a traditional 'double-imbalance' policy of being 'generous for the lower but tight for the upper' (*ha-hoo, sang-bak*). For example, it froze the wage level of political appointees and agency heads who are at the Grade 1 level in central government, while it increased the wage level of all other civil servants (by a 5.5 per cent increase in base salary and 6.7 per cent in total pay) in 2001. The government argued that the purpose of such practice was to show an example to the public at large to help overcome an economic crisis, but such symbolic politics distorts compensation policy and practices in government, making top-level public officeholders' rewards lag far behind those of the private sector. As we saw in Chapter 2 (Figure 2.6), the vertical compression ratio of the Korean civil service (highest to lowest level, in terms of base pay) was lower than that of Japan up to 2000. In the public sector, however, vertical compression is much lower than in the private sector. According to a recent study (Cho 1999: 83), such pay gap based on a new entrant's pay (100) is as follows: entry-level Executive Director (430), mid-level Executive Director (520), general Executive Director (640), Vice President (780) and the President (1060).

Life-time earnings in the public sector

In Chapter 10, the editors analyse the time-pattern of high public officeholders' rewards, highlighting the significance of the point in their careers that high public officials accumulate wealth, if any. In Korea, public servants are not impoverished during their working lifetime, but neither are they likely to become wealthy from the rewards offered by government. The public sector does, however, offer some opportunities to receive income after the end of the normal career in government. On top of the superannuation schemes available to most public employees, the better-placed public employees have other, more lucrative opportunities similar to those available to high public officials in Japan.

Elected officials such as Members of the National Assembly or Members of Local Government Council are not part of the civil service scheme. Up until the late 1990s, no pension programme was provided to them by the government. When the National Pension Corporation (NPC) scheme, designed mainly for citizens who are under the age of 60, was expanded nationwide in 2000, most members of the National Assembly became part of the NPC scheme. However, many members of the National Assembly are elderly and know they will not receive substantial benefits from it when they leave the National Assembly. Many would, however, also have private- or corporate-pension coverage. Still, such a system has provided an incentive for politicians to remain in office as long as possible, to improve their superannuation benefits.

The Prime Minister, Ministers, Vice Ministers, Chief Justice and Justices are part of the civil service superannuation scheme. If someone works in the civil service for more than 20 years, he or she is entitled to receive the civil service pension amounting to more than 50 per cent of his or her pay on retirement, with the percentage varying according to one's seniority in the civil service. (Those who work in the civil service for less than 20 years are entitled to receive a lump-sum payment.)

The President is not part of the civil service scheme, and has a special superannuation scheme. According to Article 4 in the Act of Privilege for the Former President, the President is entitled to receive 95 per cent of the total annual pay he received during his official term. In addition, the former President is also entitled to have three executive secretaries, a security service, health-care benefits, transportation and communication service and an office.

Another noticeable component of the long-term rewards for public service is the common practice of 'descent by parachute' (*nakhasan-insa*) in the public sector, which is the Korean equivalent of the pattern described for Japan by Akira Nakamura in Chapter 6. As in Japan, it functioned as a method of financial support for outgoing politicians and high public officials. Those who are defeated in elections but have been loyal to the ruler or the ruling party have a high probability of receiving patronage from the President as a head or governing board member in various kinds of public enterprises. According to a recent report (2001), more than 80 per cent of the Chief Executive Officers (CEOs) of SOEs have descended by parachute,[13] and in 2001 the presidents of nine SOEs were generals, politicians or bureaucrats. The presidents of the Korea Housing Authority and Korea Gas Safety Authority were former Congressmen, a former Naval Chief of Staff headed the Korea Petroleum Authority, the President of the Industrial Safety Corporation was a former Assistant Minister in the Ministry of Labour and several presidential positions in the banking sector were held by senior officials in the Ministry of Finance and Economy, including the Industrial Bank, the Medium and Small Business Bank and the Export and Import Bank.

Further, the President sometimes provides top jobs in the public sector for loyal supporters and those who have contributed to the ruling party but have not taken a high position in government or in the political party. This 'spoils' system has long been embedded and a number of CEO positions in SOEs and SIEs have been perceived as 'party spoils' in Korea. However, the case for merit as against 'spoils' appointments has been increasing in recent years, and the practice of 'spoils' appointments to top positions appears to have declined, because the 'spoils' tradition not only jeopardizes industrial competitiveness (as a result of appointing 'political' people who lack business experience) but have also been increasingly and heavily criticized by the media and the public at large.

Also, the lack of transparency in RHPOs has led to a substantial degree of corruption in the past. When citizens began to speak out and the Administrative Procedures Act and the Freedom of Information Act were introduced, what used to be hidden information became available to the public. Moreover, proactive leaders in well-organized NGOs investigated various issues such as details of expense accounts, descent by parachute and unlawful conduct of public office. At the same time, ethical issues have been part of an international agenda in recent years. As a result, the degree of transparency in government operations is improving. It is risky and dangerous for SOE CEOs to use expense accounts for their own personal interests because NGOs and the Independent Commission against Corruption established in 2002 scrutinize the usage of such funds. Therefore, top-officeholders have demanded substantial increases of their regular pay as a logical response to such environmental changes. In other words, as the degree of transparency and individual competition increases in government, demand for high salaries at the top also increases.

Policy implications and concluding remarks

As discussed earlier, RHPOs in Korea have been affected by political, economic and socio-cultural factors, and pay according to individual performance has been limitedly developed. Also, hidden factors such as the expense accounts and the practice of 'descent by parachute' have been obstacles to 'normalization' of the compensation system in Korea. Hence, it can be argued that a more transparent and competitive system needs to be established.

It is said that transparent and competitive government is essential for national prosperity in an era of increased international competition. The competitiveness of government is determined by the competitiveness and quality of the civil service. Pay is one of the devices that makes talented people volunteer for public service and motivates civil servants to work harder. As one of the reform measures to improve an old problem of civil servants' compensation, the President set up a five-year plan to raise civil service pay from 2000 to 2004. The main goals for this plan were to balance the civil servants' pay level with employees in the private sector; and to re-organize the pay structure rationally by continuing the trend towards absorption of allowances into base salaries, integrating similar allowances and abolishing others. According to this plan, civil service pay was expected to rise 3–4 per cent more than employee's pay in the private sector every year. Overall, it aimed at narrowing the gap in pay between the private sector and the public sector, on the basis of annual surveys of the wages paid by approximately 700 private enterprises in Korea and comparing the results with pay in the public sector.

Other directions for changing the government compensation system are individualization and decentralization of government pay. The individualization of pay needs to be employed to increase the dispersion of pay within occupations. Even where the introduction of performance-related pay initially results in a narrower dispersion of pay, tying pay to performance should ensure that subsequently there is greater dispersion of pay within each occupation. Subsequent increases would be expected to reflect the diversity of performance in a way that the uniform settlements awarded under the previous system could not. At present, the Korean government compensation system is highly centralized without flexibility and uniform without diversity. A more flexible and diverse pay scheme needs to be developed. Finally, a device for strengthening the pay system that is based on the performance-oriented principle is to improve the annual merit incremental programme and the performance bonus programme in force.

The reform of the wage system was attracting much attention at the time of writing and the Korean government was willing to give more emphasis to merit elements in determining wages. Naturally, such cultural changes could not be achieved suddenly. Nevertheless, the trend toward ability-based pay, focusing on performance and workers' abilities, with an emphasis on the evaluation of a worker's contribution, should be strengthened in the future.

Notes

1 During Japanese colonial rule, particularly in the early 1940s, the Japanese Governor in Korea issued a decree limiting company pay for employees. Because of that measure, the basic salary of company pay and government pay has been steady, while allowances as an alternative way to increase earnings were heavily utilized. Such practices have continued since Korea's independence from Japanese colonial rule to the present day.

2 Lately, NGOs made a significant contribution to enhance transparency of government operation. See *http://peoplepower21.org* for the People's Solidarity for Participatory Democracy and *http://www.ccbg.org* for the Citizens' Coalition for Better Government.

3 See *http://www.ccej.or.kr* for more details.

4 In the Korean civil service, Grade 9 is the lowest level and Grade 1 is the highest.

5 This kind of privilege for legal professionals is also observed in the civil service. Those who passed a bar examination receive a higher salary than those who passed an entrance examination of the senior civil service, even if they otherwise have the same academic and personal qualifications.

6 For the senior public servants, this also heralded the potential adoption of a pay for performance system.

7 Since 1999, the number of allowances declined as noted earlier.

8 Presidents' official terms were: Chun (1980–81 and 1981–88); Roh (1988–93); Kim, YS (1993–98) and Kim, DJ (1998–2002).

9 A direct presidential election was introduced in 1948, but it was suspended in the middle of President Park's administration through a constitutional amendment and then an indirect presidential election was utilized. The Constitution was amended in 1986 and a direct presidential election was restarted in 1987.

10 Interview with an official in charge of public unions in the Ministry of Government Administration and Home Affairs, 9 March 2001.

11 See also Weber (1951, 1965) on religious ethics.

12 In comparison, several Western countries such as the UK and Sweden have decentralized pay determination in large areas of the public sector to agencies, and the idea that linking their pay to their performance can enhance the performance of public-sector workers has gained widespread acceptance in these countries in recent years, although the pace and scale of these reforms has not been uniform (OECD 1996).

13 Proportion of 'descendants by parachute' by each regime are: 84 per cent in the Chun Doo-Hwan Administration; 90 per cent in the Roh Tae-Woo Administration; 86 per cent in the Kim Young-Sam Administration; and 82 per cent in the Kim Dae Jung Administration. For more details, see *The Chosun Daily* (*Chosun Ilbo*, 5 February 2001: 4–5).

8 Hong Kong – institutional inheritance from colony to special administrative region

Grace O. M. Lee

Introduction

Hong Kong's remarkably generous pattern of rewards to top public officeholders, described in Chapter 2, seems to be explained in large part by that variant of institutional theory that sees policy outcomes as heavily conditioned by policy legacies, by decision-making rules, traditions and routines within established organizations, as well as by the pattern of intermediary structures between state and society (Hood and Peters 1994: 4–5). Although Hong Kong has been a Special Administrative Region of China since 1997, the nature of its system of reward for high public office reflects an institutional legacy from its 156 years of British colonial rule. Under the 'one country, two systems' model, adopted in 1997, the Basic Law (Article 100) guarantees the rights of the civil servants inherited from the colonial era to retain their positions and conditions of employment. The high basic salaries enjoyed by Hong Kong's top public officeholders that was noted in Chapter 2 results from a variant of Bentham's principle that salaries should be set at a level that will attract and retain the necessary talent. This colonial legacy shapes present-day political and administrative institutions as well as the repertoire of organizational and institutional models accepted as potential solutions to modern problems of governance (Christensen 1997: 145).

The colonial legacy is illustrated by the generous perks and benefits (including housing, chauffeur-driven limousines for personal use, passages, local and overseas education allowances) enjoyed by Hong Kong's Chief Executive, Chief Justice and top bureaucrats (but not by its legislators). As in the case of Singapore, described by Jon Quah in Chapter 9, these generous pay packages were originally designed for expatriate colonial rulers under a system lacking democratic scrutiny. The perks were gradually extended to local civil servants after a long and hard-fought campaign for equal pay, particularly after acceleration of the localization policy in the final years of colonial rule. However, in addition to simple historical inertia, preservation of the colonial pay system can also be seen as means of reward maximization by public officials. Since high salaries had been institutionalized under colonial rule, preserving them presented fewer political problems than would have been presented in adopting such a reward system from scratch.

The top rewards game in Hong Kong: the major players

Hong Kong's top political executive, the successor office to that of Governor in colonial days, is appointed by the Central People's Government. The Basic Law provides for a selection process by an electoral college of 400 members drawn from various social groups.

The Hong Kong legislature, the Legislative Council, has always had much more limited powers than the parliaments of Western democracies. For most of the period of colonial rule, from 1844 to 1985, the Governor appointed all members of the Council. Only in 1995, at the very end of colonial rule, did the last Legislative Council under British rule become a fully elected legislature (Legislative Council 2001). With the introduction of representative government and popular election to the legislature in the 1980s and 1990s, there was an increase in public scrutiny, but not fully democratic scrutiny of the executive. Democratization in Hong Kong was a top–down process, dominated by Britain and China. Indeed, those two countries were 'strikingly similar in insisting on an executive-led government and in their determination to restrict reforms only to the legislative institution (the Legislative Council). The executive-led government monopolizes policy-making and control of the legislative agenda, and Hong Kong's democratization can thus be described as only partial in nature' (Lau and Kuan 2000: 706). The deliberate efforts of Chris Patten, the last Governor, to work with the legislature succeeded to some degree in elevating its symbolic status in Hong Kong's political system. However, in reality it still lacks the constitutional power to make and unmake governments, to propose and formulate policies, or to play a significant role in the appointment or dismissal of top officials. Its main role is a limited form of oversight over the administration (Lau and Kuan 2000: 707).

Under colonial administration, civil servants emerged as a ruling elite and still dominate the structure of executive government. At the time of writing, the apex of the hierarchy is the Directorate Officer Grade comprising 15 secretaries of the policy bureaux, heads and deputy heads of the 69 departments and agencies, and senior professionals like doctors, lawyers and engineers. Up to now, Hong Kong has had no Ministers as in a conventional parliamentary system, but the 15 secretaries of the policy bureaux have collectively formed the Government Secretariat. The Chief Secretary for Administration has exercised direction primarily as head of the Government Secretariat, and has been one of the Chief Executive's main advisers, along with the Financial Secretary and the Secretary for Justice.

Structure of rewards: inheritance and self-interest

As Chapter 2 showed, formal rewards for the Chief Executive, his executive aides and the Chief Justice are much higher than those applying to the legislature. For example, in 2000 the base salary of the President of the Legislative Council was less than two-thirds of the US$ 333,000 earned as base salary by the Chief Secretary for Administration. The numerous benefits and perks enjoyed by the executives were also absent for legislators. As can be seen from Tables 8.1 and 8.2, which give a simplified summary of the allowance structure for civil servants and other top public officeholders as of 2001, executive officers and the judiciary received a base salary plus money allowances, allowances on a reimbursable basis, benefits in kind, leave arrangements, medical and dental benefits and end of service benefits. But as the tables show, the president of the legislature received only a substantially lower base salary plus reimbursable office expenses. The great difference in reward packages can be largely explained by the fact, mentioned earlier, that the generous pay packages obtained by government officers originated as colonial privileges that had gradually been extended to local civil servants.

The colonial inheritance of high pay and perks in the high civil service, as summarized in Table 8.1, dates back to the establishment of the Administrative Officer Grade in 1861 by a Victorian-era Governor of Hong Kong, Sir Hercules Robinson (Lethbridge 1978: 221). Known as the 'cadet scheme' until 1960, the administrative civil service was racially exclusive, with no possibility of accepting local recruits (Miners 1986: 85). The aim was to recruit highly educated young men from professional families in the UK and offer them attractive careers as colonial civil servants, with generous perks and benefits. No serious attempt was made to increase the number of posts held by local Chinese in the Hong Kong civil service until 1930 when the desirability of replacing European staff by Chinese became a public issue after unofficial members of the Legislative Council opposed proposals for increased salaries for public servants and the new taxes needed to finance them. The then Governor, Sir William Peel, appointed a retrenchment committee to advise on financial redistribution in government staff and administration. In the interests of economy, the committee's recommendations included the replacement of Europeans with Chinese wherever possible (Miners 1986: 84).

However, progress in replacing Europeans with local staff was slow. European staff could not be dismissed to make way for Chinese before they reached retirement age, so vacancies arose only from natural wastage and new public-service positions. Some heads of departments were reluctant to employ local staff and the lower salaries offered to local appointees might also have discouraged local applicants. In 1938, the government did find it necessary to make an upward adjustment in the pay of certain Chinese medical doctors who had graduated from the University of Hong Kong, to prevent them from resigning and going into private practice. Even so, their maximum salary remained below the starting salary for a European doctor (Miners 1986: 85).

In 1951, the first Chinese Crown Counsel (a senior lawyer), Patrick Yu Shuk-siu, resigned after the Public Services Commission refused to grant him expatriate terms. As Yu put it, 'I was thus to be paid no more than a minimum flat salary without any high-cost-of-living allowance, living quarters, housing allowance, long leave with pay, or any one of a long list of miscellaneous pecuniary as well as other privileges and benefits to which all expatriate officers were automatically entitled' (Yu 1998: 125–6). In 1958, the Senior Non-Expatriate Officers' Association

Table 8.1 Monthly salaries and fringe benefits of senior civil servants in Hong Kong (2000), in HK$

Grade	D1	D2–D3	D4–D5	D6–D7	D8	D9, Financial Secretary	D10, Chief Secretary
Monthly salary	$98,250					$204,800	$216,650
Housing							
Home Financing Scheme	$32,400		$36,450		$48,600	Housing provided	
Departmental quarters	Staff contribute 7.5% of substantive salary						
Leave							
Appointed before 1.1.99	31–40.5 (maximum accumulation: 120–180)				55.5 days (maximum accumulation: 365)		
Appointed on or after 1.1.99	27–34 (maximum accumulation: 54–68)				No change		
Leave passages (staff + spouse + dependent children up to a total of five recipients)	Every 24 months				Every 12 months (rate: $41,440)		
Government car for personal use + chauffeur + running costs					Applicable (starting from D8)		
Pension	1/675 × pensionable service in months × highest annual salary (subject to a maximum of 2/3 of the highest annual pensionable salary; and optional to reduce pension up to 50 per cent for conversion into a lump-sum gratuity of 14 times the amount of the annual reduction)						
Medical, dental, hospitalization benefit	Same for all serving civil servants and pensioners; and their dependents (below age of 19 or below age of 21 if in full time education/ vocational training or dependent as a result of physical or mental infirmity)						
Children's education allowance							
Local	All civil servants except temporary staff						
Overseas	All civil servants except those appointed on or after 1.8.96 and those on Model Scale I and temporary terms of appointment						

Sources: Pay and Research Unit, Standing Commission on Civil Service Salaries and Conditions of Service.

was formed to fight colonial discrimination and concessions in one form or another were won from government from time to time, but progress was slow. Pay parity was achieved only in 1971 and overseas leave passages were extended to local directorate officers and their families a decade later. The government started

Table 8.2 Monthly salaries and fringe benefits of senior executive and judicial officers in Hong Kong (2000), in HK$

	Chief Executive	Chief Secretary	Financial Secretary	Secretary for Justice	Chief Justice	Pres. of Legislative Council
Base salary (per month)	$270,800	$216,650	$204,800	$193,050	$216,650	$118,800
Non-accountable entertainment and travel expenses (per month)	n.a.	n.a.	n.a.	n.a.	n.a.	Up to $13,720
Money allowance						
Non-accountable entertainment allowance (per annum)	$825,700	$412,900	$316,400	$206,400	344,000	$49,440
Accountable entertainment allowance (per annum)	n.a.	n.a.	n.a.	n.a.	n.a.	$115,360
Allowances on a reimbursable basis						
Accountable component for office operation (per month)	n.a.	n.a.	n.a.	n.a.	n.a.	Up to $96,120
Passage	Staff + spouse + dependent children at $42,060 per adult per year					Nil
Local education	Up to $31,950–49,238 each per annum for up to four children up to the age of 19					Nil
Overseas education allowance	Up to 90% of boarding school fees or up to approx. US$14,000 per year per child, or day school allowance of up to approx. US$2000 for specified countries					Nil
School passage allowance	$17,700–11,800 per year each for up to four children under 21 (for staff on overseas terms) or between 9 and 21 (for staff on local terms)					Nil
In-kind benefits						
Housing	An official and country residence	Official residence but subject to rent deduction of 7.5% of salary				Nil
Personal transport	A government car with all running costs, including a chauffeur, borne by the government					Nil
Medical benefit	Free medical advice and treatment at government clinics and hospitals/specialist clinics for officeholder and dependents					Nil
Dental	Free dental service at government clinics for 'conservative' treatment					Nil
Hospital	Hospital maintenance fees ranging from $241–368 per day					Nil
Club membership	Reimbursement of fees for joining professional organizations, district sports or arts associations for approved purposes					Nil
Gratuity/pension	Gratuity: 25% of base salary	Gratuity: 25% of base salary. Pension depends on terms of appointment (see Table 8.1)			Gratuity: 25% of base salary per 3-year term renewable up to age 65	Nil
Leave	55.5 days within each 12-month period	For those promoted to D4 before 1998: either 55.5 days per year with passage or 72.5 days per year without passage			55.5 days for each 12-month cycle	Nil

Source: Information supplied by Civil Service Bureau, Judiciary Administration, HKSAR Government, and Legislative Council Secretariat in 2001; Pay and Research Unit, Standing Commission on Civil Service Salaries and Conditions of Service 1999; Independent Commission on Remuneration for Members of the Executive Council and the Legislature of the HKSAR 1999.

Note
n.a. = Not applicable.

to pursue a thoroughgoing policy of localization after signing the Joint Declaration between the Chinese and British governments in 1984. The Declaration, stipulated that after 1997 the highest 'principal official' levels[1] in the Hong Kong government were to be occupied by Chinese nationals who were permanent residents of the HKSAR, and did not have the right of abode in any foreign country. Accordingly, by 1997, all 19 Secretaries were locals, compared to 8 out of 15 in 1990 and 4 out of 18 in 1985 (Huque *et al.* 1998: 69).

In the current pay structure, the Chief Executive's base salary is pegged to that of a high administrator, and is currently fixed at 125 per cent of the base salary of the Chief Secretary for Administration, as mentioned earlier. Like former Colonial Governors, the Chief Executive could have been exempted from taxation, but the present Chief Executive volunteered to subject his earnings to taxation – a sacrifice which is limited by Hong Kong's very low rate of income tax, which currently stands at a maximum of 15 per cent. In turn, the Chief Secretary for Administration is the highest-paid civil servant in Hong Kong, graded at the top of the Directorate pay scale (the Financial Secretary is one step lower), which is one of the Hong Kong civil service's 13 different pay scales. The Secretary for Justice (former Attorney General) is at the top of the Directorate Legal Pay Scale and the Chief Justice (Court of Final Appeal) is on the top scale of the Judicial Services Pay Scale, which is equivalent to the salary of the Chief Secretary for Administration. The Chief Justice is independent from the civil service, but enjoys the same benefits as civil servants.

The substantial salaries enjoyed by these individuals are largely of a fixed, status-based type, in contrast to Singapore, Australia and New Zealand. The fixed salaries incorporate a set of incremental steps within each pay grade and the system of incrementation in principle reflects performance in that 'an officer may be granted an increment only if conduct (including fidelity, obedience to orders, propriety) in the year under review have been satisfactory'. But the real situation is that 'increments are granted automatically with no regard to an officer's actual performance ... another reality is that over 50% of [the civil servants] are already at maximum pay point, as high as 88% in some groups' (Civil Service Bureau 1999: 1). Even though the Hong Kong government proposed an element of performance-based pay (Civil Service Bureau 2000a: 5), current performance pay schemes are aimed at front-line staff rather than top civil servants and heads of departments were not obliged to participate in pilot schemes for performance pay.

In contrast to the lavish salaries traditionally enjoyed by Hong Kong's civil service rulers, service on the Legislative Council was entirely unpaid until 1976 and there was not even any provision for the payment of expenses, though unofficially members could obtain clerical assistance and some help with research from the staff of the Office of the Unofficial Members of the Executive and Legislative Council. This arrangement predictably left the Council open to the criticism that only the wealthy could afford to serve on it, though discussion does not seem to have focused on the incentives for corruption provided by the absence of any salary (in contrast to the received view that the civil service's high salaries acted as an antidote to corruption). In 1976, when the Council was enlarged to include two members from the 'working classes', an allowance for expenses was established (Miners 1998: 120). From 1991, members of the Legislative Council have been paid a modest salary in recognition of the fact that service on a Council, which now meets once a week, and on its numerous panels and committees, is difficult to combine with a full-time occupation, even though its demands are modest in comparison with parliaments in Western democracies. In fact, as in Singapore, most Legislative Councillors (particularly those representing 'functional' constituencies) are in full-time employment and do not see their legislative work as a career.

As noted earlier, members of the executive and the judiciary have traditionally been entitled to a wide range of allowances on top of their lavish salaries, which were summarized earlier in Tables 8.1 and 8.2. Major reimbursable allowances have included 'leave passages' or holiday travel, and children's education allowance. Leave passages have traditionally been provided to directorate officers in the form of generous 'passage allowances' to cover themselves, their spouses and dependent children of up to five recipients at a rate of HK$ 42,060 per adult. However, those arrangements have been replaced by less generous terms for new recruits, with a cut in leave allowances for directorate officers from 1999 and a replacement of leave passage arrangements with an annual (taxable) cash allowance payable to the officer alone, and not family members (Civil Service Bureau 1999: 4).

In addition, for their children's education, all permanent civil servants have been entitled to local education allowance, for up to four children up to the age of 19. Furthermore, all permanent civil servants appointed before 1996 (and not on Model Scale I) are entitled to an overseas education allowance, for up to four children between 9 and 19, either in the UK or in the country of origin (for staff on overseas terms). These allowances, which were summarized in Table 8.2, were designed to pay most of the cost of private day or boarding school education. All civil servants appointed before 1996 are also entitled to school passages as outlined in Table 8.2. The countries covered by the overseas education allowance and school passage, coupled with the fact that the benefits were abolished in 1996, just before the end of colonial rule, shows that those strikingly generous allowances were originally intended for the benefit of the colonial masters. In contrast, the President of the legislature can only enjoy the entertainment allowance.

In addition to these allowances, there have been a set of in-kind benefits including club membership, government cars for personal use, medical, dental and hospitalization benefits, and housing as detailed in Table 8.2. For instance, in addition to an annual salary of more than US$ 400,000, the Chief Executive is provided with an official residence and a country house. The present Chief Executive, a wealthy shipping magnate, decided not to move into the former Governor's mansion, preferring his own apartment, and used the official residence for official visitors and distinguished guests. The government then leased the apartment next door to the private apartment of the Chief Executive, effectively doubling the useable area. The Chief Secretary for Administration has also been provided with an official residence (a large and luxurious house in a millionaires' district on the Peak), but subject to rent deduction of 7.5 per cent of salary. Similar arrangements traditionally applied to the Chief Justice, Financial Secretary and the Secretary for Justice. All of the official residences attached to these positions are in prestigious locations, fully furnished and staffed by a chief steward, a head chef, chefs and domestic servants. Indeed, harking back to the point made by Akira Nakamura and Kosaku Dairokuno for Japan's MPs in Chapter 6, the fact that Hong Kong's top three executive officeholders have been entitled to live in a palatial house in the city centre during their term of service can be considered a luxurious and prestigious reward when compared to the average family living space of around 500 square feet in Hong Kong.

Life-time earnings

Unlike the Japanese 'descent from heaven' pattern, Hong Kong's civil servants traditionally lived on generous non-contributory pensions in retirement. The size of the pension a civil servant could get was traditionally a function of his or her pensionable service (in months) times the highest annual salary divided by 675. This meant that top civil servants with a career spanning several decades (traditionally the normal pattern) could accumulate very large sums on retirement. To take the former Chief Secretary for Administration (Anson Chan) as an example, she was entitled to an enviable lump sum of about US$ 15 million on her official retirement date in 2000 and a pension of over US$ 9,000 a month until her death. However, from 2000, new civil service recruits have not been offered permanent and pensionable jobs and the traditional non-contributory pension system has been replaced by a contributory provident fund.

Under the terms of the pensions legislation, retiring civil servants are required to seek prior permission from the Chief Executive before they enter into business or take up employment in Hong Kong within a specified period after retirement if their business or employment is mainly carried out in Hong Kong. Retired officers at director of bureau rank or above are required to seek permission within three years after retirement, whereas other retirees have to seek approval within a two-year period.

The main aim of these rules, policed by an advisory committee set up in 1987, is 'to ensure that former civil servants do not enter into any business or outside employment which may constitute a conflict of interest with their previous employment in the Civil Service or embarrass the Government' (Advisory Committee on Post-retirement Employment 1999: 2). The public perception of the appropriateness of a retiree's taking up the proposed employment and the question of whether the proposed employment will result in the person concerned having an undesirable public profile are also important considerations. In principle, various conditions, such as a period of sanitization during which the applicant would be barred from assuming employment or restrictions on the scope of activities to be taken, may be imposed. But, in practice, none of the 28 approved applications for post-retirement employment from retired bureau secretaries between 1996 and 2000 involved a sanitization period. Information about post-retirement earnings of top civil servants is, however, elusive, unless their second jobs are within the government or quasi-government sector, such as the case of two former secretaries who started their lucrative post-retirement careers as heads of quasi-government organizations with attractive pay packages and pensions in 1995.

Institutions and pay decisions

Since the 1960s, Hong Kong has handled the issue of top public-sector pay by a linkage between top pay and that of the rest of the civil service, and by the use of special arms-length pay commissions to depoliticize the pay decision process. Separate committees were formed to review and advise on the pay of the civil service (other than the uniformed services), the judiciary and later (in 1993) on the pay of legislative councillors. Before 1993, salary adjustments were considered internally within the administration, to be endorsed by the Finance Committee of the Legislative Council if extra funding was needed. With the change in sovereignty in 1997, an Independent Commission on Remuneration for Members of the Executive Council and the Legislature of the HKSAR (the Independent Commission) was established. Its terms of reference include consideration of the pay of members of the Executive Council and the Legislative Council, and periodic reviews of remuneration packages for members of the Legislative Council. The Independent Commission considers that 'work on the legislature is a form of service to the public. Members of the legislature should be adequately remunerated in recognition of the time and effort they contribute to the legislature, and be given financial assistance to pay for staff and office expenses arising from their duties. Since public funds are involved, there should be adequate transparency and accountability in the way Members use their allowance' (Independent Commission on Remuneration for Members of the Executive Council and the Legislature of the HKSAR 1999: 1). The Independent Commission is intended to depoliticize decision-making over pay of legislators and annual adjustments in pay and allowances are made according to the cost of living index. However, each modified pay package that incurs extra expenditure needs endorsement of the Executive Council and approval by the Finance Committee of the Legislative Council and indeed the Legislative Council retains the formal power to disregard the Independent Commission's recommendations and fix its own rewards. For civil service pay, the official guiding principle is that '[c]ivil service pay is set at a level which is sufficient to attract, retain and motivate staff of a suitable calibre to provide the public with an effective and efficient service, and such remuneration should be regarded as fair by both civil servants and the public which they serve' (Civil Service Bureau 1998). Officially, broad comparability with the private sector is the main factor in setting civil service pay, involving the discovery of starting private-sector pay for jobs with certain education qualifications and using these figures to set benchmarks for starting pay in civil service jobs with similar qualifications. Yet, Hong Kong's civil service pay structure involves some degree of 'double imbalance', with some pay premium in the lower ranks of the bureaucracy relative to the private sector and a pay discount in the upper ranks (cf. Sjölund 1989, cited in Hood 1999). The civil service starting salaries review in 1999 indicated that 'the private sector pay for Degree recruits, as evidenced by the results of the pay comparison survey, is currently about 25 % lower than the civil service pay' (Hong Kong Standing Commission on Civil Service Salaries and Conditions of Service 1999: 25). In the light of this 'discovery', the starting salary for degree holders was later reduced by 23 per cent.

In contrast, government had not reviewed directorate salaries for more than a decade at the time of writing. In 1989, the Standing Committee on Directorate Salaries and Conditions of Service (the Standing Committee) commissioned two consultant companies to 'conduct a confidential survey of salaries and fringe benefits at senior management levels in the private sector' (Standing Committee on Directorate Salaries and Conditions of Service 1989: 42). The main finding of the survey was that 'the average of the most common pay increases over the four-year period 1985–86 and 1988–89 for the surveyed positions was in the region of 60%. The most common pay increase in 1988–89 was about 14.5%. These findings compare with a cumulative increase of 24.5% in directorate pay since the adjustment recommended in our last (Ninth) Review in 1985. This 24.5% has been based on the adjustments to the upper band of the non-directorate in 1986, 1987 and 1988. To bring the cumulative increase to 60% would mean an increase of 28.5% on top of the 24.5%' (Standing Committee on Directorate Salaries and Conditions of Service 1989: 43). However, the Standing Committee did not think it necessary for government to pay top public servants exactly the same as private-sector employees. The Standing Committee believed that '[w]hile private sector is important in determining rates of pay in the civil service, other factors must also be taken into account' and it quoted the first Standing Committee in 1964:

> There are many other factors and conditions of service to be considered, and we have fully in mind the differences of security of employment and other considerations of service. Moreover, commercial systems of promotion and payment in the higher ranks are much more flexible than those of the public service. In the Government service, promotion is based on qualifications, experience and merit … The salary of posts is fixed; Government pays the same salary to the holder of a post whether or not he makes a conspicuous success of it. The rewards in commerce are more unevenly distributed. The exceptionally able may rise rapidly to senior posts, while the person of average ability may remain at a relatively low level. There is no 'pay for the job' for these senior posts, and salaries may vary greatly according to the merits of the occupant. But despite these differences of method, any reasonable assessment of fair remuneration for government salaries must take into account the range of corresponding commercial salaries.
>
> (Standing Committee on Directorate Salaries and
> Conditions of Service 1989: 44)

This justification for a pay discount for top civil servants appeared in four consecutive reports published by the Standing Committee in 1980, 1982, 1985 and 1989. While the Standing Committee accepted that 'civil service directorate salaries cannot match those of some top executives in the private sector … [they] believe that some regard should be had to pay trends (as opposed to levels) of senior executives in the private sector' (the Standing Committee on Directorate Salaries and Conditions of Service 1989: 44–5). As the Deputy Secretary for the Civil Service has pointed out, it is very difficult to obtain information on the pay of directorate-equivalent staff in the private sector (Legislative Council 1998: 7). Nevertheless, Table 8.3 gives some idea that rewards at the top in the private sector are much more attractive than those of the civil service.

Traditionally, as noted earlier, most pensionable civil servants have tended only to start a second career, if any, after retirement. But there are signs that this pattern may be changing. Top bureaucrats have begun to resign from the civil service for greener pastures. For example, in 2000 a policy secretary left the civil service in his mid-40s to head a key independent public body, the Financial Services Authority, obtaining as a result an annual income of over US$ 1 million. Such high public officeholders may see their civil service job as a 'first career' to be approached in a way which maximizes earning opportunities in a subsequent career, either in the private sector or in a better-paid area in the public sector, and if this trend becomes firmly established and widespread it may produce increasing conflicts of interest (see Hood and Peters 1994: 20).

The government's long-standing policy has been one of annual consideration of the pay of the civil service as a whole, with changes broadly in line with pay adjustments in the private sector. Hence, elaborate annual pay trend surveys have been carried out among private-sector companies since 1974 by the independent Pay Survey and Research Unit of the Standing Commission on Civil Service Salaries and Conditions of Service (the Standing Commission). The pay trend survey does not apply to the directorate-level staff, but adjustments to directorate

Table 8.3 Comparison of annual salaries of selected top executive officers in government, staff enterprises and the private sector, Hong Kong (2001)

Government	Counterparts in QUANGOs and private sector

Secretary for Health and Welfare
  About $ 2.2 million
	Chief Executive of Hospital Authority
	  About $ 5 million

Secretary for Transport
  About $ 2.2 million
	Managing Director of Kowloon Motor Bus
	  About $ 8 million

Secretary for Housing
  About $ 2.2 million
	Executive Director of Hong Kong Housing Society
	  About $ 4 million

Financial Secretary
  About $ 2.4 million
	Chief Executive of Hong Kong Monetary Authority
	  About $ 8 million

Sources: *Ming Pao* and HKSAR.

salaries in practice have followed the Pay Trend Indicators of the upper pay band of the non-directorate staff of the civil service.

Other factors taken into account have included changes in the cost of living, the state of the economy, budgetary considerations, employees' pay claims and civil service morale. Each pay adjustment has been a separate annual exercise based on circumstances prevailing at the time (Civil Service Bureau 2000b).

As Chapter 2 showed, between 1980 and 2000 Hong Kong's Gross Domestic Product (GDP) almost tripled, with GDP growing at an average annual rate of about 5 per cent in real terms. In those palmy days, per capita GDP in Hong Kong more than doubled in real terms and in 1999, it reached US$ 23,200 at current market prices (HKSAR Government 2000b). Those years of 'miraculous' economic growth not only enriched the capitalists but also increased the real wages of the salaried class, so the market principle of broad comparability with the private sector described above led to a tenfold increase in the pay of Hong Kong's top political executive (Governor and later Chief Executive) from 1976 to 2001.

Readers will recall that Chapter 2 explored top public pay changes over time relative to economic performance, showing that Hong Kong was one of the cases where a long period of sharp salary rises slowed after the Asian financial crisis of 1997. In fact, in 1998 pay was frozen at Directorate Pay Scale Point 3 (D3) level and above, 'to demonstrate that senior officers responsible for policy-making in the Government understood and were prepared to share the hardship caused by the economic turmoil' (Legislative Council 1998: 7). The pay trend surveys for 1999 and 2000 indicated that pay adjustments awarded by private employers to their employees in the preceding year were either nil or marginally downward. In the light of the 'psychological impact' of public-sector pay on the economy, civil service salaries were frozen for two consecutive years (Civil Service Bureau 2000b), but the pay and allowances of members of the legislature continued to rise up to 2000, two years after top civil servants had their salaries frozen.

High pay and low corruption?

As Chapter 2 showed, Hong Kong is a case where high top public pay combines with low levels of corruption on conventional international indices, with Transparency International (1999) rating it as the second lowest-corruption Asian city behind Singapore. An internal government survey in 2000 sampled 480 directorate officers and revealed that over 87 per cent of the respondents said that corruption was 'not common' and 'never exists' in government. Only 7.9 per cent of the respondents believed that corruption was 'common' (*Ming Pao*, 29 September 2000). Indeed, government servants of Hong Kong are subject to stringent formal stipulations against corruption and conflict of interests, enforced by an Independent Commission Against Corruption. For instance, in addition to conventional prohibitions or bribery and extortion, the Prevention of Bribery Ordinance (Section 10) provides for the punishment of civil servants who receive bribes over a period of time even when the assets they possess cannot be linked to any specific corrupt deal. It stipulates that it is an offence for a civil servant to maintain a standard of living or control assets, which are not commensurate with his or her official emoluments.

Furthermore, Civil Service Regulations 461 and 466 require civil servants to avoid making private investments that may lead to real or apparent conflicts of interest. Following a revision of the declaration of investments system after a review by the Civil Service Bureau in 1998, numerous officers must declare their interests, including high-level officials such as the Chief Secretary for Administration, Financial Secretary, directors of bureaux, Commissioner of Police and other top public officeholders, as well as administrative assistants and personal secretaries in support of the upper-level positions. These individuals are required to report 'all their investments in and outside Hong Kong' (Legislative Council Secretariat 2000). In addition, higher-level officers must make an annual declaration of other financial interests, including real estate, proprietorships or directorships of companies and shareholdings of per cent or more of the issued shares in any listed company.

Convictions for corruption impose heavy penalties on a career civil servant, and may lead to instant dismissal from the job, loss of pension entitlements and jail sentences. To date, the most senior government official convicted for fraud over allowances in recent decades has been a top tax official, Deputy Inland Revenue Commissioner Sin in 1984. Ms Sin was convicted of defrauding the government of HK$ 330,000 in rental allowances and her downfall resulted from her being considered for promotion to Commissioner for Inland Revenue. Following standard operating procedures, integrity checks are made on all top officials by the police, particularly those being considered for promotion. The Commercial Crime Bureau detected the fraud and passed the case to the Independent Commission Against Corruption, which had wider powers to seize documents from the Inland Revenue Department. The judge found Sin and her husband had intended to deceive the government when they submitted an application for rental allowances that contained false information. Sin's salary was stopped after her conviction, she could have lost her pension of HK$ 6.6 million and faced a suspended jail sentence (Wong 2000).

Conclusion

As Chapter 2 showed, formal rewards for high public office in Hong Kong, the executives and the judiciary in particular, are among the highest in the world. Though these rewards appear less generous when compared to the exceptionally high rewards at the top of the private sector, the government (like that of Singapore and Korea) was traditionally able to recruit the 'cream' of university graduates to the civil service as Administrative Officers and professionals, offering secure, fairly lucrative work in a closed-career system with substantial pension and end-of-service entitlements.

With the change in sovereignty, this cosy world may be altering to some extent. After the end of the colonial era, numerous successful professionals and senior executives left lucrative private-sector careers to take up public office, including the present Chief Executive Tung Chee Hwa who owned a successful international ocean liner company before taking office, and had no public administration experience. In the colonial era, a closed-career model prevailed and it was rare for non-civil servants to enter the government as policy secretaries (*Ming Pao* 2001), but since then, there has been an increase in political appointments. Notable examples include Elsie Leung who quit a private legal practice to become the Secretary for Justice in 1997, Dr E. K. Yeoh who halved an HK$ 5 million annual income as Chief Executive of the Hospital Authority to become the Secretary for Health and Manpower in 1999, and Antony Leung Kam-chung, Asia-Pacific chairman of JP Morgan Chase, who gave up a HK$ 15 million a year pay package for HK$ 2.45 million to become Financial Secretary in 2001 (Harrison and Wan 2001).

Having served in the business sector for 28 years, the new Financial Secretary had no civil service experience. He became a member of the Executive Council in July 1997 and was made chairman of the Education Commission in 1998. While the business sector was cautiously optimistic about Leung's appointment, civil service unions expressed disappointment at a banker, instead of a career civil servant, being made financial chief. But the local deputy of the National People's Congress commented that Leung would act as a role model for 'specialists running Hong Kong'. The Executive Director of the One Country, Two Systems Research Institute added that

> The right to form his own team is essential for every Chief Executive in order to put his political platform into practice ... Theoretically, senior civil servants only serve at the pleasure of the Chief Executive. They are, in form, appointed by the sovereign government and can be removed at any time upon the suggestion of the Chief Executive.
>
> (Shiu 2001)

In fact, in his Policy Address of October 2000 the Chief Executive announced plans to introduce greater accountability for senior officials. Unlike the present system, which imposes considerable constraints on Tung picking people from outside the civil service, the Chief Executive was to be given more leeway to form a cabinet of like-minded political appointees, even though the public at large appeared to express more satisfaction with the performance of permanent civil servants than political appointees, according to a government survey carried out in 2000.

It would thus appear that a new class of high public officeholders is paving the way for what is set to be a ministerial system (in all but name) in Hong Kong, albeit not popularly elected and lacking in legitimacy. It seems likely that the political role traditionally assumed by permanent civil servants, together with their traditional perks and benefits, will fade in time. As was shown earlier, some of the colonial-era allowances, notably the overseas education allowance and the leave and passage allowances, have been wound back for new entrants, and the former pension system has also been replaced by less generous terms for new staff. Even top-level officeholders, such as the case of Antony Leung referred to earlier, are set to serve on fixed-term contracts in the future.

Hence, the Hong Kong story presents a double-edged message for understanding what drives reward systems for high public office. On the one hand, rewards for high public office in Hong Kong undoubtedly reflect its colonial past, with very high rewards for the top executives largely continuing, albeit with some reductions in colonial era allowances. Likewise, the institutional system for determining pay and parity in pay has tended to reinforce that reward structure at the top. The legacy of higher rewards at the top dies hard. But, on the other hand, the changes that have occurred since Hong Kong's handover to China demonstrate that even well-institutionalized legacies must bow before fundamental political change. The existing reward system is challenged both by the more egalitarian ideology of China and by demands for greater transparency.

Note

1 According to Article 101 of the Basic Law, the principal official-level posts are those of Chief Secretary, Financial Secretary, Attorney General, 14 policy secretaries, Commissioner of the Independent Commission Against Corruption, Director of Audit, Commissioner of Police, Director of Immigration and Commissioner of Customs and Excise.

9 Paying for the 'best and brightest'

Rewards for high public office in Singapore

Jon S. T. Quah

> … Singapore will remain clean and honest only if honest, able men are willing to fight elections and assume office. They must be paid a wage commensurate with what men of their ability and integrity are earning for managing a big corporation or successful legal or other professional practice. … If we underpay men of quality as ministers, we cannot expect them to stay long in office earning a fraction of what they could outside. With high economic growth and higher earnings in the private sector, ministers' salaries have to match their counterparts in the private sector. Underpaid ministers and public officials have ruined many governments in Asia. Adequate remuneration is vital for high standards of probity in political leaders and high officials.
>
> (Lee, K. Y. 2000: 192–3)

Introduction

A comparative analysis of the public personnel systems in Indonesia, Malaysia, Philippines, Singapore and Thailand in 1986 found that civil servants in Singapore were paid the highest salaries among the five countries (Quah 1986: 256). Seven years later, the World Bank study on *The East Asian Miracle* that was discussed in Chapter 1 noted that 'in bureaucracies, as in nearly everything else, you get what you pay for' (World Bank 1993: 175). Accordingly, 'Singapore, which is widely perceived to have the region's most competent and upright bureaucracy, pays its bureaucrats best' (World Bank 1993: 176).

The following year saw the publication of the remarkable White Paper on *Competitive Salaries for Competent and Honest Government* that we also commented on in Chapter 1 and which sought to justify pegging the salaries of ministers, top judges and civil servants to the top-level pay of six private sector professions in Singapore (Republic of Singapore 1994). Six years after that, Deputy Prime Minister Lee Hsien Loong announced a revamping of the salary structure of senior civil servants and ministers to increase the 'performance-related' component of their pay – a move which had the effect of raising the Prime Minister's salary to well over a million US dollars a year, as we saw in Chapter 2 (Lee, H. L. 2000: 52–3).

Why did the Singapore government decide to pay its senior civil servants and ministers salaries that dwarfed those paid in most of the other political systems in this study (as one saw in Chapter 2) and indeed the 'first world' democracies as well? And what have been the consequences of this extraordinarily high level of formal pay at the top? How exportable or generalizable is the Singapore model of top public pay? To answer these questions, we begin by first tracing the evolution of changes in compensation in the Singapore Civil Service (SCS), beginning with the historical antecedents during the British colonial period.

Historical antecedents

As with Hong Kong, considered in Chapter 8, the origins of today's highly paid top officials in Singapore can be traced back to its colonial past – indeed to the days before it became a British colony, when it was ruled by the British East India Company from 1819 to 1867 (Quah 1978: 416). The civil service established by the East India Company had a mixture of covenanted, uncovenanted and extra-covenanted officers.

The top officeholders at that time, covenanted civil servants, were recruited from the UK, trained at the Company's administrative school in England and signed a bond with the Company to serve for a stipulated period of years (Seah 1971: 3–4). The recruits' next of kin were required to execute very substantial penalty bonds, equivalent to several years' salary, which was intended as a check on corruption (Tan 1957: 27). Uncovenanted civil servants, who occupied the subordinate and clerical grades in the civil service, were recruited locally in the Straits Settlements from among the local people or from Europeans who had settled in the territories under the Company's jurisdiction and received much lower salaries. The pay gap between covenanted and uncovenanted civil servants, and differences in their conditions of service, predictably gave rise to animosity and jealousy (Lee 1976: 89). The extra-covenanted civil servants were people who were granted covenants locally because of exceptional administrative capabilities.

Rule by the East India Company gave way to 75 years of British Crown Colony rule from 1867 to the Japanese invasion of Singapore in 1942 (followed by three years of occupation) and during the Crown Colony period, as in Hong Kong, the top levels of the civil service were racially exclusive, being restricted to European (i.e. British) candidates and closed to local candidates even if they possessed the requisite qualifications (Seah 1971: 12). Further, as in Hong Kong, local officers were discriminated against in terms of salary and prospects for promotion. For example, a local officer had to work seven years before reaching the initial salary of a (European) Malayan Civil Service cadet (Seah 1971: 89–90).

According to Seah (1971: 14), 'the decision to pay European officers a higher salary was based on racial criteria' and indeed top Malayan civil servants were paid substantially more than their counterparts in the colonial regimes of what are now Sri Lanka, Ghana and Nigeria (Seah 1971: 15, table 1.1). The Public Services Salaries Commission of 1919 justified the necessity for remunerating

European officers higher wages thus:

> Malaya is not a suitable country for the 'poor white'; unless a European can earn a wage on which he is able to live decently as a European should, he merely brings discredit and contempt upon the European community.
>
> (quoted by Seah 1971: 15)

In short, high salaries at the top and low vertical compression – features of the Singapore case that were noted in Chapter 2 – are not a recent creation, but can be traced back to the practices of the SCS in the days of racial discrimination during the colonial period.

In the colonial era, the British government repeatedly used commissions or committees to review and recommend changes in civil servants' salaries and other rewards. Examples prior to the Japanese invasion in 1942 include the Bucknill Report of 1919 for Senior Officers (and a parallel report for junior officers a year later) and the 1937 MacGregor Commission. The same pattern applied during the 15 years of British colonial rule after the Second World War, in the form of a Wages and Cost of Living Committee of 1946, the Trusted Commission of 1947 to review civil service salaries and other rewards in Singapore and Malaya, a review of the Trusted Report's recommendations by J. V. Cowgill in 1948, and a further review of Cowgill's recommendations by a committee of the Singapore Legislative Council the following year. However, this plethora of committees after the Second World War did not produce salary raises for the topmost SCS officeholders, either because they failed to recommend such increases at the top or because such recommendations as they did make were rejected by the colonial government.

Austerity and Tocquevillian restraint 1959–71

With the ending of British colonial rule in 1959 and the emergence of Singapore as a self-governing state whose government was elected by general franchise, there was a phase of austerity and wage restraint that is consistent with Tocquevillian ideas about the effect of democracy on the salaries of top-level public officeholders. Indeed, their effect was augmented by the desire of the new indigenous government to stamp its authority on formerly colonial civil servants.

The People's Action Party (PAP) won government in the 1959 general election and has been in office ever since, having been re-elected on 10 occasions (Singapore Ministry of Information and the Arts 2001: 37; *Sunday Times*, 4 November 2001: 1). The PAP's predominance and the weak or non-existent opposition it has faced in Parliament has meant that top salaries have not been a political football among rival parties in the manner described for Australia by Martin Painter in Chapter 4, and the ruling party has had free rein in setting and revising these salaries. Nevertheless, the newly elected PAP government declared that it needed to cut the rewards of upper-level civil servants on the grounds that, as a developing country with depleted national coffers on its attainment of self-government, expenditure cuts had to be made. Accordingly, a Cabinet Budget

Committee on Expenditure recommended major cuts in public service expenditures 'including the removal of the cost of living allowance payable to civil servants in the middle and upper salary brackets' (Bogaars 1973: 80). Goh Keng Swee, the then Finance Minister, said the government's drastic decision to remove the allowance was based on an anticipated budgetary deficit of S$ 14 million of which S$ 10 million could be removed by abolition of the upper civil servants' allowances (Bogaars 1973: 80). If those allowances were not removed, the government would be compelled to increase taxes or face financial bankruptcy (Seah 1971: 90).

Table 9.1 shows that SCS Division I officers were the hardest hit by these measures, since they lost all their allowances, amounting to 35 per cent of their base salaries. Even though Division IV civil servants were not affected, the local civil servants reaction was 'one of disbelief' as they 'were not prepared for this abrupt move' (Seah 1971: 91).

As the budgetary situation improved, the government quickly restored the allowances in 1961 (Seah 1971: 94) and in 1968 a report on public sector salaries recommended pay rises of more than 25 per cent for most civil servants (though not for topmost judicial officers) (see Republic of Singapore 1968: 42–3). However, the government did not implement this recommendation until 1973 on two grounds: it was held that the economy could not support a major salary revision; and the private sector was not considered a serious threat in terms of competing for talent with the government at the top executive level (Lee 1994–95: 21–2).

This policy of salary restraint also applied to the political leaders. Recounting this experience in Parliament in March 1985, Prime Minister Lee Kuan Yew said: '... immediately after we came into office in 1959, we cut Minister's pay by $ 450. I cut my own pay to $ 3,050 and it stayed cut for two years till September 1961 when we restored it' (Republic of Singapore 1985b: col. 1207). He explained in his memoirs that he 'had frozen ministerial salaries and kept public service wage increases at a low level' after independence to ensure that 'we could cope with the expected unemployment and slowdown in the economy and to set an example of restraint' (Lee, K. Y. 2000: 194–5). When the employment situation improved in the 1970s, he raised ministers' salaries from S$ 2,500 to 4,500 per month but kept his own salary fixed at S$ 3,500 'to remind the public service that some restraint was still necessary' (Lee, K. Y. 2000: 195). In his 1985 parliamentary

Table 9.1 Reduction in variable allowances in the SCS by salary and division, June 1959 (in S$)

Division	Salary scale (Basic in S$)	Previous allowances (%)	Amount reduced (%)	Net allowance (%)
I	505 and above	35	All	None
II	251–504	30	20	10
III	220–250	25	5	20
IV	219 and below	20	None	20

Source: Adapted from Seah (1971: 91, table 4.2).

speech, Lee explained that he stayed at $3,500 'because I was nervous that the ground might misread the signal. Wage restraint might be thrown overboard by the unions and before we had fully absorbed the full impact of unemployment we would be on the rocks' (Republic of Singapore 1985b: col. 1207).

As Members of Parliament (MPs) in Singapore who are not part of the government hold full-time jobs, they do not receive a salary as such, but rather a non-taxable allowance to assist them in meeting some of their expenses. The purpose of the allowance is to help MPs cover expenses such as secretarial help and other constituency expenses. For example, if MPs are invited to a wedding dinner or funeral wake of one of their constituents, they are expected to give a present, usually in the form of money, and MPs often invite their helpers for a meal after their weekly 'meet the people' sessions in their constituencies. In line with the initial policy of salary restraint for the ministers, the MP's allowance remained at S$ 500 from June 1959 until it was doubled to S$ 1,000 eleven years later. There was no further increase in the MP's allowance until 1981, when it was raised to S$ 2,403.

Competing for talent through salary revisions (January 1972–September 1994)

As Singapore's economy grew in the 1970s, the higher salaries paid by the private sector contributed to a brain drain from the SCS, and civil service pay began to be raised to curb the loss of talent. The government set up the National Wages Council (NWC) in 1972 as an advisory body to formulate general guidelines on wage policies, recommend annual wage adjustments and advise on incentive systems for improving efficiency and productivity (Then 1998: 220–1). The NWC recommended the payment of an Annual Wage Supplement (AWS), Bonus and Annual Wage Increase (AWI). The AWS was a single annual payment to supplement base salaries. Banks and trading houses paid their employees an additional three months salary per year, but other companies and the SCS paid their employees one month's salary as the AWS, which became known as '13th month pay' in Singapore. The aim of the 13th month salary was to minimize the gap between salaries in the public and private sectors in Singapore and in 1973, the salaries of senior civil servants were increased substantially to reduce the gap with the private sector (Quah 1984: 296). Similarly, ministerial salaries were also revised upwards with the Prime Minister's monthly salary being increased to S$ 9,500, and the monthly salaries of the Chief Justice and Minister increased to S$ 7,000.

Why did the PAP government increase the salaries of civil servants in 1972, 13 years after assuming office? Arguably there was a mixture of motive and opportunity. Between 1959 and 1972, the per capita indigenous Gross National Product (GNP) had more than doubled, a civil service 'brain drain' to the private sector had started to develop, and the PAP government was overwhelmingly re-elected for the third time, winning 70 per cent of the valid votes and all the parliamentary seats, which repeated its 'clean sweep' in the 1968 election (Singapore Ministry of Information and the Arts 1998: 338).

The pattern set in 1972 and 1973 started a trend of repeated pay increases for top public officeholders. In 1979, the then Minister for Trade and Industry, Goh Chok Tong, justified a further salary increase thus:

> The terms and conditions of the Administrative Service must match the best in the private sector. The Government has compared the incomes of graduates in the public and private sectors. ... [It] has concluded that the immediate problem is ... the ... gross disparity between what the outstanding graduates are earning in the private sector compared to what the highfliers are earning in the Administrative Service. This revision of the salary structure of the Administrative Service is to put right this gap in earnings of top graduates.
>
> (Republic of Singapore 1979: cols 359–60)

Goh also announced a restructuring of the top SCS pay scales, creating more 'superscale' grades and grades above the top 'superscale' grades (Republic of Singapore 1979: col. 360). In 1981, an extensive survey of graduate earnings by the Research and Statistics Unit of the Inland Revenue Department revealed (among other things) that graduates in the private sector earned, on average, 42 per cent more than those in the public sector (*Sunday Times*, 21 February 1982: 1). The Public Service Commission produced figures to show that eight superscale and 67 timescale administrative officers resigned from the SCS between 1978 and 1981 for more lucrative jobs in the private sector (*Sunday Times*, 28 February 1982: 1). So in 1982, the government further revised the salaries of those in the Administrative Service and other Professional Services as another move to counter the two problems of wide disparity in pay between graduates in the public and private sectors, and the serious brain drain of senior civil servants from the SCS to the private sector (Quah 1984: 296–7).

In 1986, the Minister for Finance, Richard Hu, appointed a Task Force to consider how the NWC Sub-committee on Wage Reform's recommendations could be adopted in the public sector. This Task Force recommended that the public sector in Singapore should adopt a flexible wage system with four components: a basic wage; a monthly variable component; a variable 13th month non-pensionable annual allowance; and a mid-year or year-end variable bonus (Singapore Ministry of Labour 1988: 1–2; Singapore Ministry of Finance 1988: 1). The PAP government accepted the Task Force's recommendations and implemented the new flexible wage system in the SCS and statutory boards in 1988.

In the following year, the then Minister for Trade and Industry, Lee Hsien Loong, recommended a further hefty salary increase for the SCS on the grounds that the comparatively low salaries and slow advancement in the Administrative Service had contributed to its low recruitment and high resignation rates. He justified the need for this salary revision in his ministerial statement in Parliament in the following way:

> The need to revise salaries is most acute in the Administrative Service. ... Over the last 20 years, the Government has been able to identify and develop

a core of young, able administrators to succeed the older generation of Permanent Secretaries. However, we have not succeeded in maintaining this flow of talent into the Civil Service. ... Annual recruitment in the Administrative Service has declined steadily from a peak of 37 in 1974 to an average of less than 10 per year in recent years. ... There is no queue of qualified applicants seeking to join the Administrative Service. Many of those within the Service have left as soon as their bonds have expired, and some even sooner. Every one of those who were recruited in 1975 and 1976 has left. So have three-quarters of the 1977 and 1978 cohorts, and half of the 1983 cohort. As the economy boomed after the 1985 recession, able young officers quit for more attractive jobs elsewhere. ... From a peak in 1975 of 260 officers, it [the Administrative Service] has declined to 183 this year, down by 30%. ... The most successful of those who left the Service are earning 40% to 100% more than their contemporaries who stayed. ... Able civil servants are opting out and they are not being replaced fast enough. Low salaries and slow advancement are major factors in low recruitment and high resignation rates. A substantial salary rise for the key individuals in the public sector, especially the Administrative Service and related services, is therefore essential.

(Republic of Singapore 1989a: cols 378–80, 382)

Lee stressed that as the government's fundamental philosophy was to 'pay civil servants market rates for their abilities and responsibilities', it 'will offer whatever salaries are necessary to attract and retain the talent that it needs'. He pointed out that the salary revision was 'designed to catch up with several years of rising private sector incomes, and to make public service careers more competitive with the private sector'. He concluded by promising that the government 'will continue to carry out regular surveys of private sector salaries to stay competitive' because 'paying civil servants adequate salaries is *absolutely essential* to maintain the quality of public administration which Singaporeans have come to expect' (Republic of Singapore 1989a: cols 382–3, 396, emphasis added).

Six days later, the first Deputy Prime Minister, Goh Chok Tong, announced in Parliament that the government would be also revising the salaries of political, judicial, and other statutory appointments in addition to the salary revision for the civil servants. He began by emphasizing the importance of attracting the best Singaporeans to be part of the government:

If we want the right decisions to be taken for Singapore, we must continue to get the right people to do the job. ... Every one of Singapore's Ministers must come from the top of their cohorts. ... I can say that nearly every Minister in the present Cabinet was among the top students of their year.

(Republic of Singapore 1989b: cols 749–50)

However, Goh added that 'such men are increasingly difficult to recruit' because 'successful Singaporeans are seldom eager to enter politics' for the following reasons:

> Putting aside any loss in salaries, why should they give up the certainty of a good career and a good future in a profession, or a bank, or a big company or the Civil Service, for the uncertainty of ministerial office? Why should they give up their privacy and subject themselves to the glare of publicity? Why should they spend more time with voters when they need the time to spend with their families? Why should they be called upon when others can do it? Why should they do it when others are running the government so well, and they, like everyone else, are enjoying the fruits of economic progress?
>
> (Republic of Singapore 1989b: cols 750–1)

Accordingly, Goh argued that it was 'necessary to minimize the sacrifice that a person is asked to make, and minimizing the financial sacrifice is the least we

Table 9.2 Monthly base salaries of political and judicial appointments in Singapore, in 1985 and April 1989 (S$)

Appointment	Monthly base salary	
	(1985)	*(April 1989)*
President	25,000	39,425
Prime Minister	23,900	38,275
1 Deputy Prime Minister	20,600	31,875
2 Deputy Prime Minister	18,800	28,950
Chief Justice	18,800	28,950
Senior Minister	18,400	28,375
Speaker	17,400	28,100
Minister	—	27,825
	16,700	22,100
Attorney-General/Chairman PSC	15,900	21,100
Judges	13,600	19,550
Senior Minister of State	—	17,025
	—	14,550
	11,500	12,300
Minister of State	—	12,300
	9,500	10,175
	—	9,100
Permanent Secretary	9,500	10,175
Senior Parliamentary	—	8,100
Secretary	6,500	7,550
Parliamentary Secretary	6,000	7,000
Political Secretary	5,500	6,450
Member of Parliament[a]	3,000	4,000

Source: Republic of Singapore (1989b: col. 833, annex B).

Note
a Tax-free monthly allowance.

should do' (Republic of Singapore 1989b: col. 752). He concluded thus:

> If Singapore is to continue to have able men in Government, we must at least
> ensure that after having sacrificed their privacy, leisure and family time, such
> people do not also have to make too large a financial sacrifice.
>
> (Republic of Singapore 1989b: col. 753)

Table 9.2 provides a summary of the monthly basic salaries of the political and
judicial appointments before and after the 1989 revision.

In 1993, Deputy Prime Minister Lee Hsien Loong announced that the salaries
of ministers and senior civil servants would be increased the following year to
keep pace with the private sector and to compensate for the reduction in their
medical benefits (*Straits Times*, 4 December 1993: 1). While the government could
not 'match private sector incomes dollar for dollar', he stressed that it should
nevertheless not let the gap between public and private sector salaries widen.
Since private sector incomes rose much faster than public sector incomes after the
1989 salary revision, the 1994 revision was designed 'to enable the Civil Service
to catch up with the private sector, and restore the relativity between the two'
(Republic of Singapore 1993: col. 1213). There was an average salary increase of
20 per cent for the Administrative Service and superscale officers received
between 21 and 34 per cent increase in wages, including bonuses.

Institutionalizing salary revision: benchmarking with the private sector

The strategy of periodic pay rises for top public officeholders that began in 1972
moved into a quite new phase with the 1994 White Paper on *Competitive Salaries for
Competent and Honest Government* that was referred to earlier and discussed in
Chapter 1. The document justified the benchmarking of the salaries of ministers
and senior civil servants to the average salaries of the top four earners in six
private sector professions (accounting, banking, engineering, law, local manufacturing companies and multinational corporations).

The White Paper recommended the introduction of formal salary benchmarks
for ministers and senior bureaucrats, additional salary grades for political
appointments, and annual salary reviews for the SCS. More specifically, annual
revisions would be based on a formula linking a Staff Grade I Minister's salary at
'two-thirds the average principal earned income of the top four individuals' from
each of the six professions, and a Superscale G Administrative Officer to 'the
average of the principal earned income of the 15th person aged 32 years old',
belonging to the same professions (Republic of Singapore 1994: 12–13). The
adoption of the long-term formula suggested in the White Paper removed the
need to justify the salaries of ministers and senior civil servants 'from scratch with
each salary revision', and also was claimed to ensure the building of 'an efficient
public service and a competent and honest political leadership, which have been
vital for Singapore's prosperity and success' (Republic of Singapore 1994: 18).

In short, the White Paper institutionalized the government's practice of 'matching public pay to the private sector, dollar for dollar' as it enabled the government to revise automatically public sector salaries in response to increases in private sector salaries (Lee 1994–95: 26). Apart from removing the need to justify future salary revisions, the practice of benchmarking public sector salaries with those in the private sector led to less transparency, as we saw in Chapter 2, because the salary scales for civil service, political and judicial appointments were no longer published in the budget from the 1995 financial year onwards.

In 1996, the salaries of ministers and senior civil servants were raised as both benchmarks went up. However, in 1997 the Asian financial crisis and the subsequent slowing down of the Singapore economy led to a 2 per cent decrease in Superscale G and a 7 per cent decrease in Staff Grade I salaries as a result of the GDP performance link in the bonus structure, and the reduction of the employers' contribution to the Central Provident Fund (CPF) from 20 to 10 per cent for all employees, including ministers and top civil servants. The purpose of the CPF reduction was to enhance the Singapore economy's competitiveness by lowering the cost of doing business in Singapore.

With the recovery of the Singapore economy in 1999 with a growth rate of 5.4 per cent, and the reduction of retrenchments (redundancies) from 29,100 in 1998 to 14,600 in 1999, and falling unemployment, wages in the private sector began to rise again. Given the tight labour market in Singapore and the improved conditions in the private sector, Deputy Prime Minister Lee Hsien Loong revealed in Parliament in mid-2000 that eight administrative officers had already resigned in that year. Since attracting and retaining talent in the SCS was 'quickly becoming a real problem,' the government, Lee argued, had to respond quickly by changing both the salaries and terms of service, as well as the incentives and rewards for those in 'leadership' positions in the public service, namely the permanent secretaries, deputy secretaries, chief executive officers of major statutory boards and heads of key departments.

To reinforce the link between pay and individual performance, Lee proposed that a 'performance-related' component be included in the total wage package of every civil servant. The benchmark was also broadened from four to eight top earners in six professions. The variable component of annual salaries was thus to be increased from 30 to 40 per cent of the total annual pay of superscale administrative officers and ministers.

Lee concluded his address in Parliament by reiterating that 'our policy is to pay people according to their market value and contribution, in the case of political-appointment holders, with a discount. Paying officers properly is essential to recruiting the quality of talent that we need to build a first-class civil service'. This policy had been effective, Lee claimed, since foreign investors and international rating agencies had regularly rated Singapore's competitiveness highly and a key aspect of these ratings was 'their high assessments of the quality of the government and political leadership' (Lee, H. L. 2000: 53).

Table 9.3 shows the increase in the Prime Minister's monthly basic salary from the advent of self-government in 1959 up to 2000. The salary increase was

Table 9.3 Monthly base salaries (or allowances) for Singapore Prime Minister, Minister and MP, 1959–2000 (S$ at current values)

Year of office	Prime Minister		Minister		MP (allowance)	
	Monthly BS	Per cent rise from last time	Monthly BS	Per cent rise from last time	Monthly allowance	Per cent rise from last time
1959	3,050	—	2,050	—	500	—
1961	3,500	14	2,500	22		
1970			4,500	80	100	100
1973	9,500	210	7,000	55		
1978	13,695	40	10,095	44		
1981					2,403	140
1982	16,500	20	11,500	14		
1983	23,900	44	16,700	45		
1985					3,000	25
1990	38,275	60	27,825	67	4,000	33
1994	45,867	20	33,261	19	4,516	13
1995					9,100	101
1999	85,000	85	48,900	50		
2000	85,300	0.3	49,900	0.2	11,900	31

Source: Republic of Singapore (1985b, 2000).

gradual during the austerity phase (1959–71) as the Prime Minister's monthly basic salary increased by 15 per cent from S$ 3,050 in 1959 to S$ 3,500 in 1961. From 1972 to 1994, the Prime Minister's salary was further increased from S$ 3,500 to 45,867. After the benchmarking with the private sector in 1995, the monthly basic salary of the Prime Minister rose to S$ 85,300 in 2000.

Similarly, Table 9.3 traces the increase in ministerial salaries from 1959 to 2000. Except for the 1961–72 period, when the Prime Minister's monthly base salary remained at S$ 3,500, the increase in the Minister's monthly base salary was higher than that of the Prime Minister's from 1973 to 1998. During 1999–2000, the salary increase for both the Prime Minister and ministers exceeded by more than 2,600 and 2,300 per cent, respectively. The table also shows the slower pattern of increase in the monthly allowance of MPs from 1959 to 1980 and the very high rate of growth after 1995.

Explaining and justifying RHPOs Singapore-style

We must have the best people for Cabinet. Their policies and actions will determine whether Singaporeans continue to enjoy better jobs, better housing and better quality of life, or whether the country goes downhill and renders Singaporeans jobless and poor. ... Study why some countries do well and others do not. You will see that the major explanation for the difference in performance is the quality of Government – its competence, integrity and dedication to the people. If I am unable to recruit honest and able men and women into Cabinet, I cannot maintain the same high degree of honesty and competence. ... My biggest responsibility is to ensure that Singapore continues to have a proficient Government. ... It is not possible to pay a Minister as much as he can command in the private sector. ... If we do not pay Ministers adequately, we will get inadequate Ministers. If you pay peanuts, you will get monkeys for your Ministers. The people will suffer, not the monkeys. I have been in the Government long enough to know that if the Cabinet is inadequate, and worse, dishonest, disaster for the country must follow.

(Goh Chok Tong in Republic of Singapore 1993: cols 1260–4)

What is the rationale for the high level of rewards for high public offices (RHPOs) in Singapore that has been outlined earlier? There are three reasons repeatedly given by the PAP government for raising top public-sector pay and reducing the gap between the public and private sectors. First, the Singapore government has to compete with the private sector and multinational corporations for talented personnel from a relatively small labour-market pool. The economic growth in Singapore during the 1970s forced the PAP government to raise the salaries of civil servants as many of them had left for more lucrative private-sector jobs. Thus, the most important reason given by the PAP government for high RHPOs in Singapore is to minimize the brain drain of talented senior civil servants to the private sector. As we have seen earlier, this was the rationale repeatedly given for the various salary raises since 1972.

The second justification that is repeatedly given for paying senior civil servants and ministers high salaries in Singapore is to minimize corruption in the public sector. In 1985, Prime Minister Lee Kuan Yew contended that political leaders should be paid the top salaries that they deserved to ensure honest government. If ministers and senior civil servants were underpaid, they would succumb to temptation and indulge in corrupt behaviour (see Quah 1989: 848). He began a parliamentary debate on ministers' salaries by asking these questions:

How is Singapore to preserve its most precious asset, an administration that is absolutely corruption free, a political leadership that can be subject to the closest scrutiny because it sets the highest standards? Why does this island survive? Why does it attract banks, computer software, financial services, information services, manufacturing, in preference to so many countries better endowed – natural resources, manpower, markets?

(Republic of Singapore 1985b: col. 1204)

Lee's answer to these questions was unequivocal:

Every Member knows that there is no easy money on the take. That is the way we are. Nobody believes we spent money to get into this House. ... There is no pay-off here. ... Do we want to maintain our unique system? ... I am probably the highest paid in the Commonwealth if you go by official salary. But I am probably one of the poorest in the Commonwealth.... I am one of the best paid and probably one of the poorest of the Third World

Prime Ministers. ... There are ways and ways of doing things and I am suggesting our way – moving with the market is an honest, open, defensible and workable system. You abandon this for hypocrisy, you will end up with duplicity and corruption. Take your choice.

(Republic of Singapore 1985b: cols 1211–13, 1218)

The plausibility of this argument is debatable. It should be noted that Singapore initiated its anti-corruption strategy in 1960 with the reduction of opportunities for corruption by strengthening the Prevention of Corruption Act (POCA) and the Corrupt Practices Investigation Bureau (CPIB), since, as shown earlier, the government could not afford to reduce the incentive for corruption through raising salaries until after 1972 (see also Quah 2001: 33).

Finally, in line with the PAP government's emphasis on meritocracy, it claims that senior civil servants and ministers must be paid handsome salaries to attract the 'best and brightest' to join the government (Quah 1998: 111). Vogel (1989: 1052–3) has described Singapore as 'a macho-meritocracy' because 'what is unusual in Singapore is not the prominence of meritocratic administrators, but the fact that the meritocracy extends upwards to include virtually all political leaders'. The 1994 White Paper stressed the importance of attracting Singapore's 'most outstanding and committed citizens' to become ministers since 'competent political leadership is crucial to good government'. As Singaporeans 'have little incentive to take on the risks and public responsibilities of a political career,' the White Paper argued that the government should minimize the financial sacrifice they make by paying ministers salaries comparable to those in the private sector (Republic of Singapore 1994: 1–2).

In March 1985, Lee Kuan Yew referred in Parliament to the financial sacrifice made by his colleague, E. W. Barker, for embarking on a political career. He said:

I pulled the Member for Tanglin [Barker] into this House in 1963 because I told him that, if I did not get good men, everything would be lost. He came in. He lost money by coming in. By 1970 he said, 'That's enough. Things look all right. I have to leave.' If Members want to know why it [minister's salary] was altered in 1970 ... it was because he could not pay his mortgage. ... I had to up his salary from $2,500 to $4,500.

(Republic of Singapore 1985b: col. 1221)

Similarly, more than a decade later, Lee referred to the financial sacrifice made by Yong Pung How when he became the Chief Justice thus:

... if he [Yong Pung How] had stayed on in OCBC [Oversea Chinese Banking Corporation, then Singapore's largest bank] he would have earned $2.6 million for the whole of 1989. ... As a Judge of the Supreme Court, he would receive ... for the second six months of 1989 the princely sum of $177,000 less than one-seventh of his OCBC remuneration for the first six months.

(Republic of Singapore 1995: col. 234)

In sum, the PAP government repeatedly gave three reasons for its policy of high RHPOs: to minimize the brain drain of talented civil servants to the private sector; to minimize corruption in the public sector; and to reinforce its emphasis on meritocracy by attracting the most talented Singaporeans to join the government as senior civil servants or ministers.

Consequences of the high level of RHPOs

Was the brain drain to the private sector curbed?

High pay for high public office in Singapore seems to have been effective in curbing the brain drain of political leaders to the private sector, since to date none of the leaders have resigned from political office to work in the private sector before their retirement. But some of the old guard leaders were appointed as chairmen of government-linked companies or statutory boards after their retirement from politics. For example, Lim Kim San, a former Cabinet Minister, is Executive Chairman of Singapore Press Holdings, and Dr Yeo Ning Hong, another former Cabinet Minister, is Chairman of the Singapore Totalisator Board. In a sense, such a pattern could be considered a Singapore version of the Japanese *amakutari* or 'descent from heaven' or the Korean *nakhasan-insa* or 'descent by parachute' that have been discussed earlier in this book.

High pay for permanent secretaries (departmental heads) has also been effective in retaining them in the SCS, since none of them have left for private sector jobs before their retirement. However, the high level of RHPOs has been ineffective in preventing Division I officers below the head of department level from

Table 9.4 Resignation rate of Division I officers in the SCS, 1971–84

Year	No of Division I officers resigned	No. of Division I officers in SCS	Resignation rate (per cent)
1971	142	2,826	5.0
1972	163	3,621	4.5
1973	205	3,874	5.3
1974	256	4,136	6.2
1975	259	4,633	5.6
1976	326	5,249	6.2
1977	293	5,479	5.4
1978	269	6,002	4.5
1979	307	6,430	4.8
1980	322	6,634	4.9
1981	474	6,912	6.9
1982	351	7,298	4.8
1983	309	7,754	4.0
1984	272	8,396	3.2

Source: Republic of Singapore (1985a: appendix III, table 2).

leaving the SCS. Table 9.4 gives the resignation rate of Division I officers in the SCS from 1971 to 1984. As indicated earlier, Lee Hsien Loong justified the 1989 pay rise on the grounds of the Administrative Service's low recruitment and high resignation rates, but Table 9.4 shows that the various pay rises in the 1970s and 1980s did not succeed in curbing the brain drain of bureaucrats to the private sector.

Was corruption curbed?

As already argued, it seems doubtful if high RHPOs was a decisive factor in reducing corruption, because corruption had already been minimized in Singapore before 1972, when the PAP government first introduced 13th month pay. A year after the PAP government took office in 1959, POCA was enacted and the CPIB was set up to enforce the law. The strategy was thus to reduce the opportunities for corruption and to increase the penalties for corrupt behaviour. For example, political leaders and senior civil servants found guilty of corruption have been severely punished with a S$100,000 fine and up to five years of imprisonment. I have argued earlier (Quah 1978: 19) that 'the comprehensive nature of the POCA and the wide powers given to the CPIB constitute an effective combination for the eradication of corruption in Singapore'. The effectiveness of this comprehensive anticorruption strategy is reflected in Singapore's status as the least corrupt Asian country since 1995, according to the annual surveys conducted by the Political and Economic Risk Consultancy and Transparency International, and discussed in Chapter 2 (see also Quah 2001: 29). It may nevertheless be that the PAP government's policy of high RHPOs reinforces its commitment against corruption.

Did the 'best and brightest' join the government?

As with the Korean case described by Pan Suk Kim, the SCS for many years succeeded in attracting the 'best and brightest' Singaporeans as the top students of each cohort competed for the President's Scholarship and the Overseas Merit Scholarships. However, in recent years, the Public Service Commission has no longer monopolized the award of scholarships, because the Singapore Armed Forces (SAF), statutory boards, government-linked companies and multinational corporations have also offered scholarships.

An analysis of the background of the 2001 Cabinet shows that seven (44 per cent) of its 16 members at the time of writing were recruited from the SCS and the SAF. Of the seven 'bureaucrat politicians' in that cabinet, two came from the army, one from the navy and four were recruited from the Administrative Service (Chandran 1999: 72). Table 9.5 shows that the proportion of 'bureaucrat politicians' in the Cabinet from the period 1959–97 has increased from 20 to 44 per cent with a peak of 47 per cent in the 1981 Cabinet.

Although most of the Cabinet members were drawn from the private sector for all 10 Cabinets, the most prominent individual to join the 1985 Cabinet was Dr Richard Hu, who was Chief Executive Officer (CEO) of Shell Company in

Table 9.5 Proportion of 'bureaucrat politicians' in the Singapore Cabinet, 1959–97

Cabinet	Per cent of 'bureaucrat politicians'
1959	22
1963	22
1968	20
1973	23
1977	43
1981	47
1985	31
1989	31
1992	40
1997	44

Source: Chandran (1999: 43, table 3.3).

Singapore, before entering politics. Dr Hu was appointed as the Minister of Finance and retained the same portfolio up to the time of writing. Lee Kuan Yew, who was then Prime Minister, praised Richard Hu for his tremendous financial sacrifice in entering politics, since Hu was earning S$ 500,000 as Shell's CEO. Lee also referred to the example of Dr Tony Tan, who resigned from his position as General Manager of the Oversea-Chinese Banking Corporation, and became a Minister of State, 'for which he was paid less than a third of his former salary, apart from losing his perks, the most valuable of which was a car with a driver' (Lee, K. Y. 2000: 195).

Although, as we saw earlier, the 1994 White Paper argued that raising ministerial salaries would remove a key 'obstacle to able Singaporeans entering politics' (Republic of Singapore 1994: 2), the benchmarking of ministerial salaries to top earners in six professions in the private sector has not been effective in attracting successful Singaporeans in the private sector into politics. Indeed, Peter Chen, former CEO of Shell Company in Singapore, who served as Senior Minister of State for Education from 1997 to 2001, was the only person recruited from the private sector since October 1994.

Conclusions

In mid-2000, Prime Minister Goh Chok Tong asked Singaporeans to judge his government on the basis of the results it had delivered. According to his calculations, the 'price of good government' was S$ 34 million a year or S$ 11 per Singaporean a year. Conversely, the price of bad government could have been a loss of S$ 9.5 billion or S$ 3,166 per Singaporean if the economy had shrunk by 5 per cent during the Asian financial crisis. He said: 'The $6 million increase in the wage bill for the Cabinet – from $28 million – was small compared to the benefit good government could produce. If it improved GDP by just 1 per cent, it was worth $1.4 billion to Singapore' (Chua 2000: 1).

When the idea of benchmarking public sector salaries to private sector salaries was proposed in 1994, there was a great deal of criticism from the public as the great emphasis on compensation detracted from the sense of duty and service to the nation. As the 2000 pay rises were even more substantial than those of 1994, some critics argued that high salaries have cheapened moral leadership because the leaders are motivated by money (Leong 2000: 70–1). While RHPOs are important to ensure good government in Singapore, the lack of a fixed ceiling for public sector salaries can also indirectly affect the country's competitiveness if private sector salaries rise as a result and increase the cost of doing business in Singapore.

A parliamentary speech by Dr Michael Lim on the proposed 2000 pay rise conveys a sense of the negative public reaction to high salaries for top public-officeholders in Singapore:

> There is still a significant minority of households in Singapore who are low income families. Many of these will find these million dollar salaries, especially for the high officeholderlders, very mind-boggling numbers which they cannot quite fathom and understand. ... the absolute amounts that the Ministers and top civil servants will get in their remuneration package are so large compared to the average household that it will be very difficult for them to accept these numbers. These are million dollar numbers and some of them in their whole lifetime will never see these numbers.
>
> (Republic of Singapore 2000: col. 423)

Indeed, the government's decision to call a general election in 2001 probably explains why it decided to raise public sector salaries in 2000 even though Singapore had not yet fully recovered from the regional financial crisis. To deal with the adverse public reaction to the 2000 salary revision, the Prime Minister announced in his National Day Rally speech two months later, the introduction of the Children Development Co-Savings Scheme (or Baby Bonus), the extension of the Eldercare Fund 'to provide for the entire range of elderly and continuing care,' ex-gratia payment for former MPs and pensioners, a Special Housing Assistance Programme to help two-room apartment owners to upgrade to larger apartments, and a Special CPF Top-up of S$ 250 for all citizens (see Goh 2000: 35–7, 46–51).

Similarly, the election year saw a 'generous' budget, with a reduction in individual tax rates and rebates on service and conservancy charges for public housing residents (Divyanathan 2001: 1). Further, even though the PAP had securely held government for over 40 years, it did not wish to risk losing votes by recommending salary revisions for senior civil servants, judges and politicians in a general election year. This strategy proved effective because the 2000 salary revision was not a decisive issue in the 2001 general election, which the PAP won by capturing all but two of the parliamentary seats.

In the final analysis, the PAP government has been able to reward high public office in Singapore with increasingly high salaries since 1972 because of the city-state's affluence and the PAP's predominance on the Singapore political scene. In stressing the need to ensure good government in Singapore by 'recruiting good people for government and paying them properly' in his 2000 National Day Rally speech, Prime Minister Goh Chok Tong acknowledged that:

> Many Western leaders have told me in private that they envied our system of Ministers' pay. But they also said that if they tried to implement it in their own countries, they would be booted out.
>
> (Goh 2000: 44)

Hence, it seems likely that the PAP government will continue to reward high public officeholders in Singapore handsomely as long as the economy continues to perform and if its predominance in Singapore politics is not eroded. Because these two prerequisites of political predominance of the incumbent government and economic affluence are difficult to satisfy, the applicability of Singapore's experience of making ministerial and civil service salaries competitive with those in the private sector appears to be limited. Singapore's strategy of matching the salaries of ministers and senior civil servants with those at the top of the tree in the private sector has limited applicability in view of its high political and economic costs.

Part III
Conclusions

10 The top pay game and good governance – where immodest theories meet slippery facts

Christopher Hood and B. Guy Peters

We prefer having people in office whom we can spit upon, rather than a caste of officials who spit upon us ...

(Max Weber '*Politics as a Vocation*': Gerth and Mills 1948: 110)

Okay boys, bring out your cost–benefit analysis now ...

(Boulding 1970: 133)

Reprise: immodest theories, rewards to top-level public officials and good governance – the revolt of complex facts against simple theories

We began this book, by raising questions about what political conditions produce what sizes and shapes of public-sector reward structures to top officeholders and what the consequences of these reward structures might be. Readers will recall that we set out three main propositions about those causes and consequences.

One concerned the link between rewards to top-level officeholders and levels of corruption. This issue is important because authorities such as the World Bank and the Singapore government have professed to find a strong causal connection between formal rewards and corruption, as we saw in Chapter 1 and were reminded in Chapter 9.

The second proposition was Alexis de Tocqueville's classic hypothesis that democracies tend to be more parsimonious than traditional autocratic regimes in the formal rewards they allow to those in high public office. The implication of that idea is that the links between money and politics create deep tensions, even contradictions, in democratic regimes.

The third, most closely related to the 'immodest theory' of the connection between the pay of business leaders and the profitability of their companies, concerned the link between high state officeholders' rewards and the performance of the societies they rule. In Chapter 9, Jon Quah gave a graphic example of this 'immodest' theory, when he reported Singapore Prime Minister Goh Chok Tong's National Day speech in 2000 which sought to justify a S\$ 6 million raise in the wage bill for his Cabinet in that year. Goh argued that the modest cost of the pay increase could be outweighed by at least S\$ 1.4 billion of benefit to Singapore on the implied grounds that the good governance the pay rise would bring was likely to 'improve' the island-state's Gross Domestic Product (GDP) by at least 1 per cent.

In Chapter 2 we explored what light could be thrown on these three issues by assembling and analysing whatever quantitative data were available about the rewards going to top public officeholders for the seven political systems in our study, each of which can be said to represent a variant of 'yesterday's tomorrow' and which make a more varied set than the western democracies. In general, that analysis produced the weakest support for most variants of the more immodest theories about the consequences of formal reward systems to top-level officials, in terms of links between rewards to top-level officials and conventional indicators of corruption and economic performance. The chapters in Part II of the book filled out that picture. For instance, we showed that not even the Singapore story is compatible with the idea of high rewards to top-level rewards as a primary cause of corruption reduction and found that the New Zealand case even suggests that the causal connection might sometimes run the other way.

As far as the causes of reward systems to top public-sector officials are concerned – what accounts for varying size and shape of reward packages to top-level officeholders – we found some support for a rather modified form of Tocqueville's ideas. For instance, we found (as Tocqueville might have expected) that the formal base pay of the top political executive of the four political systems that scored highest on the Freedom House indices of democracy fell within a fairly narrow range as a multiple of GDP per head, while the other three systems showed more variety. But Tocqueville's idea that democracies tend to be parsimonious with top public officeholders' rewards seems to apply more to elected politicians than to bureaucrats, for whom, as we saw in Part II of the book, 'new public management' doctrines have in several cases (notably Australia and New Zealand) been used as escape routes from the levelling pressures of parsimony and transparency. We will comment later on the conditions that might make Westminster-type systems of that type a particularly favourable environment for the formation of 'breakout coalitions' over pay by senior bureaucrats.

Tocqueville's idea about democratic government exerting downward pressure on top officeholders' pay also seems to apply more to base salaries than to other forms of reward and more to rewards during office rather than to rewards after it. We cannot draw very clear conclusions about the effects of a shift from autocracy to democratization, since we only had one clear case of that type (South Korea) over the past 20 years in our seven political systems. But the Korean experience, as described by Pan-Suk Kim, suggests at the least that democratization need not always have an immediately restraining effect on top public officeholders' rewards. Indeed, as we saw in Chapters 2 and 7, Korean top public officeholders' rewards went up rather than down after democratization and also moved to greater transparency rather than the multiplication of opaque allowances and other perks that has characterized the parliamentary pay game in Australia and New Zealand. Indeed, in Korea pay parity between legislators and ministers was turned by the former into 'a point of principle' – as well as of interest, presumably – on the ending of autocratic rule.

We conclude that if Tocqueville were to be spirited back from the dead to examine the size and shape of contemporary rewards to top public officeholders in these seven political systems, he would need to modify his original ideas a little to make sense of the patterns we observed. One way of adapting Tocqueville's analysis is to see top public officeholders as in some sense reward-maximizers (as several of our contributors, notably John Burns, have argued) but operating within political and institutional constraints that they can often neither choose nor change. In that vein, Figure 10.1 offers a neo-Tocquevillian historical-institutionalist account of the variety in the 'ecology' of the income-maximizing game, which is consistent with the observed variety in the size and shape of the top-reward 'icebergs' observed in our seven cases. As that figure suggests, political systems that start with lavishly rewarded expatriate bureaucracies offer different opportunities for succeeding generations of top public officeholders than systems with a different point of departure. Further, state traditions (liberal or otherwise), elite cohesion and independent labour union organization may

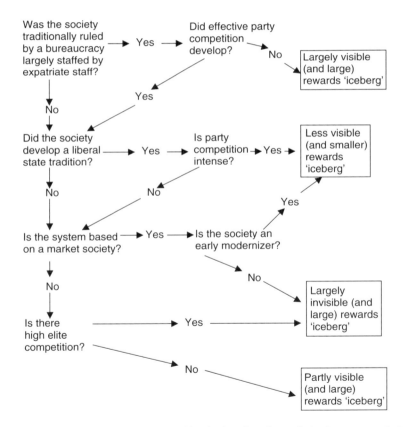

Figure 10.1 Selected aspects of historical-institutional ecology of the income-maximizing game.

also shape the size and structure of the rewards 'icebergs', as Figure 10.1 also suggests.

This analysis is consistent with our observations, but it may well be that the ecology of the top pay game may be affected by other factors not included in Figure 10.1. These other factors may include broader international-politics developments, for example, in the way that liberalizing trade regimes linked to WTO agreements may unintendedly serve to undermine some of the income-maximizing strategies that focus on the hidden parts of the top pay 'iceberg'.

When it comes to the consequences of reward patterns to top-level officeholders, the two 'immodest theory' propositions reflect doctrines that are strongly believed by their advocates, but the data presented in Chapter 2 points more to the null hypothesis or the Scottish verdict of not proven, with the possible exception of a link between high public pay and competitiveness scores. Despite the Singapore government's repeated advocacy of the doctrine of high pay for top public officeholders as a means to clean government, low levels of corruption on standard indicators seem to be consistent with relatively low levels of pay to politicians in the sort of cultural conditions possessed by the Australasian countries, while Japan, with similar or higher levels of pay, exhibits higher levels of corruption on those scales, as Nakamura and Dairokuno pointed out in Chapter 6.

Indeed, as we showed in Chapter 2 there is evidently no linear relationship between basic salary levels and the standard indicators of corruption levels. And whether the Singapore story itself demonstrates a clear causal link between high base pay for officeholders and low corruption levels is more debatable than might at first sight appear. After all, Singapore pays its elected legislators an allowance of less than one-tenth of the Prime Minister's salary – which on the face of it could be considered a recipe for high corruption on the Singapore government's own declared motivational theory, particularly since at least part of that allowance goes towards paying the expenses of office (wedding gifts to constituents and the like) and some undisclosed proportion goes as a 'tax' to the ruling PAP party. And, perhaps more important, Jon Quah's narrative account in Chapter 9 suggests that Singapore had cut its corruption levels by other measures in its post-independence austerity phase, well before the remarkable salary raises for ministers and bureaucrats that were introduced in Singapore's late-twentieth century age of 'little tiger' affluence under Lee Kuan Yew's extraordinary leadership. It seems more plausible to attribute both variations in corruption levels and variations in top pay levels (at least those that could not be explained by variation in GDP levels) to historical inheritance, leadership patterns and culture, and not to assume that they are linked in any simple or determinate relationship.

Much the same seems to apply to the other common variant of 'immodest theory', namely the idea that top pay levels are linked with economic performance (by analogy with comparable ideas for sport teams or business firms). As we saw in Chapter 2, the linkages vary in their strength according to which measure of economic performance we take. Competitiveness showed a much closer relationship with the pay of top political executives than did economic growth, where something closer to the null hypothesis seems more plausible. Indeed, in the year after the politicians' pay rises that Goh Chok Tong was defending so vigorously on the grounds that they were such a good investment by Singapore's citizens for economic performance, Singapore's GDP actually fell in all but the first quarter of the year. In a revised forecast for countries in that region that reflected the world economic fallout after the terrorist attacks on the USA in the autumn of 2001, the IMF forecast a nearly 3 per cent decline in Singapore's GDP for the year as a whole. That was a steep decline from Singapore's almost 10 per cent GDP growth in the previous year, while low-RHPO China showed economic growth of about 7 per cent, and moderate-RHPO Australia, Korea and New Zealand were forecast to turn in positive growth of about 2.5 per cent.

In the event, Goh and his ministers took a 17 per cent pay cut in the following year, to reflect Singapore's recession. That does not necessarily disprove Goh's argument about the value of high pay for top public officeholders. His words did not imply that the pay rises in 2000 would necessarily *increase* Singapore's GDP by 1 per cent – which is just as well, as events turned out. The actual word he was careful to use was 'improve', which (as is often the way with politicians' speeches) is studiedly ambiguous. The implication, presumably, is that Singapore's GDP would be at least 1 per cent higher than whatever it would have been without those ministerial pay hikes. In that particular year, it suggests Singapore's economy would have gone into even sharper decline without better-paid political talent at the top. Now this is a counterfactual that is impossible to falsify – or demonstrate. But given that other countries in the region, with quite different approaches to pay at the top, racked up much higher rates of economic growth, there is at least a case to answer.

Our analysis in Chapter 2 leads us to conclude that a high level of rewards for top public office is neither a necessary nor a sufficient condition for low corruption and high economic performance. The Singaporean pattern of high and visible rewards to top-level officials, a high level of economic performance and low levels of corruption is no doubt an important case. After all, Singapore was undoubtedly one of the world's leading economic success stories of the late-twentieth century, making it among the most recent of the 'yesterday's tomorrows' considered in this book. What is much more doubtful is whether the approach is as 'readily applicable to any society' as the World Bank claimed, or whether it reflects the far from readily imitable long-term leadership of Lee Kuan Yew that has placed such a distinctive stamp on Singapore's development over nearly half a century. As we have seen, other political systems achieve low levels of corruption or high levels of economic performance, or both, with low or limitedly visible rewards to the topmost officeholders in the state.

Moreover, the hypothesis that economic performance is related to top public-officeholders' pay depends on which dimension of performance is taken and evidently is not a linear relationship even for economic competitiveness where it fits best. Accordingly, rather more modest theories about the relationship between top-level public pay and macro-performance of political and economic systems seem to be called for, as we suggested in Chapter 2. These more modest but better-grounded theories would at the least need to allow for a large element of 'inheritance' over 'choice' in the shaping of top public pay, economic performance and corruption. They would need to allow for multi-causality and to distinguish the different sorts of jumping-off-points from which modern top reward systems emerge.

However, the level and structure of rewards for high public office may have important consequences for the quality of democracy that are not normally discussed in 'econocratic' perspectives on governance, but belong more to the preoccupations of classical political theory. For instance, there are some worrying potential effects of patterns of top public officeholders' reward that make elective politics poorly paid, unpaid or even negatively paid (as Akira Nakamura and Kosaku Dairokuno suggested for Japan in Chapter 6) relative to far more generously rewarded bureaucratic careers. This pattern, which applies to the majority of cases in our set, potentially creates a structure of incentives that makes it very expensive (in opportunity costs) for ambitious high-quality people to pursue elective politics as a full-time career. As we saw in Part II, that outcome can come about either through an executive-dominated mind-set that values elected representatives below top executive talent, or through party competition to keep legislators' visible rewards down, as Martin Painter argued for Australia in Chapter 4. Moreover, countries like Australia that have adopted superannuation systems for politicians which create strong financial incentives for ordinary legislators to quit after a few elections, may be seriously reducing the quality of executive government accountability to democratic scrutiny by thinning the ranks of experienced and long-serving legislators. Indeed, it may well be that the consequences of top reward systems for the quality of democracy are more important than any direct impact on economic growth or competitiveness. We turn to some of those issues in the next two sections.

Trends and variety in the top rewards game

When we penetrated beyond the quantitative and aggregated comparative analysis of Chapter 2 to look at the top rewards game in each of our political systems, we found a range of historical dynamics, institutional processes and cultural settings, as described in the chapters in Part II. We will comment here on only three of those qualitative aspects. The three are: the time-pattern of rewards to top-level officials; the dynamic of the top pay game (as sketched out in Chapter 1 and discussed in many of the chapters in Part II); and the place of intangible and extra-legal rewards for high public officeholders.

Time-patterns of reward for high public office: the 'when' in who gets what when how

One of the elements of variety on which the authors of the preceding chapters have commented concerns different time-patterns of rewards for those in high public office. In Chapter 1 we recalled Lasswell's (1936) famous definition of politics as 'who gets what when how', and it is the 'when' that is of particular interest here.

Table 10.1 Time, wealth and high public office: four polar types

	Reward pattern			
	Pattern (1): wealthy before high public office	Pattern (2): wealthy during high public office	Pattern (3): wealthy after high public office	Pattern (4): never wealthy (lifetime austerity)
Leading example	Hong Kong Chief Executive (to a lesser extent Singapore MPs and Hong Kong Legco members)	Public servants in Hong Kong; ministers and civil servants in Singapore	Japanese civil servants	Most New Zealand politicians (a few exceptions)

Indeed, if we look broadly at the history of government, going back before the democratic era of the last two centuries or so, the time-pattern of rewards for those at the top of the state seems to have been far from uniform. Certainly, the seven political systems explored in this book exhibit a range of different lifetime reward patterns for top public officeholders, and particularly for politicians. Table 10.1 depicts four polar types that we can identify from the discussion in the earlier chapters.

In some political systems, candidates for some or all types of high public office – but particularly politicians, insofar as they can be distinguished from judges or bureaucrats – are expected to have achieved a degree of financial success, or at least established themselves as successful professionals, *before* they go into public service. In Max Weber's famous distinction, such individuals live mainly 'for' rather than 'off' politics (Gerth and Mills 1948: 83). The extreme form of this approach (Pattern 1 in Table 10.1) is an oligarchical 'wealthy before public office' pattern, in which politics or public service is like 12-metre yachting – a cripplingly expensive luxury that is open only to the super-rich or their *protégés*. A less extreme variant requires public officeholders to have made some sort of success of another career – becoming at least comfortable, if not rich – before they engage in politics or public service.

Out of our seven cases, the clearest example of this style was that of Singapore's MPs, most of whom were expected to be successful full-time professionals in other employment, undertaking their parliamentary duties for the ruling PAP party (apart from the one or two struggling opposition party MPs) on a part-time basis. In line with those expectations, they received no salary for their work as MPs. They did, however, receive an appreciable *pourboire* in the form of a tax-free 'electoral allowance', notionally for office expenses (but actually 'taxed' by the ruling PAP for its own running costs, as already noted) and amounting to about one-third of top civil servants' basic pay, before the variable performance bonuses described by Jon Quah. The level of MP allowances (particularly after the PAP 'tax') contrast sharply with the stratospheric salaries enjoyed by the island-state's ministers, judges and top civil servants. This style was common in western parliamentary systems before the development of legislator salaries in the early years of the twentieth century. It still largely applies to the case of Switzerland, which like Singapore (but for quite different political reasons) is a rich country that is notably parsimonious in what it pays its legislators (see Hood and Peters 1994).

In our study, something similar also applied to the members of Hong Kong's Legco, the partly elected law-making assembly that governs post-colonial Hong Kong under the terms of its Basic Law with China, and perhaps for a similar political reason. The remuneration arrangements for Legco members, sharply contrasting with the telephone-number salaries paid to Hong Kong's top civil servants (who until recently had in effect to double as ministers, in the absence of a Cabinet government system, as explained by Grace Lee in Chapter 8) largely assumed that legislators would be established professionals acting as representatives on a part-time basis. Among executive positions, the only clear case of the 'wealthy before public service' pattern in our seven systems studied was that of the Chief Executive position in Hong Kong that replaced the British colonial governors after the 1997 handover. A wealthy shipping magnate with the appropriate political connections with the Beijing government, Tung Chee-Hwa, was chosen as the first holder of the position, but whether this pattern will become established for later holders of the office remains to be seen.

At the opposite extreme from the 'wealthy before public service' pattern are cases of remunerative 'life after politics' or public service. In this pattern (Pattern 2 in Table 10.1), top public officeholders graduate to high post-career rewards *after* a period of fairly modestly paid public service. As Akira Nakamura and Kosaku Dairokuno showed in Chapter 6 in Part II of the book, the Japanese civil service, with its traditional and highly institutionalized two-stage 'descent from heaven' pattern, is the classic case internationally of this 'wealthy after high public office' time-pattern. In the *amakaduri* style, public service is taken as a first career to be succeeded by a more lucrative second career in middle age. And, as Pan-Suk Kim showed in Chapter 7, the tradition of 'descent by parachute' in the Korean civil service is evidently a close if rather less well-known relative. So, if the first pattern in Table 10.1 reflects a 'try before you buy' political culture or set of official values that expects individuals to have made a success of their lives before they are entrusted with high public office, the second follows a different logic. Instead of 'live now, pay later', the logic of the second pattern is 'work now, be paid later', and consists of rewarding high public officeholders by making them rich at the end of their lives. This style might be said to reflect a culture or set of official values that rewards individuals who 'play the game' according to some sort of logic of appropriateness (and probably risk-aversion) over three decades or so.

The third type, exemplified by the civil service in colonial-era Hong Kong and Singapore after a brief period of austerity in its immediate post-independence years (as described by Jon Quah), consists of a 'wealthy during high public office' pattern. In this time-pattern (Pattern 3 in Table 10.1), high public officeholders do not need to have established themselves in another career before going into public service, but nor do they have to wait until after their public service career for a payoff. Rather, they are lavishly rewarded during their time in public office.

In Chapter 9, Jon Quah sketched out the historical inheritance that has shaped this pattern of top public officeholders' rewards in Singapore, and according to Grace Lee something similar seems to apply to post-handover Hong Kong. This 'wealthy during public office' style, in part, reflects the now long-defunct British tradition of highly paid expatriate colonial nabobs and it has been succeeded, in part, by the elites who fill the upper echelons of today's multinational corporations (against whose rewards, probably not coincidentally, the pay of top public officeholders in Singapore and Hong Kong has been benchmarked). We suggested earlier that the first reward pattern shown in Table 10.1 reflects a 'try before you buy' culture and the second a culture in which 'good things come to those who wait', in the sense that patience and loyalty are eventually rewarded, for those who manage to live long enough to enjoy the sweets stored up for the autumn of their lives. But the third reward pattern shown in Table 10.1 seems to reflect a 'pay as you go' or spot-market culture less disposed either to deferred gratification or to rule by those who have established themselves in some other career beforehand.

However, this third 'wealthy during public service' pattern can have elements of both the previous two. It is often remarked that a meritocracy can tend towards oligarchy or even a quasi-caste system if the elite schooling needed for the next generation to gain access to the top rungs of the ladder is more easily available to the offspring of the current elite than to their potential competitors. Then, it becomes a special variant of the 'wealthy before public service' pattern. The Singapore government has striven hard to achieve broad access to education, but this issue cannot be dismissed for several of our cases, and it is central to Pusey's (1991) idea of a 'new class' of elite-educated mandarins, with less egalitarian attitudes than their predecessors, who took over the Australian commonwealth public service from the 1980s. Moreover, the 'wealthy during public service' pattern can have elements of 'wealthy after public service' if the reward pattern incorporates a substantial element of deferred pay in the form of lavish non-contributory retirement pensions, as applied particularly to the colonial Hong Kong system, which was being wound back at the time of writing.

In principle, comfortable retirement pensions might seem to obviate the need to 'descend from heaven'. Indeed, such pensions have often been justified, following Bentham, as a way to prevent corruption and the conflicts of interest that are necessarily pervasive when high public officeholders make second careers in business. But as Martin Painter showed for Australia's MPs, such pensions may, in fact, provide the basis for a second career, to the point where Australia's parliament experiences a loss of experienced talent even in middle age in consequence of a much-discussed shift to 'politics as first career' in Australia (Weller and Fraser 1987). In contrast, John Burns' discussion of China's top-reward experience shows how top reward systems that do not incorporate provisions for retirement will add to the pressures for gerontocracy (since in the Chinese case the top-level leadership imposed mandatory retirement provisions on those down the line but not on themselves). Singapore is rather different, in that there is no specific retirement pension fund for civil servants and ministers, but they all pay into a partly contributory compulsory-savings Central Provident Fund arrangement, producing dramatic tax-free payouts for all high earners in their 50s (as well as being one of the main engines for development projects, particularly in the early years of independent Singapore).

The fourth polar type, perhaps best exemplified by New Zealand's politicians as described by Robert Gregory, consists of lifetime austerity, or high public office without the expectation that officeholders will ever accumulate significant wealth (either by open or corrupt means) at any point in their lives. New Zealand was by no means a pure case of this type – as Gregory noted in Chapter 5, at least two of the finance ministers who championed the post-1984 economic-rationalist government reforms found lucrative post-politics careers on the international speaking and consultancy circuits – but it comes closer to it than any other of the cases. For high public officials of this type, public service or politics must be its own reward. Any other kind of payoff will come, if at all, only in the next world.

As this image suggests, a rational-choice perspective would lead us to expect such a pattern of reward (Pattern 4 in Table 10.1) to produce a population of high public officeholders drawn disproportionately from religious zealots or those who are burning with other kinds of ideological fire. In fact, the likelihood of rule by an otherwise-unemployable 'zealocracy' is one of the standard and recurring arguments against the 'never wealthy' approach to rewards for high political office. If so, what is surprising about New Zealand is its relatively pragmatic political style, apart from the fairly short-lived but much-discussed period in the 1980s, described by Gregory, when it was ruled by Chicago-school ideologues. Perhaps the 'never wealthy' pattern reflects a culture that expects those who rule to be 'mediocre, like the rest of us', as a certain Senator Roman Hruska from Nebraska once argued should be the prime qualification for high judicial office in the United States (Hood and Jackson 1991: 40). But comparative politics has not yet reached the point of scientific development where we can readily compare the degree of mediocrity of politicians and bureaucrats across different political systems.

Varying lifetime patterns of reward have often been commented on before, particularly by labour economists interested in 'efficient wage' structures (usually interpreted as meaning higher pay in later years to reward early loyalty), but identifying these polar types, as illustrated in Table 10.1, both points to some major dilemmas for democratic government and raises some theoretical and empirical puzzles. Consider three of those puzzles. First, while the different types might be expected to reflect general patterns of political culture, they can evidently be mixed and matched within the same society, as is shown by the dramatic difference between Singapore's treatment of its MPs and its ministers, and Hong Kong's treatment of its top civil servants (becoming part of a new political class in the post-colonial handover period) and its legislators. That means we need to be cautious about offering macrocultural accounts of the differences.

Second, in spite or perhaps because of the apparent simplicity of this 'before', 'during', 'after' and 'never' categorization of time-patterns as depicted in Table 10.1, many cases remain slippery and ambiguous, particularly in the 'wealthy during high public office' category. For instance, we have already commented on the way that expensive educational qualifications for elite positions may blur the distinction between 'wealthy before' and 'wealthy during' high public office. Similarly, John Burns' account of China in Part II of the book suggests that what at first sight might appear to be a case of 'never wealthy' in terms of base pay may in fact be more appropriately classified as 'wealthy during public office'. If the part of the Chinese top-reward iceberg that is under water is taken into account, as discussed in Chapters 2 and 3, China's leaders are almost certainly much wealthier during office than their Singaporean counterparts, and in that sense, as John Burns argues, are even more successful income-maximizers. And even Singaporean ministers and civil servants do not necessarily fit the old colonial stereotype of 'wealthy during high public office' in the sense of retiring to comfortable idleness in some genteel domestic backwater after service. Jon Quah suggests that Singapore's politicians practise a low-key version of Japanese 'descent from heaven' in the form of highly paid directorships of government companies after public office (and the interpenetration of government companies with the careers of politicians and high public servants is a feature of the island-state's political economy that is often highlighted by critics of the regime). Indeed, since many of those individuals, in Jon Quah's argument, are 'bureaucrat-politicians', they may even be following a three-stage career, from bureaucracy to politics and thereafter to state companies.

Third, these time-patterns are evidently not fixed in perpetuity, again challenging any timeless culture account of the differences. As we have already noted, Akira Nakamura and Kosaku Dairokuno suggest in Chapter 6 that Japan's 'wealthy after public service' pattern of rewarding its top civil servants late in their lives seems to be coming under challenge, with changing public attitudes. New Zealand's bureaucrats, as described by Robert Gregory, used a rhetoric of managerialism to escape from the lifetime austerity pattern to one that combined much higher rewards during public office with a developing New Zealand pattern of 'descent from heaven'. As Martin Painter shows, Australian politicians have moved over a generation from a traditional pattern of politics-as-second-career (with politicians working in some other paid employment before assuming elected office) to an increasing politics-as-first-career style. Whether Singapore and Hong Kong's remarkable pattern of high rewards during public office can continue indefinitely may depend on what the future holds for these economies after the 'little tiger' years of the late-twentieth century.

Indeed, whether this variety presages a move towards some common style of 'modern' democratic politics or public service seems far from clear. Curiously, Max Weber's famous 1918 essay on 'politics as a vocation' does not discuss the time-pattern of officeholders' rewards that varies so noticeably among our cases (see Gerth and Mills 1948: 77–128), in spite of the centrality of the issue for democratic theory. But the political systems we have compared, are at least as different from one another as the early-twentieth-century states that surrounded Weber, and we share the difficulty he faced in forecasting how the management of politics as a vocation will shape itself in our seven cases.

The top rewards game: a vicious cycle of reward opacity and public cynicism?

In Part I, we introduced the idea of rewards for high public office as a game or set of strategic interactions between the rulers and those they rule. Essentially, this is an old contractarian idea in quasi-rational choice dress. The idea we introduced was one of a cooperation game in which democratic systems might be troubled (and indeed threatened in the long term) by a vicious cycle in which public cynicism about self-serving high public officeholders fuels and is fuelled by increasing tendencies by those officeholders to take rewards in increasingly hidden forms. The underlying reasoning, in a variant of median-voter theory on tax and expenditure policy, was that the median voter in a democracy would prefer high public officeholders to be paid no more than him- or herself. Moreover, the greater the degree of effective political competition, the more could these preferences be expected to be translated into public policy, forcing high public officeholders into various forms of subterfuge to make a living.

This problem was not discussed in Weber's classic account of politics as a vocation either. Evidently, it cannot be dismissed as a purely abstract possibility, but nor does it seem to be universal among our cases. We do not have indicators of legitimacy in the form of World Values Survey (WVS) trust and confidence data for all of the cases in our study, although we have WVS data for some of them from the 1981 and 1997 surveys. If we are to believe the WVS 1981 and 1997 data on trust and confidence in rulers, China appears to constitute a case that in the 'pay game' matrix introduced in Chapter 1 (Figure 1.1) would fall into the top right-hand cell [cell (2)] – with rewards to top-level officials largely invisible but comparatively high levels of trust (albeit falling from 1981 to 1997 for the civil service). Japan appears to constitute a case of the bottom left-hand cell [cell (3)] on the same matrix, with rewards at the top largely visible (mostly scoring 4 or 5 on the transparency ladder we set out in Chapter 2) but comparatively low levels of trust and confidence in rulers on WVS indicators. According to WVS data, levels of trust and confidence in politicians (MPs) fell sharply in both Korea and Australia between 1981 and 1997, suggesting a drift towards the 'dismal' bottom right-hand cell of the matrix [cell (4) of Figure 1.1 in Chapter 1]. How far the post-1997 Korean move towards more transparent pay at the top will help to arrest that decline remains to be seen.

At the least we can conclude from WVS data that not all of our cases, have reached the 'utterly dismal' bottom right-hand position in Figure 1.1, comprising a vicious cycle of devious rulers rewarding themselves in invisible ways and a cynical disaffected citizenry increasingly denying legitimacy to those rulers as a result. According to the contributors of the chapters in Part II, none of these seven political systems can be shown to be moving towards the top left-hand cell of the reward game matrix, several seem to be moving towards the bottom right-hand cell, and several seem to be in the top right or bottom left-hand cells. The Australian story, as told by Martin Painter in Chapter 4 is the case among our seven political systems that most clearly seems to follow the dismal logic of a drift towards less transparent politician rewards accompanied by apparently rising public cynicism and declining trust in politicians over two decades. Robert Gregory's account in Chapter 5 of New Zealanders' responses to the higher and more opaque pattern of their top civil servants' rewards suggests that a similar dynamic might be at work in that case as well.

However, whether the Australian (and possibly New Zealand) pattern turns out to be the future for other political systems in the region – particularly if democratization develops further – remains to be seen. There are several caveats that should be made about such a possibility. One is that the apparent decline in trust and confidence in Australian politicians that are revealed by WVS responses might have occurred for other reasons than as a response to politicians' attempts to make a living for themselves. For instance, the change might simply reflect the development of the kind of democratic ethic Max Weber associated with the early-twentieth-century USA, as noted in the first epigraph to this chapter – an egalitarian preference for politicians that ordinary voters can 'spit upon' to a superior mandarin class more attuned to a hierarchist society. Issues of reward might be at most a subsidiary irritant to such a development.

The second caveat relates to the distinctive (though not unique) Australian starting point. It is noticeable that the Australian dynamic starts from a historical base of remarkably high trust and confidence in state and democratic institutions and even at the end of our period Australian scores for trust and confidence in government are still slightly higher than their Japanese equivalents, in spite of Martin Painter's remarks about how cynical Australians are about their rulers. Political systems that begin with low expectations of politicians and government institutions, such as the Japanese case, do not seem to experience a similar fall in trust and confidence levels.

Indeed – and this is the third caveat – the earlier discussion suggests it is not clear that such a dynamic is to be found in the other five political systems that we have investigated in this study. For some (notably Singapore, a critical case for the 'top rewards game' sketched out in Chapter 2, and to a lesser extent Hong Kong and Korea) we do not have over-time data on trust and confidence in government to make an assessment. But China, with almost the whole of its top public office-holders' reward 'iceberg' under water, scores remarkably (one might say suspiciously) high on WVS questions about trust and confidence in government. (Suspiciously, because John Burns in Chapter 4 suggests there are reasons to believe that citizen trust in government may be falling.) And at the opposite pole, the Japanese case, with mostly higher reward transparency than the Australian one and rewards that are little higher, scores markedly lower on WVS trust and confidence responses. We can conclude that the dismal logic of the top reward game that we sketched out in Chapter 1 fits the Australian story and perhaps part of the New Zealand one. But in the latter case, most commentators appear to relate increased public distrust of politicians and the political process with perceived abuse of executive power in the 1980s and early 1990s (leading to the adoption of a PR electoral system to stop the 'crashing through' tactics described by Gregory in Chapter 5) rather than with politicians' rewards alone. So, there appear to be more ways for politicians to earn low and falling public confidence than finding more devious ways to reward themselves.

The fourth and related caveat is that the top reward game as sketched out in Chapter 1 seems most obviously applicable to elected politicians rather than bureaucrats or judges. The latter may find themselves in a quite different rewards game in some political systems; the level and direction of their trust and confidence ratings in several systems differ from those of politicians, and they may need to follow other income-maximizing strategies. (As indeed Australian and New Zealand bureaucrats did over the period of our study, with marked success.) However, in the political systems examined in this book, the distinction between 'politicians' and 'bureaucrats' can be quite variable. These two categories of top public officeholders are rigidly separated in our Australasian cases, but this distinction does not apply to all of the Asian ones. It makes little sense in the case of China, and even for Singapore and Hong Kong, the two categories are not wholly distinct. For instance, Jon Quah shows in Chapter 9 that over 40 per cent of Singapore's politicians are 'politician-bureaucrats' and Hong Kong, with its semi-appointed legislative body and top bureaucrats acting in the role of ministers (even the changes towards a new class of political appointees at the top, described by Grace Lee in Chapter 8, was still not formally described as a 'ministerial' system at the time of writing), might be considered an even more extreme case of 'politician-bureaucrats'.

Indeed, as we noted at the outset of this chapter, the professional distance between politicians and bureaucrats seems to be a key factor in the way that the top rewards game plays out, because of its effects on alliances among top public officeholders. In our Australasian cases, professional distance between politicians and bureaucrats is high, but politicians have a strong interest in trying to link their rewards to those of top bureaucrats in an attempt to escape from the levelling logic of their egalitarian cultures (and the party competition that forces them to keep their own salaries low) for their own rewards. However, for bureaucrats such a coupling in conditions where politicians' pay faces strong egalitarian challenges can be perceived as the kiss of death, condemning them to low and highly politicized rewards. So, for Australasian bureaucrats the logic of reward maximization has been to organize a 'breakout coalition' to decouple themselves from politicians' rewards by adopting individually variable packages in the name of a 'performance pay' ideology of managerialism and using the doctrine of commercial confidentiality and individual rights to privacy to counter the Benthamite doctrine of transparency over rewards. (By breakout coalition, we mean a bureaucratic group with sufficiently cohesive self-interest vis-à-vis the elected politicians to burst the traditional pay relativity between politicians and bureaucrats and move top officials' pay way above that of their nominal masters.) Indeed, Westminster-type systems where there is a tradition of a social divide between senior bureaucrats and elected politicians (unlike the politician-bureaucrats described by Jon Quah and their analogues in Hong Kong and Japan) may provide particularly favourable conditions for a 'breakout coalition' over pay by senior bureaucrats.

However, where professional distance between politicians and bureaucrats is low and cultures of egalitarianism are less entrenched, bureaucrats have less to lose in settling for a grand 'rewards coalition' with politicians. Hence, in Singapore, the archetypical 'administrative state', the relatively large number of bureaucrats leaving in mid-career has been used as a reason for dramatically raising the pay of senior politicians, for whom retention in employment has – to put it mildly – hardly been a problem in the country's half-century of post-independence history. (The same apparently goes for the bureaucrats at the very top, according to Jon Quah in Chapter 9.) And as we saw in earlier chapters, top Korean bureaucrats along with politicians saw their traditionally complex structure of allowances dramatically cut back in 2000 to produce a simpler and more transparent pay structure – exactly the opposite of the pay strategy pursued by their Australasian counterparts. Whether or how far top Japanese bureaucrats will be driven to alter their rewards strategy in the face of changing public attitudes towards 'descent from heaven' and pressures for greater economic transparency associated with international trade liberalization, remains to be seen. But both the Korean and the Australasian strategies seem to be compatible with egalitarian pressures in some conditions.

Intangible and extra-legal rewards: who wants to be a millionaire?

In Chapter 1, we introduced Nakamura and Dairokuno's distinction between tangible and legal rewards, and intangible and extra-legal ones. Our discussion in Chapter 2 necessarily focused on the tangible and legal, but the chapters in Part II looked beyond these categories. Those chapters suggested that what Nakamura and Dairokuno call the informal (and often extra-legal) but tangible benefits played a larger part in the rewards obtained by high public officeholders in China, Japan and Korea than in the other four cases. What counted as 'sleaze' (or 'rorts' in the evocative Australian term used by Martin Painter) varied from case to case, and the previous chapters pointed to some of the varying traditions, attitudes and beliefs on that issue.

One example is Australians' apparently low 'indignation threshold' for relatively petty abuses of public office that would scarcely count as remarkable in many other political systems. Another is the focus on family units rather than individuals that is pervasive in Chinese reward-maximizing strategies, as discussed by John Burns in his account of the various attempts that have been made to prevent spouses and family members from using top officeholders' positions to create new earning opportunities. The third is the group machine-politics ethic that seems to shape Japanese attitudes to financial corruption. How far such variety will continue is debatable. It may be that relatively casual approaches to conflict-of-interest issues and the use of privileged information by high public officeholders for personal gain in Japan and some of the other Asian cases may come under increasing challenge if a global regime of economic liberalization continues to develop. But, even if it does, we need to recall that the 'market' for high public office is a political market, not one of global supply and demand. Our analysis in Chapter 2 showed no sign of a shift towards a general 'going rate' for rewards for high public office among our seven cases, and it is hard to imagine the qualitative differences over informal rewards disappearing overnight.

The intangible features of reward for high public office are even harder to assess. We have already noted Max Weber's famous distinction between living 'off' politics and living 'for' politics, and Weber pointed to some of the dilemmas involved in combining the two. Most of the high public officeholders in our study were probably living 'for' politics in one way or another, although some of the PAP's MPs in Singapore do not seem to have embraced the political life with very much enthusiasm. But, most of our high public officeholders were also living 'off' politics, and following John Burns' analysis, we cannot dismiss the possibility that they were following income-maximizing strategies of a kind, albeit against different institutional constraints.

Even so, we are left with several puzzles. For example, Akira Nakamura and Kosaku Dairokuno (Chapter 6) stressed the pride that Japanese legislators feel in wearing the exclusive lapel pin signifying their office and refer to their aspirations to social pre-eminence in officiating at weddings and the like. But how can we square that story of pride and respect with the strikingly low scores returned by Japanese voters in WVS 'trust and confidence' polls? Conversely, why do Australians still return rather higher scores if, as Martin Painter tells us, they increasingly treat their politicians as 'spit upon' material? And, can we really take seriously Goh Chok Tong's claim, as reported by Jon Quah, that able Singaporeans regard representing a political party that has governed their state for over 40 years without interruption or any serious political challenge, as a riskier occupation than riding the roller-coaster of global big business?

It seems as unlikely to us today as it did to Max Weber nearly a century ago that politicians in the seven political systems we have explored are set to adopt a uniform professional style and a going rate for the job. We began – perhaps unfairly – by characterizing our seven political systems, as 'yesterday's tomorrows', in the sense that each has been presented as a political, economic or organizational model for the rest of the world over the past half-century. But it is far from clear that they are heading for a common tomorrow over rewards for high political office. Australia's salaried politicians, with their trade-union approach to perks and allowances, represent one possible tomorrow, but Singapore and Hong Kong represent another. Nor is it clear that transnational corporations will come to form the salary benchmarks for top bureaucrats everywhere in the way that they do for Singapore and Hong Kong. The Japanese alternative, of making the private sector pay part of the cost of drawing top talent into the state bureaucracy (through descent from heaven) has equal *prima facie* plausibility. And given that top public officeholders tend to live for politics as well as off it, the supply of such individuals is not likely to dry up whatever their formal rewards. But (recalling Napoleon Bonaparte's aphorism that we quoted in Part II of the book) top public rewards are likely to remain a mirror of political life.

References

Aberbach, J. and Christensen, T. (2001). Radical reform in New Zealand: crisis, windows of opportunity, and rational actors. *Public Administration*, 79: 403–22.

Advisory Committee on Post-Retirement Employment [Hong Kong] (1999). *Eleventh Report on the Work of the Advisory Committee on Post-Retirement Employment*. Hong Kong: Government Printer.

Andjelkovic, A., Boyle, G. and McNoe, W. (2000). Public disclosure of executive compensation: do shareholders need to know? *Working Paper*, Department of Finance and Quantitative Analysis. Dunedin: University of Otago.

ANAO (Australian National Audit Office) (1997). *Report No. 23 1997/1998, Ministerial Travel Claims*. Canberra: ANAO.

—— (2001). *Report No. 5 2001–2002, Parliamentarians' Entitlements: 1999–2000*. Canberra: ANAO.

Aucoin, P. (1990). Administrative reform in public management: paradigms, principles, paradoxes and pendulums. *Governance*, 3(2): 115–37.

Bagehot, W. (1964). *The English Constitution*. London: C.A. Watts (original 1867).

Bao, X. (1993). Letter from Beijing: China's democracy as viewed from the election of leading bodies, *Liaowang* (overseas edn) in US Department of Commerce, Foreign Broadcast Information Service, *Daily Report: China* [hereafter abbreviated as FBIS-CHI] (Washington, DC), 93-034 February: 16–17.

Bates (1999). Comparative politics and rational choice: a review essay. *American Political Science Review*, 1997(3): 699–704.

Bentham, J. (1825). The rationale of reward, reproduced in Bowring (ed.), *The Works of Jeremy Bentham*. New York: Russell and Russell Inc. 1962, Book II: 192–252.

Berman, E. M., Bowman, J. S., West, J. P. and Van Wart, M. (2001). *Human Resource Management in Public Service*. Thousand Oaks, CA: Sage.

Bogaars, G. E. (1973). Public services, in *Towards Tomorrow: Essays on Development and Social Transformation in Singapore*. Singapore: National Trades Union Congress.

Boston, J., Martin, J., Pallot, J. and Walsh, P. (1996). *Public Management: The New Zealand Model*. Auckland: Oxford University Press.

Boston, J., Church, S., Levine, S., McLeay, E. and Roberts, N. (2000). *Left Turn: The New Zealand General Election of 1999*. Wellington: Victoria University Press.

Boulding, K. (1970). *Economics as a Science*. New York: McGraw-Hill.

Brooks, E. B. and Brooks, A. T. (1998). *The Original Analects: Sayings of Confucius and His Successors*. New York: Columbia University Press.

Broom, L. and Cushing, R. (1977). A modest test of an immodest theory. *American Sociological Review*, 42: 157–69.

Burns, J. P. (1999). The People's Republic of China at 50: national political reform. *The China Quarterly*, 159: 580–94.

CCH Asia Pacific (1999). *China Tax and Customs Law Guide*. Hong Kong: CCH Asia Pacific Ltd.

CCP Organization Department (1993). Implementation Opinion on Chinese Communist Party Organs Participating in the Implementation of the 'State Civil Servants Provisional Regulations' [Central Committee Document No. 8] (September 13) in Ministry of Personnel (ed.), *Selection of Personnel Work Documents (Renshi gongzuo wenjian xuanbian)*, vol. 16.

Central Commission for Discipline Inspection (2000). Communique of the Fifth Plenary Session of the Central Commission for Discipline Inspection of the Chinese Communist Party, in FBIS-CHI, 2000–1227, 27 December.

Chan, K.-M. (1999). Corruption in China: a principal–agent perspective, in H. K. Wong and H. S. Chan (eds), *Handbook of Comparative Public Administration in the Asia-Pacific Basin*. New York: Marcel Dekker, pp. 299–324.

Chandran, D. C. (1999). *Bureaucrats and politicians in a one-party dominant system: a case study of Singapore*. B.Soc.Sci. Honours Thesis, Department of Political Science, National University of Singapore.

Cho, W. H. (1998). An analysis of the public–private earnings differentials in Korea. *Korean Economics Review*, 46(3): 169–95.

Christensen, J. G. (1994). Denmark: institutional constraint and the advancement of individual self-interest in HPO, Ch. 4, in C. Hood and B. G. Peters (eds), *Rewards at the Top*. London: Sage, pp. 70–89.

Christensen, J. G. (1997). Interpreting administrative change: bureaucratic self interest and institutional inheritance in government. *Governance*, 10(2): 143–74.

Chua, M. H. (2000). Judge my Govt by its Results, Says PM, *Straits Times*, 1 July.

Civil Service Bureau (HK) (1998). *Review of Pay Scales of Individual Grades*. Hong Kong: Government Printer.

—— (1999). *Civil Service Reform Newsletter*. Hong Kong: Government Printer.

—— (2000a). *Civil Service Reform Newsletter*. Hong Kong: Government Printer.

—— (2000b). *Brief for the Legislative Council: Civil Service Pay Adjustment 2000*. Hong Kong: Government Printer.

Civil Service Commission (CSC) (Korea) (2000). *The compensation system of the Korean government* (unpublished mimeo). Seoul: Civil Service Commission.

Condrey, S. E. (ed.) (1998). *Handbook of Human Resource Management in Government*. San Francisco, CA: Jossey-Bass.

Constitution of the People's Republic of China (1982). In: Kenneth Lieberthal (1995) *Governing China: From Revolution Through Reform*. New York: Norton, pp. 355–82.

Contemporary China Editorial Committee (1994). *Contemporary China's Personnel Management* [Dangdai zhongguode renshi guanli] (in Chinese), vol. 2, Beijing: Contemporary China Press, pp. 82–3.

Controller and Auditor-General (NZ) (2001). *Parliamentary Salaries, Allowances and other Entitlements*. Wellington: Controller and Auditor-General.

Curtis, G. L. (1999). *The Logic of Japanese Politics*. New York: Columbia University Press.

Dalziel, P. and Lattimore, R. (1999). *The New Zealand Macroeconomy: A Briefing on the Reforms*, 3rd edn. Greenlane, NZ: Oxford University Press.

Ding, W. (2001). Zhu Rongji's salary increases by 100 per cent his general internal duties, *Xinbao* (in Chinese) (Hong Kong), 15 January.

Divyanathan, D. (2001). Something For Everyone In 'Most Generous Budget', *Straits Times*, 24 February.

Douglas, M. (1982). *In the Active Voice*. London: Routledge and Kegan Paul.

Easton, B. (1989). The unmaking of Roger Douglas, in B. Easton (ed.), *The Making of Rogernomics*. Auckland: Auckland University Press.

Elayan, F., Lau, J. and Meyer, T. (2000). Executive incentive compensation schemes and their impact on corporate performance: evidence from New Zealand since legal disclosure requirements became effective. *Working Paper Series 00.22*, Department of Commerce, College of Business, Albany: Massey University, October.

Frank, R. and Cook, P. (1995). *The Winner-Take-All Society: Why the Few at the Top Get So Much More than the Rest of Us*. New York: Penguin.

Gerth, H. H. and Mills, C. W. (1948). *From Max Weber: Essays in Sociology*. London: Routledge and Kegan Paul.

Goh, C. T. (2000). *National Day Rally Speech by Prime Minister Goh Chok Tong, 20 August 2000*, Singapore, Ministry of Information and the Arts *(http://www.gov.sg/mita)*.

Goldfinch, S. (1998). Remaking New Zealand's economic policy: institutional elites as radical innovators, 1984–1993. *Governance*, 11(2): 177–207.

Harding, H. (1971). Maoist theories of policy-making and organization, in T. W. Robinson (ed.), *The Cultural Revolution in China*. Berkeley, CA: University of California Press, pp. 113–64.

—— (1981). *Organizing China: The Problem of Bureaucracy 1949–1976*. Stanford: Stanford University Press.

—— (1987). *China's Second Revolution: Reform after Mao*. Washington, DC: Brookings Institution.

Harrison, S. and Wan, W.-K. (2001). Decision today on top reshuffle. *South China Morning Post*, 15 February.

Hays, S. W. and Reeves, T. Z. (1989). *Personnel Management in the Public Sector*. Dubuque, IO: Wm. C. Brown.

Healy, M. (1999). Increases in parliamentary salaries, Parliamentary Library Research Note 23, 1999–2000. Canberra: Parliament of Australia.

Healy, M. and Winter, G. (2000). Remuneration of members of the parliament of Australia, Background Paper 30, 1999–2000. Canberra: Parliament of Australia.

Henderson, A. (1990). *The Quest for Efficiency: The Origins of the State Services Commission*. Wellington: State Services Commission.

Higher Salaries Commission (HSC) (NZ) (1981). *General Review as at 1 April 1981*. Wellington: Higher Salaries Commission.

—— (1999). *Parliamentary Salaries and Allowances Determination 1999*. Wellington: Higher Salaries Commission.

Hills, J. (1995). *Inquiry into Income and Wealth*, vol. 2. London: Joseph Rowntree Foundation.

Hirsch, F (1977). *Social Limits to Growth*. London: Routledge and Kegan Paul.

HKSAR Government (2000a). *Hong Kong 1999*. Hong Kong: Government Printer.

—— (2000b). *Press Release*. Hong Kong: Government Information Service.

—— (2001). *Financial Secretary's Transcript*. Hong Kong: Government Information Service, 5 June.

Hon, M. (2001). Civil Service Pay Rise Backed. *South China Morning Post*, 6 June.

Hong Kong Standing Commission on Civil Service Salaries and Conditions of Service (1999). *Civil Service Starting Salaries Review 1999*. Hong Kong: Government Printer.

Hood, C. (1998). *The Art of the State*. Oxford: Clarendon Press.

—— (1999). Changing the pay structure of the civil service in Hong Kong: an outsider's perspective. *Public Administration and Policy* (Hong Kong), 8(2): 71–6.

Hood, C. and Jackson, M. (1991). *Administrative Argument*. Aldershot: Dartmouth.

Hood, C. and Peters, B. G. (1994) Understanding RHPOs, in C. Hood and B. G. Peters (eds), *Rewards at the Top: A Comparative Study of High Public Office*. London: Sage, chapter 1.

Horn, M. J. (1995). *The Political Economy of Public Administration: Institutional Choice in the Public Sector*. Cambridge: Cambridge University Press.

Hu, A. (2001). *China: Fighting Against Corruption* [Zhongguo: tiaozhan fubai] (in Chinese). Hangzhou: Zhejiang People's Press.

Huang, C. (1997). *The Analects of Confucius (Lun Yu): A Literal Translation with an Introduction and Notes*. Oxford: Oxford University Press.

Huque, A. S., Lee, G. O. M. and Cheung, A. B. L. (1998). *The Civil Service in Hong Kong: Continuity and Change*. Hong Kong: Hong Kong University Press.

IMD (International Institute for Management Development) (2001). The World Competitiveness Scoreboard, *http://www.imd.ch/wcy/rankings/pasteresults.html*.

Independent Commission on Remuneration for Members of the Executive Council and the Legislature of the HKSAR (1999). *Review of Remuneration Package for Members of the Legislature*. Hong Kong: Government Printer.

Inose, N. (1997). *Nihon Koku no Kenkyu* (A Study of Japan). Tokyo: Bungei Shunju.

Johnson, C. (1982). *MITI and the Japanese Miracle*. Stanford, CA: Stanford University Press.

Kim, B. W. and Kim, P. S. (1997). *Korean Public Administration: Managing the Uneven Development*. Seoul: Hollym.

Kim, P. S., Kim, T. I. and Kim, M. Y. (1999). Globalization of human resource management: a cross-cultural perspective for the public manager. *Public Personnel Management*, 28(2): 227–43.

Kim, P. S. (2000a). Human resource management reform in the Korean Civil Service. *Administrative Theory and Praxis*, 22(2): 326–44.

—— (2000b). Administrative reform in the Korean Central Government: a case study of the Kim Dee Jung administration. *Public Performance and Management Review*, 24(2): 145–60.

—— (2000c). Improving ethical conduct in public service: Korean anticorruption initiatives in an international context. *Public Integrity*, 2(2): 157–71.

Kim, P. S., Kim, T. I. and Kim, M. Y. (2001). Wage differences between the public and private sectors. *Korean Public Administration Review*, 34(4): 115–38.

Kim, S. H. and Bae, B. D. (2000). Analysis of pay increase determinants in the Korean civil service. *Korean Public Administration Review*, 34(2): 253–68 (in Korean).

Kingdon, J. (1984). *Agendas, Alternatives, and Public Policies*. Boston, MA: Little, Brown.

Kryger, T. (1999). Private sector executive salaries. Parliamentary Library Research Note 24 1998–99. Canberra: Parliament of Australia.

Lasswell, H. (1936). *Politics: Who Gets What When How*. New York: McGraw-Hill.

Lau, S.-K. and Kuan, H.-C. (2000). Partial democratization, 'Foundation Moment' and political parties in Hong Kong. *The China Quarterly*, 163(1): 705–20.

Lee, B. H. (1976). *The Singapore Civil Service and its Perceptions of Time*. PhD dissertation, Department of Political Science, University of Hawaii.

Lee, H. Y. (1991). *From Revolutionary Cadres to Party Technocrats in Socialist China*. Berkeley, CA: University of California Press.

Lee, H. L. (2000). Paying What It Takes For A First-Class Civil Service. *Straits Times*, 30 June.

Lee, K. Y. (2000). *From Third World to First: The Singapore Story, 1965–2000*. Singapore: Times Media Ptd Ltd.

Lee, M. K. W. (1994–95). *Competing for the best and brightest: the strategic use of compensation in the Singapore Administrative Service*. B.Soc.Sci. Honours Thesis, Department of Political Science, National University of Singapore.

Legislative Council (1998). *Minutes of the Third meeting of the Finance Committee Held at the Legislative Council Chamber on Friday, 17 July 1998, at 2:30 pm*.

Legislative Council (2001). *History of the Legislature. http://www.legco.gov.hk/general/english/intro/hist_lc.htm*.

Legislative Council Secretariat (2000). *Declaration of Interests by Senior Civil Servants in Some Overseas Countries*. Hong Kong: Legislative Council Secretariat.

Lethbridge, D. (1978). *Hong Kong: Stability and Change*. Hong Kong: Oxford University Press.

Leong, C. (2000). Will High Pay Cheapen Moral Leadership? *Straits Times*, 8 July.

Lieberthal, K. (1995). *Governing China: From Revolution Through Reform*. New York: Norton.

Lipson, L. (1948). *The Politics of Equality: New Zealand's Adventures in Democracy*. Chicago, IL: University of Chicago Press.

Lynn, J. and Jay, A. (1986). *Yes Prime Minister: The Diaries of the Rt. Hon. James Hacker*. London: BBC Books.

McAllister, I. and Painter, M. (2000). The interpenetration of political, bureaucratic and business elites in Australia. Paper presented at the XVII World Congress of IPSA, August 2000, Quebec City.

MacFarquhar, R. (1974). *The Hundred Flowers Campaign and the Chinese Intellectuals*. New York: Octagon Books.

—— (1997). *The Origins of the Cultural Revolution: The Coming of the Cataclysm 1961–1966*. London: Oxford University Press.

Manion, M. (1993). *Retirement of Revolutionaries in China: Public Policies, Social Norms, Private Interests*. Princeton. NJ: Princeton University Press.

Massey University (1997). *The Role of Government and Work Orientation: International Social Survey Programme*, Department of Marketing, October.

—— (2000). Social Equality in New Zealand: International Social Survey Programme, Department of Marketing, March.

Mercer, Cullen, Egan Dell (2000a). *APS SES Remuneration Survey, Revised Version April 2000*. Canberra: Department of Employment, Workplace Relations and Small Business.

—— (2000b). *Broader Market Comparison – SES Remuneration*. Canberra: Department of Employment, Workplace Relations and Small Business.

Mercer, Cullen, Egan Dell (2001). *APS SES Remuneration Survey, Revised Version May 2001*. Canberra: Department of Employment, Workplace Relations and Small Business.

Miao, L. (ed.) (2000). *Most Recent Beijing Property Guide* [*Cuixin Beijing maifang baodian*]. Beijing: Xintong Press.

Miners, N. (1986). *The Government and Politics of Hong Kong*, 4th edn. Hong Kong: Oxford University Press.

—— (1998). *The Government and Politics of Hong Kong*, 5th edn. Hong Kong: Oxford University Press.

Ming Pao, 16 February 2001.

Ministry of Personnel (1993). *Provisional Regulations on State Civil Servants*. Beijing: Ministry of Personnel, mimeo.

—— (1994). *Personnel Work Documents* (*Renshi gongzuo wenjian xuanbian*), vol. 16. Beijing: China Personnel Press.

—— (1998). *Personnel Work Documents* (*Renshi gongzuo wenjian xuanbian*), vol. 20. Beijing: China Personnel Press.

Ministry of Personnel and Ministry of Finance (1990). Implementation plan for the adjustment of the wage standard for government organs in *Personnel Policy and Law Gazette* (*Renshi zhengzi fagui zhuankan*), no. 10: 4.

—— (1999). Implementation plan for the adjustment of the wage standard for government employees, State Council Document No. 78 31 August, in Ministry of Personnel (ed.), *Personnel Policy and Regulation Gazette* (*Renshi zhengci fagui zhuankan*), no. 10: 4.

Ministry of Personnel and Ministry of Finance (2001). Implementation plan for the adjustment of the wage standard for government employees, in Ministry of Personnel General

Office, *Gazette of the Ministry of Personnel of the People's Republic of China [Zhonghua renmin gongheguo renshibu gongbao]* (Beijing), no. 5, May, pp. 8–9.

Morgan, E. P. (1996). Analyzing fields of change: civil service systems in developing countries, in H. A. G. M. Bekke, J. L. Perry and T. A. J. Toonen (eds), *Civil Service Systems in Comparative Perspective*. Bloomington: Indiana University Press, pp. 227–43.

Morgan, Roy and Associates (2000). Nurses, doctors, pharmacists most respected professions. http://www.roymorgan.com.au/polls/2000/3349.

Nathan, A. J. and Tianjian Shi (1993). Cultural requisites for democracy in China: findings from a survey. *Daedalus*, 122(2): 95–123.

Nethercote, J. (1999). Public sector executive salaries. Parliamentary Library Research Note 23, 1998–99. Canberra: Parliament of Australia.

Nishimura, M. (1999). *Nihon no Komuin Kyuyo Seido* (The Wage System in Japan's National Government). Tokyo: University of Tokyo Press.

Niskanen, W. (1971). *Bureaucracy and Representative Government*. Chicago, IK: Aldine Atherton.

North, D. (1981). *Structure and Change in Economic History*. New York: Norton.

O'Dea, D. (2000). The changes in New Zealand's income distribution. *Treasury Working Paper 00/13*. Wellington: The Treasury.

OECD (1992). *National Accounts 1960–1990*, Volume 2. Paris: OECD.

—— (1996). *Pay Reform in the Public Service*. Paris: OECD.

Painter, M. (1987). *Steering the Modern State*. Sydney: Sydney University Press.

—— (1990). Values in the history of public administration, in J. Power (ed.), *Public Administration in Australia: A Watershed*. Sydney: Hale and Iremonger.

Palmier, L. (1985). *The Control of Bureaucratic Corruption: Six Cases Studies in Asia*. New Delhi: Allied Publishers.

Papadakis, E. (1999). Constituents of confidence and mistrust in Australian institutions. *Australian Journal of Political Science*, 34(1): 75–94.

Perry, P. and Webster, A. (1999). *New Zealand Politics at the Turn of the Millennium: Attitudes and Values about Politics and Government*. Auckland: Alpha Publications.

Peters, B. G. and Hood, C. (1994). Conclusion: what have we learned? in C. Hood and B. G. Peters (eds), *Rewards at the Top: A Comparative Study of High Public Office*. London: Sage.

—— (1995). Erosion and variety in pay for high public office. *Governance*, 8(2): 171–94.

Peters, B. G. (1995a). What works?: sorting out contradictions in fifteen years of reform. *Canadian Center for Management Development: Research Paper*, January.

—— (1995b). Introducing the topic, in B. G. Peters and D. J. Savoie (eds), *Governance in a Changing Environment*. Montreal: Canadian Center for Management Development, pp. 3–19.

Podder, N. and Chatterjee, S. (1998). Sharing the national cake in post-reform New Zealand: income inequality in terms of income sources. Paper presented at the New Zealand Association of Economists Conference, August.

Polaschek, R. (1958). *Government Administration in New Zealand*. London: Oxford University Press.

Pusey, M. (1991). *Economic Rationalism in Canberra*. Cambridge: Cambridge University Press.

Putnam, R., Leonardi, R. and Nanetti, R. (1993). *Making Democracy Work: Civic Traditions in Modern Italy*. Princeton, NJ: Princeton University Press.

Quah, J. S. T. (1978). The origins of the public bureaucracies in the ASEAN Countries. *Indian Journal of Public Administration*, 24(2): 400–29.

Quah, J. S. T. (1984). The public bureaucracy in Singapore, 1959–1984, in You Poh Seng and Lim Chong Yah (eds), *Singapore: Twenty-five Years of Development*. Singapore: Nan Yang Xing Zhou Lianhe Zaobao.

Quah, J. S. T. (1986). Toward productivity and excellence: a comparative analysis of the public personnel systems in the ASEAN countries, in Suchitra Punyaratabandhu-Bhakdi *et al.* (eds), *Delivery of Public Services in Asian Countries: Cases in Development Administration.* Bangkok: National Institute of Development Administration.

—— (1989). Singapore's experience in curbing corruption, in A. J. Heidenheimer, M. Johnston and V. T. LeVine (eds), *Political Corruption: A Handbook.* New Brunswick: Transaction Publishers.

Quah, J. S. T. (1998). Singapore's model of development: is it transferable?' in H. S. Rowen (ed.), *Behind East Asian Growth: The Political and Social Foundations of Prosperity.* London: Routledge.

—— (1999). Corruption in Asian countries: can it be minimized? *Public Administration Review*, 59: 483–94.

—— (2001). Combating corruption in Singapore: what can be learned? *Journal of Contingencies and Crisis Management*, 9(1): 29–36.

Remuneration Tribunal (1990). *Report and Determinations May 1990.* Canberra: Australian Government Printing Service.

—— (1992). *1992 Review.* Canberra: Australian Government Printing Service.

Remuneration Tribunal (1994). *1993 Review.* Canberra: Australian Government Printing Service.

—— (1995). *1994 Decisions and Report.* Canberra: Australian Government Printing Service.

—— (1999). *Report 1999/01. http://www.dofa.gov.au/tribunal/MPs/ 199901r.html*, accessed 22/1/2001.

Republic of Singapore (1968). *Report of the Civil Service Salaries Commission of Singapore 1967.* Singapore. Government Printing Office.

—— (1979). *Parliamentary Debates Singapore Official Report*, vol. 39, no. 5 (15 May).

—— (1985a). *Parliamentary Debates Singapore Official Report*, vol. 45, no. 8 (18 March).

—— (1985b). *Parliamentary Debates Singapore Official Report*, vol. 45, no. 12 (22 March).

—— (1989a). *Parliamentary Debates Singapore Official Report*, vol. 53, no. 6 (17 March).

—— (1989b). *Parliamentary Debates Singapore Official Report*, vol. 53, no. 10 (23 March).

—— (1993). *Parliamentary Debates Singapore Official Report*, vol. 61, no. 13 (3 December).

—— (1994). *Competitive Salaries for Competent and Honest Government: Benchmarks for Ministers and Senior Public Officers.* Singapore; Prime Minister's Office.

—— (1995). *Parliamentary Debates Singapore Official Report*, vol. 65, no. 2 (2 November).

—— (2000). *Parliamentary Debates Singapore Official Report*, vol. 72, no. 5 (29 June).

Roberts, J. (1987). *Politicians, Public Servants and Public Enterprise.* Wellington: Victoria University Press for the Institute of Policy Studies.

Roper, B. (1997). New Zealand's postwar economic history, in C. Rudd and B. Roper (eds), *The Political Economy of New Zealand.* Auckland: Oxford University Press.

Rothacher, A. (1993). *The Japanese Power Elite.* New York: St Martin's Press.

Sampson, A. (1995). *Company Man: The Rise and Fall of Corporate Life.* London: Harper Collins.

Schleifer, A. and Vishny, R. W. (1998). *The Grabbing Hand: Government Pathologies and their Cures.* Cambridge, MA: Harvard University Press.

Schurmann, F. (1969). *Ideology and Organization in Communist China.* Berkeley, CA: University of California Press.

Scott, G. (2001). *Public Management in New Zealand: Lessons and Challenges.* Wellington: New Zealand Business Roundtable.

Seah, C. M. (1971). *Bureaucratic evolution and political change in an emerging nation: a case study of Singapore.* PhD thesis, Faculty of Economic and Social Studies, Victoria University of Manchester.

Senate Select Committee on Superannuation (1997). *The Parliamentary Contributory Superannuation and the Judge's Pension Scheme.* Canberra: Parliament of the Commonwealth of Australia.

Senate Finance and Public Administration Reference Committee (2000). *Australian Public Service Employment Matters, First Report: Australian Workplace Agreements.* Canberra: Parliament of the Commonwealth of Australia.

Shiu, S.-P. (2001). Our Entrenched Civil Service. *South China Morning Post*, 6 February.

Singapore Ministry of Finance (1988). *Public Sector Wage Reform.*

Singapore Ministry of Information and the Arts (1998). *Singapore 1998.*

—— (2001). *Singapore 2001.*

Singapore Ministry of Labour (1988). Report of the Task Force on Public Sector Wage Reform.

Standing Committee on Directorate Salaries and Conditions of Service [Hong Kong] (1989). *Tenth Report of the Standing Committee on Directorate Salaries and Conditions of Service.* Hong Kong: Government Printer.

State Sector Standards Board (NZ) (2001). *A Report to the Minister of State Services on: The Ethos of the State Sector*, 29 June, Wellington.

State Services Commission (NZ) (1998). *Annual Report of the State Services Commission for the Year Ended 30 June 1998.* Wellington: State Services Commission.

—— (2000). *Annual Report of the State Services Commission for the Year Ended 30 June 2000.* Wellington: State Services Commission.

State Statistical Bureau (1995). *State Statistical Yearbook 1995.* Beijing: China Statistics Press.

—— (1989). *China Statistical Yearbook 1989.* Beijing: China Statistical Press

—— (1999). *China Statistical Yearbook 1999.* Beijing: China Statistical Press

—— (2000). *China Statistical Yearbook 2000.* Beijing: China Statistics Press.

Steinmo, S., Thelen, K. and Longstreth, F. (1991). *Structuring Politics.* Cambridge: Cambridge University Press.

Stephens, R. (2000). The social impact of reform: poverty in Aotearoa/New Zealand. *Social Policy and Administration*, 34(1): 64–86.

Tan, L. K. F. (1957). *The Development of the Straits Settlements Civil Services*, 1867–1896. B.A. Honours Academic Exercise, Department of History, University of Malaya in Singapore.

Then Y. T. (1998). The National Wages Council and the wage system in Singapore, in C. Y. Lim and R. Chew (eds), *Wages and Wages Policies: Tripartism in Singapore.* Singapore: World Scientific Publishing Company.

Tocqueville, A. de (1946). *Democracy in America.* Oxford: Oxford University Press.

Transparency International (1999). *http://www.transparency.de/documents/cpi/index.*

Vogel, E. F. (1989). 'A little dragon tamed,' in S. Kernial, S. Sandhu and P. Wheatley (eds), *Management of Success: The Moulding of Modern Singapore.* Singapore: Institute of Southeast Asian Studies.

Wade, R. (1990). *Governing the Market: Economic Theory and the Role of Government in East Asian Industrialization.* Princeton, NJ: Princeton University Press.

Wage Management Institute (Japan) (1997). *Rewards for Top Executives in Private Sector.* Tokyo: Wage Management Institute.

Weber, M. (1948). Politics as a vocation, in H. H. Gerth and C. W. Mills (eds), *From Max Weber: Essays in Sociology.* London: Routledge and Kegan Paul, pp. 77–128.

—— (1951). *The Religion of China: Confucianism and Taoism.* Translated by H. H. Gerth, Glencoe, IL: Free Press.

—— (1965). *The Protestant Ethic and the Spirit of Capitalism.* Translated by T. Parsons, London: Unwin University Books.

Wei, J. (2000). Work report delivered to the 5th Plenary Session of the Central Discipline Inspection Commission, 25 December in *FBIS-CHI-2001-0103*. January 3, 2001.

Weller, P. and Fraser, S. (1987). The younging of Australian politics or politics as first career, *Politics (Journal of the Australian Political Studies Association)*, 22: 76–83.

Weller, P. and Wood, T. (1999). The Departmental Secretaries: a profile of a changing profession'. *Australian Journal of Public Administration*, 58(2): 21–32.

Wong, C. (2000). Tax Chief faces jail over scam; 'High-flier brought down by own success. *South China Morning Post*, 15 December.

World Bank (1993). *The East Asian Miracle: Economic Growth and Public Policy*. Oxford: Oxford University Press.

—— (1997). *Sharing Rising Incomes*. Washington, DC: World Bank.

Xinhua (2000). *3 October in FBIS-CHI-2000-1003*. 3 October.

Yu, P. S. (1998). *The Seventh Child and the Law*. Hong Kong: Hong Kong University Press.

Index